Prentice Hall Essentials of Management Series
Stephen P. Robbins, Editor

Stephen E. Barndt
and Davis W. Carvey

Essentials of Operations Management

Rogene A. Buchholz

Essentials of Public Policy for Management

Joseph L. Massie

Essentials of Management, 4th ed.

Mitchell S. Novit

Essentials of Personnel Management, 2nd ed.

Stephen P. Robbins

Essentials of Organizational Behavior, 2nd ed.

W9-CGV-265

ESSENTIALS OF ORGANIZATIONAL BEHAVIOR

second edition

Stephen P. Robbins
San Diego State University

PRENTICE HALL, ENGLEWOOD CLIFFS, N.J. 07632

Library of Congress Cataloging-in-Publication Data

Robbins, Stephen P.
Essentials of organizational behavior / Stephen P. Robbins.—2nd ed.
p. cm.
Includes index.
ISBN 0-13-286485-1
1. Organizational behavior. I. Title.
HD58.7.R6   1988
658.3—dc19   87-19876
CIP

Parts of this book first appeared in Robbins, *Organizational Behavior,*
3rd ed. (Prentice Hall, 1986)

Editorial/production supervision: Nancy Benjamin
Interior and cover design: Christine Gadekar
Manufacturing buyer: Ed O'Dougherty

© 1988, 1984 by Prentice Hall
A Division of Simon & Schuster
Englewood Cliffs, New Jersey 07632

10 9 8 7 6 5 4 3 2

Printed in the United States of America.

ISBN 0-13-286485-1 01

Prentice-Hall International (UK) Limited, *London*
Prentice-Hall of Australia Pty. Limited, *Sydney*
Prentice-Hall Canada Inc., *Toronto*
Prentice-Hall Hispanoamericana, S.A., *Mexico*
Prentice-Hall of India Private Limited, *New Delhi*
Prentice-Hall of Japan, Inc., *Tokyo*
Simon & Schuster Asia Pte. Ltd., *Singapore*
Editora Prentice-Hall do Brasil, Ltda., *Rio de Janeiro*

to
my "brother" Harold—
just a reminder that we now have, between us,
over 250 million copies in print!

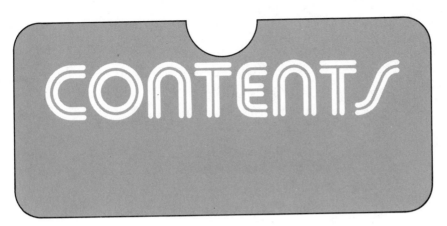

CONTENTS

3

UNDERSTANDING MOTIVATION

4

DESIGNING MOTIVATING JOBS

5

INDIVIDUAL DECISION MAKING

PART
3

GROUPS IN THE ORGANIZATION

6

FOUNDATIONS OF GROUP BEHAVIOR

Contents

10

CONFLICT

PART
4

THE ORGANIZATION SYSTEM

11

FOUNDATIONS OF ORGANIZATIONAL STRUCTURE

12

PERFORMANCE APPRAISAL AND REWARD SYSTEMS

13

ORGANIZATIONAL CULTURE

Contents

14

ORGANIZATIONAL CHANGE AND DEVELOPMENT

PREFACE

Essentials of Organizational Behavior extracts the key concepts ordinarily found in a 600- or 700-page textbook on organizational behavior (OB) and condenses them into a more concise volume. This text includes discussions of those topics usually identified as the core of OB. They are presented in a straightforward and conversational style, with an extensive use of examples to illustrate concepts. Of course, "essentials" books have to make some compromises and this one is no exception. Some interesting but less relevant OB topics have had to be excluded. Pedagogical aids such as end-of-chapter discussion questions and cases have been omitted. In addition, although the findings in this book are based on hundreds of research studies, there is a bare minimum of formal footnoting of the literature within the chapters. The result is a streamlined model of the more deluxe OB textbooks.

The above description may prompt the question: Why the need for an essentials of organizational behavior book? The answer is: It opens up options. Adopters of the first edition tell me that they used it alone in short courses and combined it with experiential, skill development, case, or readings books in organizational behavior to create unique teaching-learning packages.

There are several changes to be found in this revision. They are largely the result of feedback from instructors and students and a valuable review of the first edition by Charles W. Kroen in *Personnel Psychology* (Winter 1984, pp. 741–43). The following highlights these changes:

- New material on values (Chapter 2).
- A completely revised chapter on groups, with new material on why people join groups, stages of group development, how norms develop, contingency variables that affect group behavior, the effects of cohesiveness on group productivity, and an improved group behavior model (Chapter 6).
- More focused discussion of Fiedler's leadership model (Chapter 8).
- Revised and updated material on power plus the addition of a section on political behavior (Chapter 9).

- Introduction of structural options, a guide to use, and the addition of an integrative organization structure model (Chapter 11).
- A full chapter on performance appraisal and reward systems (Chapter 12).
- A completely revised and updated discussion of organizational culture (Chapter 13).

A personal note of thanks goes out to those users of the first edition who took the time to write and offer thoughtful suggestions on how the revision could be improved. Please feel free to drop me a note with any of your ideas or comments that could make the third edition better.

Stephen P. Robbins
San Diego, California

1

INTRODUCTION TO
ORGANIZATIONAL BEHAVIOR

When I ask managers to describe their most frequent or troublesome problems, the answers I get tend to exhibit a common theme. The managers most often describe *people* problems. They talk about their bosses' poor communication skills, subordinates' lack of motivation, conflicts between employees in their department, overcoming employee resistance to a departmental reorganization, and similar concerns.

Since a manager's job is inherently one of working with and through other people—bosses, peers, and subordinates—to solve these problems, good "people skills" become a valuable, even an essential, asset. This book has been written to help managers, and potential managers, develop these people skills.

THE FIELD OF ORGANIZATIONAL BEHAVIOR The study of people at work is generally referred to as the study of organizational behavior. Let's begin, then, by defining the term *organizational behavior* and briefly reviewing its origins.

1

Definition   *Organizational behavior (OB) is the systematic study of the actions and attitudes that people exhibit within organizations.* Let's look at the key parts of this definition.

Each of us regularly uses intuition or our "gut feelings" in trying to explain phenomena. For instance, a friend catches a cold and we're quick to remind him that he "didn't take his vitamins," "doesn't dress properly," or that "it happens every year when the seasons change." We're not really sure why he caught cold, but that doesn't stop us from offering our intuitive analysis. The field of OB seeks to replace intuitive explanations with systematic study; that is, the use of scientific evidence gathered under controlled conditions and measured and interpreted in a reasonably rigorous manner to attribute cause and effect. The objective, of course, is to draw more accurate conclusions. So the field of OB—its theories and conclusions—is based upon a large number of systematically designed research studies.

What does OB systematically study? Actions (or behaviors) and attitudes! But not *all* actions and attitudes. There are three types of behavior that have proven to be important determinants of employee performance. These are *productivity, absenteeism,* and *turnover*. The importance of productivity is obvious. Managers are clearly concerned with the quantity and quality of output that each employee generates. But absence and turnover—particularly excessively high rates—can adversely affect this output. In terms of absence, it's hard for an employee to be productive if he or she isn't at work. In addition, high rates of employee turnover increase costs and tend to place less experienced people into jobs.

OB is also concerned with employee job satisfaction, which is an attitude. The reasons managers should be concerned with their employees' job satisfaction are threefold. First, there may be a link between satisfaction and productivity. Second, satisfaction appears to be negatively related to absenteeism and turnover. Finally, it can be argued that managers have a humanistic responsibility to provide their employees with jobs that are challenging and intrinsically rewarding.

The last part of our OB definition that needs elaboration is the term *organization*. The fields of psychology and sociology are well-known disciplines that study behavior, but they do not concentrate solely on work-related issues. OB, in contrast, is specifically concerned with work-related behavior—and *that* takes place in organizations. An organization is a formal structure of planned coordination, involving two or more people, in order to achieve a common goal. It is characterized by authority relationships and some degree of division of labor. So OB encompasses the behavior of people in such diverse organizations as manufacturing and service firms; schools; hospitals; churches; military units; charitable organizations; and local, state, and federal government agencies.

Contributing Disciplines   Organizational behavior is applied behavioral science, and as a result is built upon contributions from a number of behavioral disciplines. The predominant areas are psychology, sociology, social psychology, anthropology, and political science. As we shall learn, psychology's contributions have been mainly at the individual or micro level of analysis, while the latter disciplines have contributed to our understanding of macro concepts—group processes and organization. Figure 1-1 overviews the contributions made toward a distinct field of study: Organizational Behavior.

a.   *Psychology.*   Psychology is the science that seeks to measure, explain, and sometimes change the behavior of humans and other animals. Psychologists concern themselves with studying and attempting to understand individual behavior. Those who have contributed and continue to add to the knowledge of OB are learning theorists, personality theorists, counseling psychologists, and, most important, organizational psychologists. Early organizational psychologists concerned themselves with problems of fatigue, boredom, and any other factor relevant to working conditions that could impede efficient work performance. More recently, their contributions have been expanded to include learning, perception, personality, individual decision making, training, leadership effectiveness, needs and motivational forces, job satisfaction, performance appraisals, attitude measurement, and the shaping of behavior among organizational members to facilitate repetition of desirable behaviors.

b.   *Sociology.*   Whereas psychologists focus their attention on the individual, sociologists study the social system in which individuals fill their roles; that is, people in relation to their fellow human beings. Sociologists have made their greatest contribution to OB through their study of group behavior in organizations, particularly formal and complex organizations. Areas within OB that have received valuable input from sociologists include group dynamics, the socialization process, formal organization theory and structure, bureaucracy, communications, status, power, and conflict.

c.   *Social Psychology.*   A relatively new field in its own right, social psychology examines interpersonal behavior. While psychology and sociology attempt to explain individual and group behavior respectively, social psychology seeks to explain how and why individuals behave as they do in group activities. One of the major areas receiving considerable investigation by social psychologists has been *change*—how to implement it and how to reduce barriers to its acceptance. In addition, we find social psychologists making significant contributions in measuring, understanding, and changing attitudes, communication patterns, group decision making, and the ways in which group activities can satisfy individual needs.

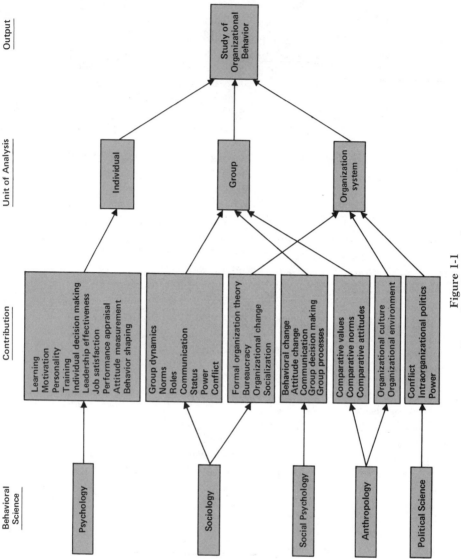

Figure 1-1
Toward an OB Discipline

4

Anthropology. Anthropologists study societies, particularly primitive ones, to learn about human beings and their activities. Recognition that how we behave is a function of our culture, for example, dramatizes the contribution that social anthropologists have made to OB. Differences in fundamental values, attitudes, and norms of acceptable behavior affect the way people act and explain to a considerable degree differences in behavior between, for example, Americans and East Indians, New Englanders and Southerners, or urbanites and those who have spent all their lives in rural or farm communities.

Our individual value systems—our priorities and sense of right and wrong—will affect our attitudes and behavior on the job. The work that anthropologists have done with animals, especially in the ape family, has been valuable in drawing generalizations about individual and group behavior.

2. *Political Science.* Although frequently overlooked, the contributions of political scientists are significant to the understanding of behavior in organizations. Political scientists study the behavior of individuals and groups within a political environment. Specific topics of concern to political scientists include structuring conflict, allocation of power, and how people manipulate power for individual self-interest.

GOALS OF ORGANIZATIONAL BEHAVIOR

What does OB seek to do? We know it is concerned with developing people skills, but what precisely are its goals? The goals of OB are to help you to *explain, predict,* and *control* human behavior.

1. Explanation

When we seek answers to *why* an individual or a group of individuals did something, we are pursuing the explanation objective. It is probably the least important of the three goals, from a management perspective, because it occurs after the fact. Yet if we are to understand a phenomenon, we must begin by trying to explain it. We can then use this understanding to determine a connective cause. For example, if a number of valued employees resign, we undoubtedly want to know why, in order to determine if it was something that could have been prevented. Obviously, employees quit their jobs for many reasons, but if the explanation for a high quit rate is inadequate pay or boring jobs, managers often can take actions that will correct this behavior in the future.

5

2. Prediction

The goal of prediction focuses on future events. It seeks to determine what outcomes will result from a given action. When the manager of an accounting department attempts to assess how department members will respond to the installation of a new computer system, that manager is engaging in a predictive exercise. Based on a knowledge of OB, the manager can predict certain behavioral responses to the change. Of course, there are a number of ways to implement a major change, so the manager is likely to assess employee responses to a number of change interventions. In this way, the manager can anticipate which approaches will generate the least degree of employee resistance and use that information in making his or her decision.

3. Control

The most controversial goal is using OB knowledge to control behavior. When a manager asks, for instance: "What can I do to make Dave put out more effort on his job?", that manager is concerned with control.

Why is control controversial? A democratic society is built upon the concept of personal freedom. Therefore the idea that one person should attempt to get others to behave in some premeditated way, when the subjects of that control may be unaware that their behavior is being manipulated, has been viewed in some circles as unethical and/or repugnant. That OB offers technologies that facilitate the control of people is a fact. Whether these technologies should be used in organizations becomes an ethical question that is beyond the scope of this book. However, you should be aware that the control objective is frequently seen by managers as the most valuable contribution that OB makes toward their effectiveness on the job.

THE PLAN OF THIS BOOK

Our approach to OB will follow a building-block process. As pictured in Figure 1-2, there are three levels of analysis in OB. As we move from the individual level through to the organization system level, we increase in an additive fashion our understanding of behavior in organizations.

Chapters 2 through 5 deal with the individual in the organization. We begin by looking at the foundations of individual behavior—values, attitudes, personality, perception, and learning. Then we move to motivation issues and the topic of individual decision making.

The behavior of people in groups is something more than the sum total of each individual acting in his or her own way. People's behavior in groups is different from their behavior when they are alone. Chapters 6 through 10 address group behavior. We introduce a group behavior model,

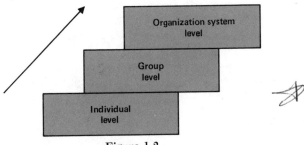

Figure 1-2
Levels of OB Analysis

consider communication issues and group decision making, and then investigate the important topics of leadership, power, politics, and conflict.

Organizational behavior reaches its highest level of sophistication when we add the formal organizational system to our knowledge of individual and group behavior. Just as groups are more than the sum of their individual members, organizations are not necessarily merely the summation of the behavior of a number of groups. In Chapters 11 through 14, we discuss how an organization's structure has an impact on behavior, the effect that an organization's formal performance appraisal and reward system has on people, how each organization has its own culture that acts to mold the behavior of its members, and the various organizational change and development techniques that managers can use to affect behavior for the organization's benefit.

SELECTED REFERENCES

CUMMINGS, LARRY L., "Organizational Behavior in the 1980s," *Decision Science,* Fall 1981, pp. 365–77.

MOHR, LAWRENCE B., *Explaining Organizational Behavior*. San Francisco: Jossey-Bass, 1982.

REITZ, H. JOSEPH, *Behavior in Organizations* (3rd ed.). Homewood, Ill.: Richard D. Irwin, 1987.

ROBBINS, STEPHEN P., *Organizational Behavior: Concepts, Controversies, and Applications* (3rd ed.). Englewood Cliffs, N.J.: Prentice-Hall, 1986.

STAW, BARRY M., "Organizational Behavior: A Review and Reformulation of the Field's Outcome Variables," in *Annual Review of Psychology*, eds. M.R. Rosenzweig and L.W. Porter, Vol. 35, pp. 627–66. Palo Alto, Calif.: Annual Reviews, 1984.

SZILAGYI, ANDREW D., AND MARC J. WALLACE, JR., *Organizational Behavior and Performance* (4th ed.). Glenview, Ill.: Scott, Foresman, 1987.

2

FOUNDATIOΠ/ OF IΠDIVIDUAL BEHAVIOR

An understanding of individual behavior begins with a review of the major psychological contributions to OB. These contributions are subdivided into the following five concepts: values, attitudes, personality, perception, and learning.

VALUES   Is capital punishment right or wrong? How about engaging in sexual relations before marriage—is it right or wrong? If a person likes power, is that good or bad? The answers to these questions are value laden. Some might argue, for example, that capital punishment is right because it is an appropriate retribution for crimes like murder or treason. However, others may argue, just as strongly, that no government has the right to take anyone's life.

Values represent basic convictions that "a specific mode of conduct or end-state of existence is personally or socially preferable to an opposite

8

or converse mode of conduct or end-state of existence."[1] They contain a moral flavor in that they carry an individual's ideas as to what is right, good, or desirable. *Value systems* represent a prioritizing of individual values in relation to their relative importance. In other words, we all have a set of values that form a value system. This system is identified by the relative importance we assign to such values as freedom, pleasure, self-respect, honesty, obedience, equality, and so forth. We all have values and, as you will see, what we think is important influences our attitudes and our behavior.

Importance of Values

Values are important to the study of organizational behavior because they lay the foundation for the understanding of attitudes, perceptions, personality, and motivations. Individuals enter an organization with preconceived notions of what "ought" and what "ought not" to be. Of course, these notions are not value-free. On the contrary, they contain interpretations of right and wrong. Further, they imply that certain behaviors or outcomes are preferred over others. As a result, values cloud objectivity and rationality.

Values generally influence behavior. Suppose you enter an organization with the view that allocating pay on the basis of performance is right, while allocating pay on the basis of seniority is wrong or inferior. How are you going to react should you find that the organization you have just joined rewards seniority and not performance? Would your behavior be different if your values aligned with the organization's pay policies?

Characteristics of Values

A person's values are relatively stable and enduring. The values you hold today are likely to be very similar to those you held last year and the ones you will hold in future years.

The stability and enduring characteristics of values can be explained in terms of the way in which they were originally learned. As children, we are told that a certain behavior or outcome is *always* desirable or *always* undesirable. There are no gray areas. You were told, for example, that you should be honest and responsible. You were never taught to be just a little bit honest or a little bit responsible. It is this learning of values as absolute or "black-or-white" that more or less assures their stability and endurance.

The process of questioning our values, of course, may result in a change. We may decide that these underlying convictions are no longer acceptable. More often, however, our questioning merely acts to reinforce those values we hold.

1. Milton Rokeach, *The Nature of Human Values* (New York: Free Press, 1973), p. 5.

Value Hierarchy   We can categorize individuals by their values. For instance, we can identify a seven-level hierarchy that describes personal values and life styles:[2]

Level 1: Reactive. These individuals are unaware of themselves or others as human beings and react to basic physiological needs. Such individuals are rarely found in organizations. This is most descriptive of newborn babies.

Level 2: Tribalistic. These individuals are characterized by high dependence. They are strongly influenced by tradition and the power exerted by authority figures.

Level 3: Egocentric. These persons believe in rugged individualism. They are aggressive and selfish. They respond primarily to power.

Level 4: Conforming. These individuals have a low tolerance for ambiguity, have difficulty in accepting people whose values differ from their own, and desire that others accept their values.

Level 5: Manipulative. These individuals strive to achieve their goals by manipulating things and people. They are materialistic and actively seek higher status and recognition.

Level 6: Sociocentric. These individuals consider it more important to be liked and to get along with others than to get ahead. They are repulsed by materialism, manipulation, and conformity.

Level 7: Existential. These individuals have a high tolerance for ambiguity and people with differing values. They are outspoken against inflexible systems, restrictive policies, status symbols, and arbitrary use of authority.

The value hierarchy can be used to analyze the problem of disparate values in organizations. Table 2-1 proposes that employees can be segmented by the era in which they entered the work force. Because most people start work between the ages of 18 and 23, the eras also correlate closely with the chronological age of employees.

Workers who grew up during the Great Depression and World War II entered the work force in the 1940s and 1950s believing in the Protestant Work Ethic. Once hired, they tended to be loyal to their employer. Levels 2 and 4 in the value hierarchy characterize these older workers in today's work force.

Employees who entered the work force during the 1960s and 1970s brought with them a large measure of the "hippie ethic" and existential philosophy. They were more concerned with the quality of life than the material quantity of money and possessions. Their desire for autonomy

---

2. Clare W. Graves, "Levels of Existence: An Open System Theory of Values," *Journal of Humanistic Psychology*, Fall 1970, pp. 131–55.

Table 2-1
Dominant Values in Today's Work Force

Stage	Entered the Work Force	Approximate Current Age	Dominant Work Values	Level in the Value Hierarchy
I. Protestant Work Ethic	1940s–1950s	45–70	Hard work, conservative. Loyalty to the organization.	Levels 2 and 4
II. Existentialism	1960s–1970s	30–45	Quality of life. Nonconforming. Seeks autonomy. Loyalty to self.	Levels 6 and 7
III. Pragmatism	1980s	Under 30	Success, achievement, ambition, hard work. Loyalty to career.	Level 5

directed their loyalty toward themselves rather than any organization that employed them. These values align well with levels 6 and 7.

Finally, individuals who entered the work force in the 1980s reflect a return to more traditional values, but with far greater emphasis on achievement and material success. Today's younger worker is a pragmatist. He or she believes that ends can justify means. They see the organizations that employ them merely as vehicles that will propel their careers. The manipulative values of level 5 appear to most closely match this group of employees.

An understanding that people's values differ but tend to reflect the times and societal values of when they grew up can be a valuable aid for explaining and predicting behavior. Employees in their 20s and 50s, for instance, are more likely to be conservative and accepting of authority than their existential peers. Yet, when workers under 30 perceive that their contributions are not being immediately rewarded by their employer, they are more likely to quit their jobs and seek bigger and quicker payoffs somewhere else.

ATTITUDES

Attitudes are evaluative statements—either favorable or unfavorable—concerning objects, people, or events. They reflect how one feels about something. When I say "I like my job," I am expressing my attitude about work.

Attitudes are not the same as values. Values are the broader and more encompassing concept. Attitudes are more specific than values. Values connote a morality, a sense of rightness or desirability. The statement that "discrimination is bad" reflects one's values. "I favor the implementation of an affirmative action program to recruit and develop women for managerial positions in our organization" is an attitude.

A person can have thousands of attitudes, but OB focuses on a very limited number of job-related attitudes. These include job satisfaction; job involvement (the degree to which a person identifies with his or her job and actively participates in it); and organizational commitment (an indicator of loyalty to, and identification with, the organization). Without question, however, job satisfaction has received the bulk of attention.

Job satisfaction refers to an individual's general attitude toward his or her job. A person with a high level of job satisfaction holds positive attitudes toward the job, while a person who is dissatisfied with his or her job holds negative attitudes about the job. When people speak of employee attitudes, more often than not they mean job satisfaction. In fact, the two terms are frequently used interchangeably.

People Seek to Reduce Dissonance

One of the most relevant findings pertaining to attitudes is the fact that individuals seek consistency. The theory of cognitive dissonance suggests that people seek to minimize dissonance.[3] Individuals will attempt to reduce dissonance and hence the discomfort that occurs when there are inconsistencies between two or more of their attitudes, or between their behavior and their attitudes.

Of course, no individual can avoid dissonance completely. You know "honesty is the best policy" but say nothing when a store clerk gives you back too much change. Or you tell your children to brush after every meal, but *you* don't. So how do people cope? A person's desire to reduce dissonance is determined by the importance of the elements creating the dissonance, the degree of influence the individual believes he or she has over the elements, and the rewards that may be involved in dissonance.

If the elements creating the dissonance are relatively unimportant, the pressure to correct this imbalance will be low. However, say a corporate manager—Mrs. Smith, who has a husband and several children—believes strongly that no company should pollute the air or water. Unfortunately, because of the requirements of her job, Mrs. Smith is placed in the position of having to make decisions that would trade off her company's profitability against her attitudes on pollution. She knows that dumping the company's sewage into the local river (which we shall assume is legal) is in the best economic interest of her firm. What will she do? Clearly, Mrs. Smith is experiencing a high degree of cognitive dissonance. Because of the importance of the elements in this example, we cannot expect Mrs. Smith to ignore the inconsistency. There are several paths that she can follow to deal with her dilemma. She can change her behavior (stop polluting the river). Or she can reduce dissonance by concluding that the dissonant behavior is not so important after all ("I've got to make a living and, in my role as a corporate decision maker, I often have to place the good of my company above that of the environment or society"). A third alternative would be for Mrs. Smith to change her attitude ("There is nothing wrong in polluting the river"). Still another choice would be to seek out more consonant elements to outweigh the dissonant ones ("The benefits to society from manufacturing our products more than offset the cost to society of the resulting water pollution").

The degree of influence that individuals believe they have over the elements will have an impact on how they will react to the dissonance. If they perceive the dissonance to be an uncontrollable result—something over which they have no choice—they are less likely to be receptive to attitude change. If, for example, the dissonance-producing behavior was required as a result of the boss's directive, the pressure to reduce dissonance would be less than if the behavior were performed voluntarily. Although dissonance exists, it can be rationalized and justified.

3. Leon Festinger, *A Theory of Cognitive Dissonance* (Stanford, Calif.: Stanford University Press, 1957).

Rewards also influence the degree to which individuals are motivated to reduce dissonance. The tension inherent in high dissonance may be reduced when accompanied by a high reward. The reward acts to reduce dissonance by increasing the consistency side of the individual's balance sheet. Since people in organizations are given some form of reward or remuneration for their services, employees often can deal with greater dissonance on their jobs than off their jobs.

These moderating factors suggest that just because individuals experience dissonance, they will not necessarily move directly toward consistency; that is, toward reduction of this dissonance. If the issues underlying the dissonance are of minimal importance, if an individual perceives that the dissonance is externally imposed and is substantially uncontrollable by him, or if rewards are significant enough to offset the dissonance, the individual will not be under great tension to reduce the dissonance.

What are the organizational implications of the theory of cognitive dissonance? It can help to predict the propensity to engage in both attitude and behavioral change. For example, if individuals are required, by the demands of their job, to say or to do things that contradict their personal attitude, they will tend to modify their attitude in order to make it compatible with the cognition of what they have said or done. Additionally, the greater the dissonance—after it has been moderated by importance, choice, and reward factors—the greater the pressures to reduce the dissonance.

The Attitude-Behavior Relationship The early research on the relationship between attitudes and behavior assumed them to be causally related; that is, the attitudes people hold determine what they do. Common sense, too, suggests a relationship. Is it not logical that people watch television programs that they say they like or that employees try to avoid assignments they find distasteful?

However, in the late 1960s, this assumed relationship between attitudes and behavior (A-B) was challenged by a review of the research.[4] Based on an evaluation of a number of studies that investigated the A-B relationship, the reviewer concluded that attitudes were unrelated to behavior or, at best, only slightly related. More recent research has demonstrated that there is indeed a measurable relationship if moderating contingency variables are taken into consideration.

One thing that improves our chances of finding significant A-B relationships is the use of both specific attitudes and specific behaviors. It is one thing to talk about a person's attitude toward "being socially responsi-

---

4. A. W. Wicker, "Attitude versus Action: The Relationship of Verbal and Overt Behavioral Responses to Attitude Objects," *Journal of Social Issues*, Autumn 1969, pp. 41–78.

ble" and another to speak of her attitude toward "donating $25 to the National Multiple Sclerosis Society." The more specific the attitude we are measuring and the more specific we are in identifying a related behavior, the greater the probability that we can show a relationship between A and B.

Another moderator is social constraints on behavior. Discrepancies between attitudes and behavior may occur because the social pressures on the individual to behave in a certain way may hold exceptional power. Group pressures, for instance, may explain why an employee who holds strong anti-union attitudes attends pro-union organizing meetings.

Of course, A and B may be at odds for other reasons. Individuals can and do hold contradictory attitudes at a given time, though, as we have noted, there are pressures toward consistency. Additionally, other things besides attitudes influence behavior. But it is fair to say that, in spite of some attacks, most A-B studies yield positive results—in other words, attitudes *do* influence behavior.

PERSONALITY

Some people are quiet and passive, while others are loud and aggressive. When we describe people in terms of characteristics such as quiet, passive, loud, aggressive, ambitious, loyal, or sociable, we are categorizing them in terms of personality traits. An individual's *personality*, therefore, is the combination of psychological traits we use to classify that person.

Psychologists have studied personality traits extensively, resulting in the identification of sixteen primary personality traits.[5] They are shown in Table 2-2. Notice that each trait is bi-polar; that is, each has two extremes (e.g., reserved-outgoing). These sixteen traits have been found to be generally steady and constant sources of behavior, allowing prediction of an individual's behavior in specific situations by weighing the characteristics for their situational relevance. Unfortunately, the relevance of these traits for understanding behavior in organizations is far from clear.

Key Personality Attributes

Four personality attributes have been identified that appear to have more direct relevance for explaining and predicting behavior in organizations. These are: locus of control, authoritarianism, Machiavellianism, and risk propensity.

Some people believe that they are masters of their own fate. Other people see themselves as pawns of fate, believing that what happens to them in their lives is due to luck or chance. *Locus of control* in the first

5. Raymond B. Cattell, "Personality Pinned Down," *Psychology Today*, July 1973, pp. 40–46.

Table 2-2
Sixteen Primary Traits

1.	Reserved	Outgoing
2.	Less intelligent	More intelligent
3.	Affected by feelings	Emotionally stable
4.	Submissive	Dominant
5.	Serious	Happy-go-lucky
6.	Expedient	Conscientious
7.	Timid	Venturesome
8.	Tough-minded	Sensitive
9.	Trusting	Suspicious
10.	Practical	Imaginative
11.	Forthright	Shrewd
12.	Self-assured	Apprehensive
13.	Conservative	Experimenting
14.	Group-dependent	Self-sufficient
15.	Uncontrolled	Controlled
16.	Relaxed	Tense

case is internal; these people believe they control their destiny. Those who see their life controlled by outsiders are externals.[6] The evidence shows that employees who rate high in externality are less satisfied with their jobs, more alienated from the work setting, and less involved on their jobs than are internals. A manager might also expect to find that externals blame a poor performance evaluation on their boss's prejudice, their co-workers, or other events outside their control. Internals would probably explain the same evaluation in terms of their own actions.

Authoritarianism is the belief that there should be status and power differences among people in organizations. The extremely high authoritarian personality is intellectually rigid, judgmental of others, deferential to those above and exploitative of those below, distrustful, and resistant to change. Of course, few people are extreme authoritarians, so conclusions must be guarded. It seems reasonable to postulate, however, that possessing a high authoritarian personality would be related negatively to performance where the job demands sensitivity to the feelings of others, tact, and the ability to adapt to complex and changing situations. On the other hand, where jobs are highly structured and success depends on close conformity to rules and regulations, the high authoritarian employee should perform quite well.

Closely related to authoritarianism is *Machiavellianism* (Mach), named after Niccolo Machiavelli, who wrote in the sixteenth century on

---

6. Paul Spector, "Behavior in Organizations as a Function of Employee's Locus of Control," *Psychological Bulletin*, May 1982, pp. 482–97.

how to gain and manipulate power. An individual exhibiting strong Machia-vellian tendencies is pragmatic, maintains emotional distance, and believes that ends can justify means.[7] "If it works, use it" is consistent with a high Mach perspective. Do high Machs make good employees? That answer depends on the type of job and whether you consider ethical implications in evaluating performance. In jobs that require bargaining skills (such as labor negotiator) or where there are substantial rewards for winning (as in commissioned sales), high Machs will be productive. But if the ends can't justify the means or if there are no absolute standards of performance, our ability to predict a high Mach's performance will be severely curtailed.

People differ in their willingness to take chances. Individuals with a high *risk propensity* make more rapid decisions and use less information in making their choices than low risk propensity individuals.[8] Managers might use this information to align employee risk-taking propensity with specific job demands. For instance, a high risk-taking propensity may lead to more effective performance for a stock trader in a brokerage firm. This type of job demands rapid decision making. On the other hand, this personality characteristic might prove a major obstacle to an accountant who performs auditing activities. This latter job might be better filled by someone with a low risk-taking propensity.

Matching Personalities and Jobs   Obviously, individual personalities differ. So, too, do jobs. Following this logic, efforts have been made to match the proper personalities with the proper jobs. The most researched personality job-fit theory is the six-personality-types model. This model states that an employee's satisfaction with and propensity to leave his or her job depends on the degree to which the individual's personality matches his or her occupational environment.[9] Six major personality types have been identified. They are listed in Table 2-3, along with their compatible occupations.

A Vocational Preference Inventory questionnaire has been developed that contains 160 occupational titles. Respondents indicate which of these occupations they like or dislike and their answers are used to form personality profiles. Utilizing this procedure, research strongly supports the hexagonal diagram in Figure 2-1. This figure shows that the closer two fields or orienta-tions are in the hexagon, the more compatible they are. Adjacent categories are quite similar, while those diagonally opposite are highly dissimilar.

7. R. G. Vleeming, "Machiavellianism: A Preliminary Review," *Psychological Reports*, February 1979, pp. 295–310.

8. R. N. Taylor and M. D. Dunnette, "Influence of Dogmatism, Risk-Taking Propensity, and Intelligence on Decision-Making Strategies for a Sample of Industrial Managers," *Journal of Applied Psychology*, August 1974, pp. 420–23.

9. Arnold R. Spokane, "A Review of Research on Person-Environment Congruence in Holland's Theory of Careers," *Journal of Vocational Behavior*, June 1985, pp. 306–43.

Table 2-3
Personality Types and Compatible Occupations

Personality Types	Occupations
1. *Realistic*—involves aggressive behavior, physical activities requiring skill, strength, and coordination	Forestry, farming, architecture
2. *Investigative*—involves activities requiring thinking, organizing, and understanding rather than feeling or emotion	Biology, mathematics, news reporting
3. *Social*—involves interpersonal rather than intellectual or physical activities	Foreign service, social work, clinical psychology
4. *Conventional*—involves rule-regulated activities and sublimation of personal needs to an organization or person of power and status	Accounting, finance, corporate management
5. *Enterprising*—involves verbal activities to influence others, to attain power and status	Law, public relations, small business management
6. *Artistic*—involves self-expression, artistic creation, or emotional activities	Art, music, writing

What does all this mean? The theory argues that satisfaction is highest and turnover lowest where personality and occupation are in agreement. Social individuals should be in social jobs, conventional people in conventional jobs, and so forth. A realistic person in a realistic job is in a more congruent situation than a realistic person in an investigative job. A realistic person in a social job is in the most incongruent situation possible. The key points of this model are that (1) there do appear to be intrinsic personality differences among individuals; (2) there are different types of jobs; and (3) people in job environments congruent with their personality type should be more satisfied and less likely to resign voluntarily than people in incongruent jobs.

PERCEPTION   *Perception* is a process by which individuals organize and interpret their sensory impressions in order to give meaning to their environment. Research on perception consistently demonstrates that different individuals may look at the same thing, yet perceive it differently. The fact is that none of us sees reality. What we do is interpret what we see and call it reality.

Factors Influencing Perception   How do we explain the fact that people perceive the same thing differently? A number of factors operate to shape and sometimes distort perception. These factors can reside in the *perceiver*, in the object or *target* being perceived, or in the context of the *situation* in which the perception is made.

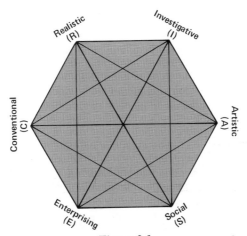

Figure 2-1
**Hexagonal Diagram of the Relationship
among Occupational Personality Types**

Source: From John L. Holland, *Making Vocational Choices:
A Theory of Careers* (Englewood Cliffs, N.J.: Prentice-Hall,
1973), p. 23. Used by permission. [This model originally
appeared in J.L. Holland et al., "An Empirical Occupational
Classification Derived from a Theory of Personality and Intended for Practice and Research," ACT Research Report
No. 29 (Iowa City): The American College Testing Program,
1969.]

When an individual looks at a target and attempts to interpret what
he or she sees, that interpretation is heavily influenced by personal characteristics of the individual perceiver. Personal characteristics affecting perception include attitudes, personality, motives, interests, past experiences,
and expectations.

Characteristics of the target being observed can affect what is perceived. Loud people are more likely to be noticed in a group than quiet
ones. So, too, are extremely attractive or unattractive individuals. Because
targets are not looked at in isolation, the relationship of a target to its
background influences perception, as does our tendency to group close
things and similar things together.

The context in which we see objects or events is also important. The
time at which an object or event is seen can influence attention, as can
location, light, heat, or any number of situational factors.

Attribution Theory

Much of the research on perception
is directed at inanimate objects. But
OB is concerned with human beings, so our discussion of perception
should focus on person perception.

Our perceptions of people differ from our perceptions of inanimate objects like desks, machines, or buildings because we make inferences about the actions of people that we don't make about inanimate objects. Nonliving objects are subject to the laws of nature, but they have no beliefs, motives, or intentions. People do. The result is that when we observe people, we attempt to develop explanations of why they behave in certain ways. Our perception and judgment of a person's actions, therefore, will be significantly influenced by the assumptions we make about the person's internal state.

Attribution theory has been proposed to develop explanations of how we judge people differently depending on what meaning we attribute to a given behavior. Basically, the theory suggests that when we observe an individual's behavior, we attempt to determine whether it was internally or externally caused. That determination, however, depends on three factors: (1) distinctiveness, (2) consensus, and (3) consistency. First, let's clarify the differences between internal and external causation, then elaborate on each of the three determining factors.

Internally caused behaviors are those that are believed to be under the personal control of the individual. Externally caused behavior results from outside causes; that is, the person is seen as forced into the behavior by the situation. If one of your employees were late for work, you might attribute his lateness to his partying into the wee hours of the morning and then oversleeping. This would be an internal interpretation. But if you attributed his arriving late to a major automobile accident that tied up traffic on the road that your employee regularly uses, then you would be making an external attribution. As observers, we have a tendency to assume that others' behavior is internally controlled, while we tend to exaggerate the degree to which our own behavior is externally determined. But this is a broad generalization. There still exists a considerable amount of deviation in attribution, depending on how we interpret the distinctiveness, consensus, and consistency of the actions.

Distinctiveness refers to whether or not an individual displays different behaviors in different situations. Is the employee who arrives late today also the source of complaints by co-workers for being a "goof-off"? What we want to know is if this behavior is unusual or not. If it is, the observer is likely to give the behavior an external attribution. If this action is not unique, it will probably be judged as internal.

If everyone who is faced with a similar situation responds in the same way, we can say the behavior shows *consensus*. Our tardy employee's behavior would meet this criterion if all employees who took the same route to work were also late. From an attribution perspective, if consensus is high you would be expected to give an external attribution to the employee's tardiness; whereas if other employees who took the same route made it to work on time, your conclusion for causation would be internal.

Finally, an observer looks for *consistency* in a person's actions. Does the person respond the same way over time? Coming in ten minutes late for work is not perceived in the same way if for one employee it represents an unusual case (she hasn't been late for several months), while for another it is part of a routine pattern (she is regularly late two or three times a week). The more consistent the behavior, the more the observer is inclined to attribute it to internal causes.

The above explains what you have seen operating for years. All similar behaviors are not perceived similarly. We look at actions and judge them within their situational context. If you have a reputation as a good student yet blow one test in a course, the instructor is more likely to disregard the poor exam. Why? He or she will attribute the cause of this unusual performance to external conditions. It may not be your fault! But for the student who has a consistent record of being a poor performer, it is unlikely the teacher will ignore the low test score. Similarly, if everyone in class blew the test, the instructor might attribute the outcome to external causes rather than to causes under the students' own control. (He or she might conclude that the questions were poorly written, the room was too warm, or that the students didn't have the necessary prerequisites.)

Shortcuts to Judging Others

Making judgments about others is done all the time by people in organizations. For example, managers regularly evaluate the performance of their employees, and operatives assess whether their co-workers are putting forth their full effort or not. But making judgments about others is difficult. To make the task easier, individuals take shortcuts. Some of these shortcuts are valuable—they allow us to make accurate perceptions rapidly and provide valid data for making predictions. However, they can also result in significant distortions.

Individuals cannot assimilate all they observe, so they engage in *selectivity*. They take in bits and pieces. But these bits and pieces are not chosen randomly; rather, they are selectively chosen depending on the interests, background, experience, and attitudes of the observer. Selective perception allows us to "speed read" others, but not without the risk of drawing an inaccurate picture.

It is easy to judge others if we assume they are similar to us. *Assumed similarity*, or the "like me" effect, results in an individual's perception of others being influenced more by what the observer is like than by what the person being observed is like. If you want challenge and responsibility in your job, you may assume others want the same. People who assume others are like them will be right some of the time, but only in those cases when they judge someone who is actually like them. The rest of the time, they're wrong.

When we judge someone on the basis of our perception of the group to which he or she belongs, we are using the shortcut called *stereotyping*. "Married people are more stable employees than singles" or "union people expect something for nothing" are examples of stereotypes. To the degree that a stereotype is a factual generalization, it helps in making accurate judgments. But many stereotypes have no foundation in fact. In these latter cases, stereotypes distort judgments.

When we draw a general impression about an individual based on a single characteristic such as intelligence, sociability, or appearance, a *halo effect* is operating. It is not unusual for the halo effect to occur during selection interviews. A sloppily dressed candidate for a marketing research position may be perceived by an interviewer as an irresponsible person with an unprofessional attitude and marginal abilities, when in fact the candidate may be highly responsible, professional, and competent. What has happened is that a single trait—appearance—has overridden other characteristics in the interviewer's general perception about the individual.

LEARNING The final concept introduced in this chapter is learning. It is included for the obvious reason that almost all complex human behavior is learned. If we want to explain, predict, or control behavior, we need to understand how people learn.

The psychologist's definition of learning is considerably broader than the lay person's view that "it's what we did when we went to school." In actuality, each of us is continuously going "to school." Learning is going on all the time. A more correct definition of *learning*, therefore, is any relatively permanent change in behavior that occurs as a result of experience.

How do we learn? Figure 2-2 summarizes the learning process. First, learning helps us to adapt to, and master, our environment. By changing our behavior to accommodate changing conditions, we become responsible citizens and productive employees. But learning is built upon the *law of effect*, which says that behavior is a function of its consequences.[10] Behavior that is followed by a favorable consequence tends to be repeated; behavior followed by an unfavorable consequence tends not to be repeated. Consequence, in this terminology, refers to anything a person considers rewarding (i.e., money, praise, promotions, a smile). If your boss compliments you on your sales approach, you're likely to repeat that behavior. Conversely, if you're reprimanded for your sales approach, you're less likely to repeat it. But the keys to the learning process are the two the-

---

10. Edward L. Thorndike, *Educational Psychology: The Psychology of Learning* (New York: Columbia University Press, 1913); and B.F. Skinner, *Beyond Freedom and Dignity* (New York: Knopf, 1971).

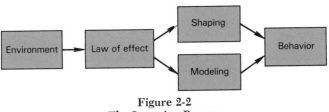

Figure 2-2
The Learning Process

ories, or explanations, of how we learn. One is *shaping* and the other is *modeling*.

When learning takes place in graduated steps, it is shaped. Managers shape employee behavior by systematically reinforcing, through rewards, each successive step that moves the employee closer to the desired behavior. Much of our learning has been done by shaping. When we speak of "learning by mistakes," we are referring to shaping. We try, we fail, and we try again. Through such series of trial-and-error, most of us have mastered such skills as riding a bicycle, performing basic mathematical computations, taking classroom notes, and answering multiple-choice tests.

In addition to shaping, much of what we have learned is the result of observing others and modeling our behavior after them. While trial-and-error is usually a slow learning process, modeling can produce complex behavioral changes quite rapidly. For instance, most of us, at one time or another, when having trouble in school or in a particular class, look around to find someone who seems to have the system down pat. Then we observe that person to see what he or she is doing that is different from our approach. If we find some differences, we then incorporate them into our behavior repertoire. If our performance improves (a favorable consequence), we're likely to make a permanent change in our behavior to reflect what we've seen work for others. The process is the same at work as it is in school. A new employee, who wants to be successful on her job, is likely to look for someone in the organization who is well-respected and successful, and then try to imitate that person's behavior.

IMPLICATIONS FOR MANAGERS This chapter has introduced a number of psychological concepts. Let's now turn toward putting them together and demonstrating their importance for the manager who is trying to understand organizational behavior.

Figure 2-3 summarizes our discussion of individual behavior. In very simplified terms, we can say that an individual enters an organization with

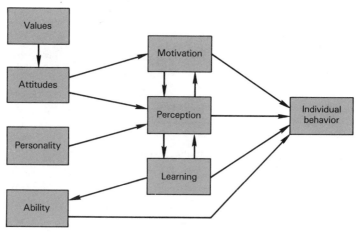

Figure 2-3
Key Variables Affecting Individual Behavior

a relatively entrenched set of values and attitudes, and a substantially established personality. While not permanently fixed, an employee's values, attitudes, and personality are essentially "givens" at the time he or she enters an organization. How employees interpret their work environment (perception) will influence their level of motivation (the topic of the next chapter), what they learn on the job, and, eventually, their individual work behavior. We've also added *ability* to our model to acknowledge that an individual's behavior is influenced by the talents and skills that person holds when he or she joins the organization. Learning, of course, will alter this variable over time.

Values Why should a manager seek to know an individual's values? Though they don't directly have an impact on behavior, values strongly influence a person's attitudes. So knowledge of an individual's value system can provide insight into his or her attitudes.

In general terms, knowledge of when an individual entered the work force can be used to predict his or her basic values and responses to certain managerial practices. For instance, employees who joined the labor force in the late 1960s are more likely to value autonomy in their jobs. Therefore, you should expect them to be more receptive to management's efforts to reduce rules and regulations, decentralize decision making, and give employees more say in how they do their jobs than their co-workers who entered the work force twenty years earlier. On a more individual level, managers can use the seven-level value hierarchy to characterize potential employees and determine if their values align with the dominant values of the organization. An employee's performance and satisfaction are likely to be higher if his or her values fit well with the organization. For instance, the egocentric individualist is poorly matched with an organization that seeks conformity from its employees. Managers are more likely to appreciate employees who fit in; and employees are more likely to be satisfied if they perceive that they fit in.

Attitudes

Managers should be interested in their employees' attitudes because attitudes influence behavior. Satisfied employees, for instance, have lower rates of turnover and absenteeism. Given that managers want to keep resignations and absences down—especially among their more productive employees—they will want to do those things that will generate positive job attitudes.

Managers should also be aware that employees will try to reduce cognitive dissonance. More importantly, dissonance can be managed. If employees are required to engage in activities that appear inconsistent to them or that are at odds with their attitudes, the pressures to reduce the resulting dissonance are lessened when the employee perceives that the dissonance is externally imposed and is beyond his or her control, or if the rewards are significant enough to offset the dissonance.

Personality

The major value of a manager's understanding personality differences probably lies in selection. You are likely to have higher-performing and more satisfied employees if consideration is given to matching personality types with compatible jobs. In addition, there may be other benefits. For instance, managers can expect that individuals with an external locus of control may be less satisfied with their jobs than internals and also that they may be less willing to accept responsibility for their actions.

Perception

Managers need to recognize that their employees react to perceptions, not reality. So whether a manager's appraisal of an employee is *actually* objective and unbiased or whether the organization's wage levels are *actually* among the highest in the industry is less relevant than what employees perceive. If individuals perceive appraisals to be biased or wage levels as low, they will behave as if these conditions actually exist. Employees organize and interpret what they see; this creates the potential for perceptual distortion.

The message to managers should be clear: They need to pay close attention to how employees perceive both their jobs and management practices. Remember, the competent employee who quits for an invalid reason is just as "gone" as one who quits for a valid reason.

Learning   The issue isn't whether employees continually learn on the job or not. They do! The only issue is whether managers are going to let employee learning occur randomly or whether they are going to manage learning—through the rewards they allocate and the examples they set. If marginal employees are rewarded with pay raises and promotions, they will have little reason to change their behavior. If managers want behavior A, but reward behavior B, it shouldn't surprise them to find employees learning to engage in behavior B. Similarly, managers should expect that employees will look to them as models. Managers who are constantly late to work, or take two hours for lunch, or help themselves to company office supplies for personal use, should expect employees to read the message they're sending and model their behavior accordingly.

SELECTED REFERENCES

COOPER, JOEL, AND ROBERT T. B. CROYLE, "Attitudes and Attitude Change," in *Annual Review of Psychology*, eds. M.R. Rosenzweig and L.W. Porter, Vol. 35, pp. 395–426. Palo Alto, Calif.: Annual Reviews, 1984.

FELDMAN, DANIEL C., AND HUGH J. ARNOLD, "Personality Types and Career Patterns: Some Empirical Evidence on Holland's Model," *Canadian Journal of Administrative Science*, January 1985, pp. 192–210.

IAFFALDANO, MICHELLE T., AND PAUL M. MUCHINSKY, "Job Satisfaction and Job Performance: A Meta-Analysis," *Psychological Bulletin*, March 1985, pp. 251–73.

KELLEY, HAROLD H. AND J. L. MICHELA, "Attribution Theory and Research," in *Annual Review of Psychology*, eds. M.R. Rosenzweig and L.W. Porter, Vol. 31, pp. 457–501. Palo Alto, Calif.: Annual Reviews, 1980.

LUTHANS, FRED, AND ROBERT KREITNER, *Organizational Behavior Modification and Beyond: An Operant and Social Learning Approach.* Glenview, Ill.: Scott, Foresman, 1984.

WEISS, HAROLD, AND SEYMOUR ADLER, "Personality and Organizational Behavior," in *Research in Organizational Behavior*, eds. B. M. Staw and L. L. Cummings, Vol. 6, pp. 1–50. Greenwich, Conn.: JAI Press, 1984.

3

UNDERSTANDING MOTIVATION

⟸ **IDEAS TO BE FOUND** ⟹
IN THIS CHAPTER

- Motivation
- Hierarchy of needs
- Theory X and Y
- Hygiene factors
- Achievement need
- Goal-setting theory
- Reinforcement theory
- Equity theory
- Expectancy theory

Referring to their son or daughter, parents have said it for so many years that it has achieved cliché status: "He/she has the ability but just won't apply him/herself." Few of us work to, or even near, our potential, and most of us will admit to that. Einstein underscored his belief in the importance of hard work for achieving success when he said that "genius is 10 percent inspiration and 90 percent perspiration." The fact is that some people work harder or exert more effort than others. The result is that individuals of lesser ability can, and do, outperform their more gifted counterparts. For this reason, an individual's performance at work or otherwise depends not only on ability but on motivation as well. This chapter will consider various explanations of why some people exert more effort on their jobs than do others. We'll also extract from these explanations a set of general guidelines to help you motivate others more effectively.

WHAT IS MOTIVATION?   We might define motivation in terms of some outward behavior. People who are motivated exert a greater effort to perform than those who are not

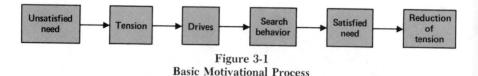

Figure 3-1
Basic Motivational Process

motivated. However, such a definition is relative and tells us little. A more descriptive but less substantive definition would say that motivation is the willingness to do something, and is conditioned by this action's ability to satisfy some need for the individual. A need, in our terminology, means a physiological or psychological deficiency that makes certain outcomes appear attractive. This motivation process can be seen in Figure 3-1.

An unsatisfied need creates tension, which stimulates drives within the individual. These drives generate a search to find particular goals that, if attained, will satisfy the need and lead to the reduction of tension.

Motivated employees are in a state of tension. In order to relieve this tension, they engage in activity. The greater the tension, the more activity will be needed to bring about relief. Therefore, when we see employees working hard at some activity, we can conclude that they are driven by a desire to achieve some goal that they value.

EARLY THEORIES OF MOTIVATION

The decade of the 1950s was a fruitful period in the development of motivation concepts. Three specific theories were formulated during this period, which, though now heavily attacked and their validity called into question, are probably still the best-known explanations for employee motivation. These are: the hierarchy of needs theory, Theory X and Y, and the motivation-hygiene theory. As you'll see later in this chapter, we have since developed more valid explanations of motivation, but you should know these early theories for at least two reasons: (1) they represent a foundation from which contemporary theories have grown, and (2) practicing managers regularly use these theories and their terminologies in explaining employee motivation.

Hierarchy of Needs Theory

It's probably safe to say that the best-known theory of motivation is Abraham Maslow's hierarchy of needs.[1] He hypothesized that within every human being there exists a hierarchy of five needs. These needs are:

1. Abraham Maslow, *Motivation and Personality* (New York: Harper & Row, 1954).

1. **Physiological**—includes hunger, thirst, shelter, sex, and other bodily needs
2. **Safety**—includes security and protection from physical and emotional harm
3. **Social**—includes affection, a sense of belonging, acceptance, and friendship
4. **Esteem**—includes internal factors such as self-respect, autonomy, and achievement; and external factors such as status, recognition, and attention
5. **Self-actualization**—the drive to become what one is capable of becoming; includes growth, achieving one's potential, and self-fulfillment

As each of these needs becomes substantially satisfied, the next need becomes dominant. In terms of Figure 3-2, the individual moves up the hierarchy. From the standpoint of motivation, Maslow's theory would say that although no need is ever fully gratified, a substantially satisfied need no longer motivates.

Maslow separated the five needs into higher and lower orders. Physiological and safety needs were described as lower-order; social, esteem, and self-actualization were categorized as higher-order needs. The differentiation between the two orders was made on the premise that higher-order needs are satisfied internally, whereas lower-order needs are predominantly satisfied externally (by such things as wages, union contracts, and tenure). In fact, the natural conclusion to be drawn from Maslow's classification is that, in times of economic plenty, almost all permanently employed workers will have their lower-order needs substantially met.

Figure 3-2
Maslow's Hierarchy of Needs

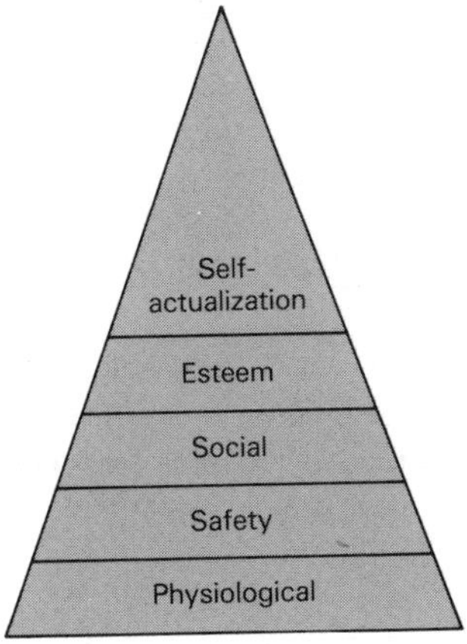

29

Maslow's need theory has received wide recognition, particularly among practicing managers. This can be attributed to the logic and ease with which the theory is intuitively understood. Unfortunately, however, research does not generally validate the theory. For instance, little support is found for the prediction that need structures are organized along the dimensions proposed by Maslow or the prediction that the substantial satisfaction of a given need leads to the activation of the next higher need. So, although the need hierarchy is well known and undoubtedly used by many managers as a guide toward motivating their employees, there is little substantive evidence to indicate that following the theory will lead to a more motivated work force.

Theory X and Y

Douglas McGregor proposed two distinct views of human beings: one basically negative, labeled Theory X, and the other basically positive, labeled Theory Y.[2] After viewing the way managers dealt with employees, McGregor concluded that a manager's view of the nature of human beings is based on a certain grouping of assumptions, and that he or she tends to mold his or her behavior toward subordinates according to these assumptions.

Under Theory X, the four assumptions held by the manager are:

1. Employees inherently dislike work and, whenever possible, will attempt to avoid it.
2. Since employees dislike work, they must be coerced, controlled, or threatened with punishment to achieve desired goals.
3. Employees will shirk responsibilities and seek formal direction whenever possible.
4. Most workers place security above all other factors associated with work, and will display little ambition.

In contrast to these negative views toward the nature of human beings, McGregor listed four other assumptions that he called Theory Y:

1. Employees can view work as being as natural as rest or play.
2. A person will exercise self-direction and self-control if he is committed to the objectives.
3. The average person can learn to accept, even seek, responsibility.
4. Creativity—that is, the ability to make good decisions—is widely dispersed throughout the population, and not necessarily the sole province of those in management functions.

2. Douglas McGregor, *The Human Side of Enterprise* (New York: McGraw-Hill, 1960).

What are the motivational implications if you accept McGregor's analysis? The answer is best expressed in the framework presented by Maslow. Theory X assumes that lower-order needs dominate individuals. Theory Y assumes that higher-order needs dominate individuals. McGregor, himself, held to the belief that Theory Y assumptions were more valid than Theory X. Therefore, he proposed ideas like participation in decision making, responsible and challenging jobs, and good group relations as approaches that would maximize an employee's job motivation.

Unfortunately, there is no evidence to confirm that either set of assumptions is valid, or that acceptance of Theory Y assumptions and altering one's actions accordingly will lead to more motivated workers. As will become evident later in this chapter, either Theory X or Theory Y assumptions may be appropriate in a particular situation.

Motivation-Hygiene Theory

The motivation-hygiene theory was proposed by psychologist Frederick Herzberg.[3] In the belief that an individual's relation to his work is a basic one and that his attitude to his work can very well determine his success or failure, Herzberg investigated the question, "What do people want from their jobs?" He asked people to describe, in detail, situations in which they felt exceptionally good or bad about their jobs. These responses were tabulated and categorized. Factors affecting job attitudes, as reported in twelve investigations conducted by Herzberg, are illustrated in Figure 3-3.

From the categorized responses, Herzberg concluded that the replies people gave when they felt good about their jobs were significantly different from the replies given when they felt bad. As seen in Figure 3-3, certain characteristics tend to be consistently related to job satisfaction, and others to job dissatisfaction. Intrinsic factors, such as achievement, recognition, the work itself, responsibility, and advancement seem to be related to job satisfaction. When those questioned felt good about their work, they tended to attribute these characteristics to themselves. On the other hand, when they were dissatisfied, they tended to cite extrinsic factors, such as company policy and administration, supervision, interpersonal relations, and working conditions.

The data suggest, says Herzberg, that the opposite of satisfaction is not dissatisfaction, as was traditionally believed. Removing dissatisfying characteristics from a job does not necessarily make the job satisfying. Herzberg proposes that his findings indicate the existence of a dual continuum: the opposite of "Satisfaction" is "No Satisfaction," and the opposite of "Dissatisfaction" is "No Dissatisfaction."

3. Frederick Herzberg, B. Mausner, and B. Snyderman, *The Motivation to Work* (New York: John Wiley and Sons, 1959).

Factors characterizing 1,844 events on the job that led to *extreme dissatisfaction*

Factors characterizing 1,753 events on the job that led to *extreme satisfaction*

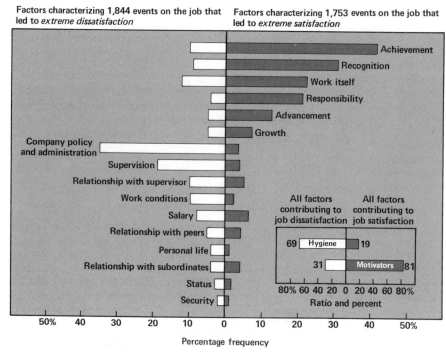

Figure 3-3
Comparison of Satisfiers and Dissatisfiers
Source: Frederick Herzberg, "One More Time; How Do You Motivate Employees?" *Harvard Business Review*, January-February 1968, p. 57. With permission. Copyright © 1967 by the President and Fellows of Harvard College; all rights reserved.

According to Herzberg, the factors leading to job satisfaction are separate and distinct from those that lead to job dissatisfaction. Therefore, managers who seek to eliminate factors that can create job dissatisfaction may bring about peace, but not necessarily motivation. They will be placating their work force rather than motivating them. As a result, such characteristics as company policy and administration, supervision, interpersonal relations, working conditions, and salary have been characterized by Herzberg as hygiene factors. When they are adequate, people will not be dissatisfied; however, neither will they be satisfied. If we want to motivate people on their jobs, Herzberg suggests emphasizing achievement, recognition, the work itself, responsibility, and growth. These are the characteristics that people find intrinsically rewarding.

The motivation-hygiene theory is not without its detractors. The criticisms of the theory include:

1. The procedure that Herzberg used is limited by its methodology. When things are going well, people tend to take credit themselves. Contrarily, they blame failure on the extrinsic environment.

2. The reliability of Herzberg's methodology is questioned. Since raters have to make interpretations, it is possible that they may contaminate the findings by interpreting one response in one manner while treating a similar response differently.

3. No overall measure of satisfaction was utilized. A person may dislike part of his or her job, yet still think the job is acceptable.

4. The theory is inconsistent with previous research. The motivation-hygiene theory ignores situational variables.

5. Herzberg assumes that there is a relationship between satisfaction and productivity, but the research methodology he used looked only at satisfaction, not at productivity. To make such research relevant, one must assume a strong relationship between satisfaction and productivity.

Regardless of criticisms, Herzberg's theory has been widely popularized and few managers are unfamiliar with his recommendations. As a case in point, much of the enthusiasm in the late 1960s and early 1970s for vertically expanding jobs to allow workers greater responsibility in planning and controlling their work (which we will discuss in Chapter 4) can probably be attributed largely to Herzberg's findings and recommendations.

CONTEMPORARY THEORIES OF MOTIVATION The previous theories are well known but, unfortunately, have not held up well under close examination. However, all is not lost. We have a number of contemporary theories that have one thing in common—to date, each has a reasonable degree of valid supporting documentation. Of course, this doesn't mean that the theories we are about to introduce are necessarily right. Maybe they just haven't been disproved yet. Nevertheless, the following theories represent the "state of the art" in explaining employee motivation.

Three Needs Theory David McClelland and others have proposed that there are three major relevant motives or needs in the workplace:[4]

4. David C. McClelland, *The Achieving Society* (New York: Van Nostrand Reinhold, 1961); John W. Atkinson and Joel O. Raynor, *Motivation and Achievement* (Washington, D. C.: Winston, 1974); and David C. McClelland, *Power: The Inner Experience* (New York: Irvington, 1975).

1. The need for achievement (*nAch*)—the drive to excel, to achieve in relation to a set of standards, to strive to succeed.
2. The need for power (*nPow*)—the need to make others behave in a way that they would not have behaved otherwise.
3. The need for affiliation (*nAff*)—the desire for friendly and close interpersonal relationships.

Some people have a compelling drive to succeed, but they are striving for personal achievement rather than the rewards of success. They have a desire to do something better or more efficiently than it has been done before. This drive is the need for achievement. From research into the need for achievement, McClelland found that high achievers differentiate themselves from others by their desire to do things better. They seek situations where they can attain personal responsibility for finding solutions to problems, where they can receive rapid and unambiguous feedback on their performance so they can tell easily whether they are improving or not, and where they can set moderately challenging goals. High achievers are not gamblers; they dislike succeeding by chance. They prefer the challenge of working at a problem and accepting the personal responsibility for success or failure, rather than leaving the outcome to chance or the actions of others. They avoid what they perceive to be very easy or very difficult tasks.

High achievers perform best when they perceive their probability of success as being 0.5; that is, when they estimate that they have a 50-50 chance of success. They dislike gambling with high odds because they get no achievement satisfaction from happenstance success. Similarly, they dislike low odds (high probability of success) because then there is no challenge to their skills. They like to set goals that require stretching themselves a little. When there is an approximately equal chance of success or failure, there is the optimum opportunity to experience feelings of accomplishment and satisfaction from their efforts.

The need for power is the desire to have impact, to be influential, and to control others. Individuals high in *nPow* enjoy being in charge, strive for influence over others, prefer to be placed in competitive and status-oriented situations, and tend to be more concerned with gaining influence over others and prestige than with effective performance.

The third need isolated by McClelland is affiliation. This need has received the least attention of researchers. Affiliation can be likened to Dale Carnegie's goals—the desire to be liked and accepted by others. Individuals with a high *nAff* strive for friendship, prefer cooperative situations rather than competitive ones, and desire relationships involving a high degree of mutual understanding.

How do you find out if someone is, for instance, a high achiever? All three motives are typically measured through a projective test in which subjects respond to a set of pictures. Each picture is briefly shown to the subject and then he or she writes a story based on the picture. As an example, the picture may show a male sitting at a desk in a pensive position, looking at a picture of a woman and two children which sits at the corner of the desk. The subject will then be asked to write a story describing what is going on, what preceded this situation, what will happen in the future, and the like. The stories become, in effect, projective tests that measure unconscious motives. Each story is scored and a subject's rating on each of the three motives is obtained.

Based on an extensive amount of research, some reasonably well-supported predictions can be made based on the relationship between achievement need and job performance. Though less research has been done on power and affiliation needs, there are consistent findings here too. First, individuals with a high need to achieve prefer job situations with personal responsibility, feedback, and an intermediate degree of risk. When these characteristics are prevalent, high achievers will be strongly motivated. The evidence consistently demonstrates, for instance, that high achievers are successful in entrepreneurial activities such as running their own business, managing a self-contained unit within a large organization, and many sales positions. Second, a high need to achieve does not necessarily lead to being a good manager, especially in large organizations. High *nAch* sales people do not necessarily make good sales managers, and the good manager in a large organization does not typically have a high need to achieve. Third, the needs for affiliation and power tend to be closely related to managerial success. The best managers are high in the need for power and low in their need for affiliation. Lastly, employees have been successfully trained to stimulate their achievement need. If the job calls for a high achiever, management can select a person with a high *nAch* or develop its own candidate through achievement training.

Goal-Setting Theory   There is considerable evidence to support the theory that intentions—expressed as goals—can be a major source of work motivation. We can say, with a considerable degree of confidence, that specific goals lead to increased performance and that difficult goals, when accepted, result in higher performance than easy goals.[5]

Specific, difficult-to-achieve goals produce a higher level of output than a generalized goal of "do your best." The specificity of the goal itself acts as an internal stimulus. For instance, when a trucker commits to making eighteen round-trip hauls between Baltimore and Washington,

---

5. Mark E. Tubbs, "Goal-Setting: A Meta-Analysis Examination of the Empirical Evidence," *Journal of Applied Psychology*, August 1986, pp. 474–83.

D.C. each week, this intention gives him a specific objective to reach for. We can say that, all things being equal, the trucker with a specific goal will out-perform his counterpart who operates either with no goals or with the generalized goal of "do your best."

If factors such as ability and acceptance of the goals are held constant, we can also state that the more difficult the goals, the higher the level of performance. However, it's logical to assume that easier goals are more likely to be accepted. But once an employee accepts a hard task, he or she will exert a high level of effort until the goal is achieved, lowered, or abandoned.

If employees have the opportunity to participate in the setting of their own goals, will they try harder? The evidence is mixed regarding the superiority of participation over assigned goals. In some cases, goals that have been set participatively have elicited superior performance, while in other cases individuals have performed best when assigned goals by their boss. A major advantage of participation may be in increasing acceptance of the goal, itself, as a desirable one to work toward. As we noted earlier, resistance is greater when goals are difficult. If people participate in goal setting, they are more likely to accept even a difficult goal than if it is arbitrarily assigned to them by their boss. The reason is that individuals are more committed to choices in which they have a voice. Thus, although participative goals may have no superiority over assigned goals when acceptance is taken as a given, participation does increase the probability that more difficult goals will be agreed to and acted upon.

Studies on goal setting have demonstrated the superiority of specific and challenging goals as motivating forces. While we can't conclude that having employees participate in the goal-setting process is *always* desirable, participation is probably preferable to assignment when you expect resistance to more difficult challenges. As an overall conclusion, therefore, we have significant evidence that intentions—as articulated in terms of goals—are a potent motivating force.

The observant reader may have noted what appears to be a contradiction between the findings on achievement motivation and goal setting. Is it a contradiction that achievement motivation is stimulated by moderately challenging goals, while goal-setting theory says motivation is maximized by difficult goals? The answer is "No!" The explanation is twofold. First, goal-setting theory deals with people in general. The conclusions on achievement motivation are based only on people who have a high *nAch*. Given that probably not more than 10 to 20 percent of North Americans are naturally high achievers, difficult goals are still recommended for the majority of workers. Second, goal setting's conclusions apply to those who accept, and are committed to, the goals. Difficult goals will only lead to higher performance if they are accepted.

Reinforcement Theory   A counterpoint to goal-setting theory is reinforcement theory. The former is a cognitive approach, proposing that an individual's purposes direct his or her actions. In reinforcement theory we have a behavioristic approach, which argues that reinforcement conditions behavior. The two theories are clearly at odds philosophically. Reinforcement theorists see behavior as environmentally caused; internal cognitive events are not matters for concern. What controls behavior are reinforcers—any consequences which, when immediately following a response, increase the probability that the behavior will be repeated.

Reinforcement theory ignores the inner state of the individual and concentrates solely on what happens to a person when he or she takes some action. Because it does not concern itself with what initiates behavior, it is not, strictly speaking, a theory of motivation. However, it does provide a powerful means of analysis of what controls behavior, and it is for this reason that it is typically considered in discussions of motivation.

The last chapter introduced the law of effect as it relates to learning and showed that reinforcers condition behavior and help to explain how people learn. But the law of effect and the concept of reinforcement also have a wide following as an explanation of motivation. There is a large amount of supportive research indicating that people will exert higher levels of effort in tasks that are reinforced.[6] Reinforcement *is* undoubtedly an important influence on work behavior. What people do on their jobs and the amount of effort they allocate to various tasks is affected by the consequences that follow their behavior. But reinforcement is not the single explanation for differences in employee motivation. Goals, for instance, have an impact on motivation; so, too, do levels of achievement motivation, inequities in rewards, and expectations.

Equity Theory   Employees don't work in a vacuum. They make comparisons. If someone offered you $40,000 a year for your first job upon graduation from college, you'd probably grab at the offer and report to work enthused and certainly satisfied with your pay. How would you react, however, if you found out a month or so into the job that a co-worker—another recent graduate, your age, with comparable grades from a comparable college—was getting $45,000 a year? You'd probably be upset! Even though, in absolute terms, $40,000 is a lot of money for a new graduate to make (and you know it!), that suddenly isn't the issue. The issue now centers around relative rewards and what you believe is fair. There is considerable evidence for us to

6. Fred Luthans and Robert Kreitner, *Organizational Behavior Modification and Beyond: An Operant and Social Learning Approach* (Glenview, Ill: Scott, Foresman, 1984).

conclude that employees make comparisons of their job inputs and out-comes relative to others and that inequities can influence the degree of effort that employees exert.[7]

Equity theory says that employees perceive what they get from a job situation (outcomes) in relation to what they put into it (inputs), and then compare their input-outcome ratio with the input-outcome ratio of relevant others. If they perceive their ratio to be equal to the relevant others with whom they compare themselves, a state of equity is said to exist. They feel their situation is fair, that justice prevails. If the ratios are unequal, in-equity exists; that is, the employees tend to view themselves as under-rewarded or overrewarded. When inequities occur, employees will attempt to correct them.

The referent that employees choose to compare themselves against is an important variable in equity theory. The three referent categories have been classified as "other," "system," and "self." The "other" category in-cludes other individuals with similar jobs in the same organization, and also includes friends, neighbors, or professional associates. Based on informa-tion that employees receive through word of mouth, newspapers, and magazines, on such issues as executive salaries or a recent union contract, employees can compare their pay to that of others.

The "system" category considers organizational pay policies and procedures, as well as the administration of this system. It considers orga-nization-wide pay policies, both implied and explicit. Precedents set by the organization in terms of allocation of pay would be a major determinant in this category.

The "self" category refers to input-outcome ratios that are unique to the individual. This category is influenced by such criteria as past jobs or family commitments.

The choice of a particular set of referents is related to the information available about referents as well as to their perceived relevance. Based on equity theory, when employees envision an inequity, they may make one or more of five choices:

1. Distort either their own or others' inputs or outcomes
2. Behave in some way so as to induce others to change their inputs or outcomes
3. Behave in some way so as to change their own inputs or outcomes
4. Choose a different comparison referent
5. Quit their job

7. Robert P. Vecchio, "Models of Psychological Inequity," *Organizational Behavior and Human Performance*, October 1984, pp. 266–82.

Equity theory recognizes that individuals are concerned not only with the absolute amount of rewards they receive for their efforts, but also with the relationship of this amount to what others receive. They make judgments based on the relationship between their inputs and outcomes and the inputs and outcomes of others. Inputs, such as effort, experience, education, and competence, can be compared to outcomes such as salary levels, raises, recognition, and other factors. When people perceive an imbalance in their input-outcome ratio relative to others, tension is created. This tension provides the basis for motivation, as people strive for what they perceive as equity and fairness.

Specifically, the theory establishes four propositions relating to inequitable pay: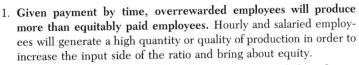

1. **Given payment by time, overrewarded employees will produce more than equitably paid employees.** Hourly and salaried employees will generate a high quantity or quality of production in order to increase the input side of the ratio and bring about equity.

2. **Given payment by quantity of production, overrewarded employees will produce fewer but higher-quality units than equitably paid employees.** Individuals paid on a piece-rate basis will increase their effort to achieve equity, which can result in greater quality or quantity. However, increases in quantity will only increase inequity since every unit produced results in further overpayment. Therefore, effort is directed toward increasing quality rather than quantity.

3. **Given payment by time, underrewarded employees will produce less or a poorer quality of output.** Effort will be decreased, which will bring about lower productivity or poorer quality of output than equitably paid subjects.

4. **Given payment by quantity of production, underrewarded employees will produce a large number of low-quality units in comparison with equitably paid employees.** Employees on piece-rate pay plans can bring about equity because trading off quantity of output for quality will result in an increase in rewards with little or no increase in contributions.

A review of the recent research tends to consistently confirm the equity thesis: Employee motivation is influenced significantly by relative rewards as well as absolute rewards. When employees perceive inequity, they will act to correct the situation. The result might be lower or higher productivity, improved or reduced quality of output, increased absenteeism, or voluntary resignation.

The above does not mean that equity theory is without problems. The theory leaves some key issues unclear. For instance, how do employees select who is included in the "other" referent category? How do they define inputs and outcomes? How do they combine and weight their inputs and outcomes to arrive at totals? When and how do the factors change over time? However, regardless of these problems, equity theory has an impressive amount of research support and offers us some important insights into employee motivation.

Expectancy Theory

The most comprehensive explanation of motivation is expectancy theory.[8] Though it, too, has its critics, most of the research evidence is supportive of the theory.

Essentially, expectancy theory argues that the strength of a tendency to act in a certain way depends on the strength of an expectation that the act will be followed by a given outcome, and on the attractiveness of that outcome to the individual. Therefore, it includes three variables:

1. **Attractiveness**—the importance that the individual places on the potential outcome or reward that can be achieved on the job. This considers the unsatisfied needs of the individual.
2. **Performance-reward linkage**—the degree to which the individual believes that performing at a particular level will lead to the attainment of a desired outcome.
3. **Effort-performance linkage**—the probability perceived by the individual that exerting a given amount of effort will lead to performance.

While this may sound pretty complex, it really is not that difficult to visualize. Whether or not one has the desire to produce at any given time depends on one's particular goals and one's perception of the relative worth of performance as a path to the attainment of these goals.

Figure 3-4 is a considerable simplification of expectancy theory, but expresses its major contentions. The strength of a person's motivation to perform (effort) depends on how strongly she believes that she can achieve what she attempts. If she achieves this goal (performance), will she be adequately rewarded and, if she is rewarded by the organization, will the reward satisfy her individual goals? Let us consider the four steps inherent in the theory.

First, what perceived outcomes does the job offer the employee? Outcomes may be positive: pay, security, companionship, trust, fringe benefits, a chance to use talent or skills, congenial relationships. On the other

8. Victor H. Vroom, *Work and Motivation* (New York: John Wiley and Sons, 1964).

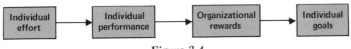

Figure 3-4
Simplified Expectancy Model

hand, employees may view the outcomes as negative: fatigue, boredom, frustration, anxiety, harsh supervision, threat of dismissal. Importantly, reality is not relevant here; the critical issue is what the individual employee *perceives* the outcome to be, regardless of whether or not her perceptions are accurate.

Second, how attractive do employees consider these outcomes? Are they valued positively, negatively, or neutrally? This is obviously an internal issue to the individual and considers her personal attitudes, personality, and needs. The individual who finds a particular outcome attractive—that is, positively valued—will prefer attaining it to not attaining it. Others may find it negative and, therefore, prefer not to attain it. Still others may be neutral.

Third, what kind of behavior must the employee exhibit in order to achieve these outcomes? The outcomes are not likely to have any effect on the individual employee's performance unless the employee knows, clearly and unambiguously, what she must do in order to achieve them. For example, what is "doing well" in terms of performance appraisal? On what criteria will the employee's performance be judged?

Fourth and last, how does the employee view her chances of doing what is asked of her? After the employee has considered her own competencies and her ability to control those variables that will determine her success, what probability does she place on successful attainment?

Let's highlight some of the issues that expectancy theory has brought forward. First, it emphasizes payoffs or rewards. As a result, we have to believe that the rewards the organization is offering align with what the employee wants. It is a theory based on self-interest, wherein each individual seeks to maximize his or her expected satisfaction. We have to be concerned with the attractiveness of rewards; this requires an understanding and knowledge of what value the individual puts on organizational payoffs. We want to reward individuals with those things they value positively. Second, expectancy theory emphasizes expected behaviors. Does the person know what is expected of her and how she will be appraised? Finally, the theory is concerned with the individual's expectations. What is realistic is irrelevant. An employee's own expectations of performance, reward, and goal satisfaction outcomes, not the objective outcomes themselves, will determine her level of effort.

IMPLICATIONS FOR MANAGERS We've presented a number of theories in this chapter, many of which have demonstrated reasonably strong predictive value. If you're a manager, concerned with motivating your employees, how do you apply these theories? While there is no simple, all-encompassing set of guidelines, the essence of what we know about motivating employees in organizations is distilled in the following suggestions. They consider and integrate personal variables, job variables, and system variables.

a. *Recognize Individual Differences.* Almost every contemporary motivation theory recognizes that employees are not homogeneous. People have different needs. They also differ in terms of attitudes, personalities, and other important individual variables. For instance, expectancy predictions tend to be more accurate with individuals who have an internal rather than external locus of control. Why? Such individuals believe that events in their lives are influenced by themselves, consistent with expectancy theory's assumptions that people rationally pursue their individual goals.

b. *Match People to Jobs.* There is abundant evidence to support the idea that motivational benefits accrue from carefully matching people to jobs. For example, if the job involves running a small business or an autonomous unit within a larger business, high achievers should be sought. However, if the job to be filled is a managerial slot in a large bureaucratic organization, a candidate high in *nPow* and low in *nAff* should be selected. Along these same lines, don't put a high achiever into a job that is inconsistent with his or her needs. Achievers will do best where the job provides opportunities to set goals participatively, and where there is autonomy and feedback. But keep in mind that not everybody will be motivated by jobs with increased autonomy, variety, and responsibility.

c. *Use Goals.* The goal-setting literature gives us considerable confidence in suggesting that managers should ensure that employees have hard and specific goals, as well as feedback on how well they are doing in pursuit of those goals. For those with high achievement needs—typically a minority in any organization—the existence of external goals is of less importance because these people are already internally motivated.

Should the goals be assigned by a manager or should they be participatively set in conjunction with the employee? The answer to that question depends on your perception of goal acceptance and the organization's culture. If you expect resistance to goals, the use of participation should increase acceptance. If participation is inconsistent with the culture—that is, if the organization is formal and strongly authority-oriented—use assigned goals. Where participation and the culture are incongruous, employees are likely to perceive the participative process as manipulative and distrust it.

d. *Ensure that Goals Are Perceived as* Regardless of whether goals are actu-
Attainable. ally attainable and well within management's perceptions of the employees' ability, if employees see them as unattainable, they will reduce their effort. Managers must be sure, therefore, that employees feel confident that their effort *can* lead to performance goals. For managers, this means that employees must have the capability to do the job and employees must perceive the appraisal process by which their performance will be evaluated as both reliable and valid.

e. *Individualize Rewards.* Since employees have different needs, what acts as a reinforcer for one may not work for another. Managers should use their knowledge of individual differences to individualize the rewards over which they have control. Some of the more obvious rewards that managers allocate include pay, promotions, autonomy, and the opportunity to participate in goal setting and decision making.

f. *Link Rewards to Performance.* In both reinforcement theory and expectancy theory, managers need to make rewards contingent on performance. To reward factors other than performance will only act to reinforce those other factors. Key rewards such as pay increases and promotions should be allocated for the attainment of the employee's specific goals. As they maximize the impact of the reward contingency, managers should look for ways to increase the visibility of rewards. Eliminating the secrecy surrounding pay by openly communicating everyone's compensation, publicizing performance bonuses, and allocating annual salary increases in a lump sum rather than spreading them out over the entire year are examples of actions that will make rewards more visible and potentially more motivating.

g. *Check the System for Equity.* Rewards or outcomes should be perceived by employees as equaling the inputs they give. At a simplistic level, this should mean that experience, abilities, effort, and other obvious inputs should explain differences in pay, responsibility, and the other obvious outcomes. The problem, however, is complicated by the fact that there are dozens of inputs and outcomes, and that employee groups place different degrees of importance on them. This suggests that one person's equity is another's inequity, so an ideal reward system should probably weight inputs differently in order to arrive at the proper rewards for each job.

h. *Don't Ignore Money!* It's easy to get so caught up in setting goals or providing opportunities for participation that one can forget that money is a major reason why most people work. So the allocation of performance-based wage increases, piece-work bonuses, and other pay incentives are important in determining employee motivation. Maybe the best case for "money as a motivator" is a recent review of eighty studies evaluating motivational methods and their impacts on employee productivity.[9] Goal setting alone produced, on average, a 16 percent increase in productivity; efforts to redesign jobs in order to make them more interesting and challenging yielded 8 to 16 percent increases; employee participation in decision making produced a median increase of less than one percent; while monetary incentives led to an average increase of 30 percent.

SELECTED REFERENCES

EVANS, MARTIN G., "Organizational Behavior: The Central Role of Motivation," *Journal of Management*, Summer 1986, pp. 203–22.

LAWLER, EDWARD E. III, *Motivation in Work Organizations*. Monterey, Calif.: Brooks/Cole, 1973.

LOCKE, EDWIN A., AND GARY P. LATHAM, *Goal Setting: A Motivational Technique That Works!* Englewood Cliffs, N.J.: Prentice-Hall, 1984.

MITCHELL, TERENCE R., "Motivation: New Directions for Theory, Research and Practice," *Academy of Management Review*, January 1982, pp. 80–88.

PINDER, CRAIG C., *Work Motivation: Theory, Issues, and Applications*. Glenview, Ill.: Scott, Foresman, 1984.

STEERS, RICHARD M., AND LYMAN W. PORTER, *Motivation and Work Behavior* (4th ed.). New York: McGraw-Hill, 1987.

9. Edwin A. Locke, D.V. Feren, V.M. McCaleb, K.N. Shaw, and A.T. Denny, "The Relative Effectiveness of Four Methods of Motivating Employee Performance," in *Changes in Working Life*, eds. K.D. Duncan, M.M. Gruneberg, and D. Wallis (London: John Wiley, Ltd., 1980), pp. 363–83.

4

DE/IGNING MOTIVATING JOB/

One of the more important factors that influence an employee's motivational level is the structure of his or her work. Is there a lot of variety or is the job repetitive? Is the work closely supervised? Does the job allow the employee discretion? The answers to questions like these will have a major impact on the motivational properties inherent in the job and hence the level of productivity that an employee can expect to achieve. In this chapter, we shall demonstrate how a job's content and structure affect the level of effort exerted. In addition, we will offer some options for redesigning jobs to make them more attractive and motivational to employees.

DESIGNING JOBS AND MOTIVATING EMPLOYEES   The previous chapter demonstrated the central role that needs play in motivation. Employees have needs, which they seek to satisfy. Obviously, some of these needs can be, and should be, satisfied *off* the job. Since the time a person puts into his job represents about 35 percent of his waking hours, there are ample opportunities for finding fulfillment and satisfaction from non-job-related activities. It can be argued that if jobs are a bore, there are sufficient opportunities for finding excitement off the job. On the other hand, it can also be argued that jobs that are intrinsically rewarding—those that offer challenge and greater freedom, and that employees find interesting—will provide motivation in themselves, and will require substantially less reliance upon externally initiated motivators.

The importance that job design plays in motivation can be seen in the results of a study of over 56,000 people who were asked to rate the most important factor in a job.[1] Interesting work was rated *the* most important factor—ahead of security, advancement opportunities, pay, a fair and considerate boss, or pleasant co-workers. So, if management can design jobs that employees find interesting, the jobs themselves can provide a major source of motivation.

CLARIFYING TERMINOLOGY The term "job design" is closely associated with "quality of work life" programs and "job *re*design." In this section, we want to define each of these concepts.

Job Design The term *job design* refers to the way that tasks are combined to form complete jobs. Some jobs are routine because the tasks are standardized and repetitive; others are nonroutine. Some require a large number of varied and diverse skills; others are narrow in scope. Some jobs constrain the employee by requiring him or her to follow very precise procedures; others allow employees substantial freedom in how they do their work. Some jobs are most effectively accomplished by groups of employees working as a team, while other jobs are best done by individuals essentially acting independently. The point is that jobs differ in the way tasks are combined and these different combinations create a variety of job designs.

Quality of Work Life The content and design of jobs have interested engineers and economists for centuries. Adam Smith, for instance, wrote on the economies of specialization—dividing jobs into smaller and smaller pieces—over 200 years ago. At the turn of this century, Frederick Taylor introduced scientific management that strongly advocated the systematizing and proceduring of jobs. In fact, up until the 1950s, job design was substantially synonymous with job specialization.

1. Clifford E. Jergensen, "Job Preferences (What Makes a Job Good or Bad?)," *Journal of Applied Psychology*, June 1978, pp. 267–76.

However, during the last thirty-five years or so, psychologists, sociologists, and other social scientists have begun to shift their attention to consider the human needs of employees, which has led to the consideration of human issues in job content and alternative methods, besides specialization, of job design. Today we describe these alternatives as part of *quality of work life* (QWL) programs. QWL has become a label to describe system-wide change programs that improve the work environment and satisfy the needs of individual employees. Job design changes that humanize the workplace and respond to employees' personal needs are central elements in many QWL programs.

Job Redesign

Job redesign is concerned with change. For the most part, job redesign programs seek to make jobs more interesting, diverse, and challenging.

We start with the assumption that designing jobs around high specialization offers many economic advantages for managers. The wide popularity of specialization attests to the validity of this assumption. Yet, specialization has created jobs that, to many workers, are repetitive, boring, stressful, and generally lacking in meaningfulness. Job redesign, therefore, refers to the alteration of specific jobs or interdependent groups of jobs for the purpose of increasing both the quality of an employee's work experience and on-the-job productivity. The following pages consider the major job redesign options available to managers.

INDIVIDUAL REDESIGN OPTIONS

The first set of options is concerned with redesigning individual tasks. Among the individual redesign options that managers may want to consider are job rotation, work modules, job enlargement, and job enrichment.

Job Rotation

Job rotation allows workers to diversify their activities to offset boredom. There are actually two types of rotation: vertical and horizontal. Vertical rotation relates to promotions and demotions. When we talk about job rotation, however, we are referring to the horizontal variety, or what may be more accurately called a lateral transfer.

Horizontal job transfers can be instituted on a planned basis—that is, by means of a training program whereby the employee spends, say, two or three months in an activity and is then moved on. This approach, for example, is common among large Wall Street law firms where new associates work for many different partners before choosing an area of specialization. Horizontal transfers can also be made based on individual situations—moving someone to another activity when the first is no longer challenging or when the needs of the work schedule dictate it. In other words, people may be put in a continual transfer mode. Many large organizations employ rotation in their programs to develop managerial talent. This approach may include moving people between line and staff positions, often allowing an employee to understudy a more experienced organizational member.

The advantages of job rotation are clear. It broadens employees and gives them a range of experiences. Boredom and monotony, which develop after a person has acquired the skills to perform his or her task effectively, are reduced when transfers are made frequently. Finally, since a broad experience permits a greater understanding of other activities within the organization, people are prepared more rapidly to assume greater responsibility, especially at the upper echelons. In other words, as one moves up the organization, it becomes increasingly necessary to understand the intricacies and interrelationships of activities; and these skills can be more quickly acquired by moving about within the organization.

On the other hand, job rotation is not without its drawbacks. Training costs are increased and productivity is reduced by moving a worker into a new position just when his or her efficiency at the prior job created organizational economies. An extensive rotation program can result in having a vast number of employees situated in positions where their experience is very limited. And even though there may be significant long-term benefits from the program, the organization must be equipped to deal with the day-to-day problems that result when inexperienced personnel perform new tasks, and when rotated managers make decisions based on little experience in the activity at hand. Job rotation can also demotivate intelligent and aggressive trainees who seek specific responsibility in their chosen speciality. Finally, rotation that is imposed involuntarily on employees can reduce job satisfaction and increase absenteeism rates.

Work Modules

If you can conceive of extremely rapid job rotation, in which a worker assumes new activities every few hours, you can comprehend the option of work modules. This approach has been suggested as a solution to meet the problem of fractionated, boring, and standardized work. It can be accomplished at an acceptable price, with undiminished quality and quantity of output.

A work module is defined as a time task unit equal to approximately two hours of work at a given task. A normal forty-hour-a-week job would then be defined in terms of four modules a day, five days a week, for between forty-eight and fifty weeks per year.

Modules can increase work diversity and give employees a greater opportunity to determine the nature of their jobs. Employees could request a set of modules which, together, would constitute a day's work. Additionally, those tasks that are characteristically seen as undesirable could be spread about, for example, by having everyone take a module or two each day. The result would be that people would change activities by changing work modules. Or, as we noted previously, it could be viewed as a very rapid job rotation system.

There are benefits to work modules: letting employees pick their work tasks, thus taking into account individual job preferences; providing a way for the more boring and undesirable tasks to be completed without seriously demoralizing those people who must do them; and allowing employees some say in the choice of modules, thus constructing the job to meet the needs of the individual rather than forcing people to fit a job.

However, work modules would present the same cost and disruption obstacles as job rotation. Considerable time and money are involved in planning and executing the changeover. Bookkeeping and payroll-computation costs increase. Conflicts can also develop over the question of equity and allocation of modules.

Job Enlargement

Job enlargement expands jobs horizontally. It increases *job scope*; that is, it increases the number of different operations required in a job and the frequency with which the job cycle is repeated. By increasing the number of tasks an individual performs, job enlargement increases diversity. Instead of only sorting the incoming mail by department, for instance, a mail sorter's job could be enlarged to include physically delivering the mail to the various departments or running outgoing letters through the postage meter.

Efforts at job enlargement have met with less than enthusiastic results. As one employee who experienced such a redesign on his job remarked, "Before, I had one lousy job. Now, through enlargement, I have three!" So, while job enlargement attacks the problem of lack of diversity in over-specialized jobs, it has done little to instill challenge or a sense of meaningfulness to a worker's activities. Job enrichment has proven effective at dealing with the shortcomings of enlargement.

Job Enrichment

Job enrichment expands jobs vertically. While job enlargement increases job scope, job enrichment increases *job depth*. What this means is that job enrichment allows the employee to have greater control over his or her work. He or she is allowed to assume some of the tasks typically done by a supervisor—he or she has greater influence over the planning, executing, and evaluating of the job. The tasks in an enriched job should allow workers to complete an activity with increased freedom, independence,

49

and responsibility; this type of job should also provide feedback so that individuals can assess and correct their own performance.

How jobs can be enriched is illustrated by a program implemented at Travelers Insurance in their keypunch operations.[2] The company's management was displeased with the performance of its keypunch operators. Output seemed inadequate, the error rate excessive, and absenteeism too high. As a result, the following changes were introduced:

1. The random assignment of work was replaced by assigning to each operator continuing responsibility for certain accounts.
2. Some planning and control functions were combined with the central task of keypunching.
3. Each operator was given several channels of direct contact with clients. When problems arose, the operator, not the supervisor, took them up with the client.
4. Operators were given the authority to set their own schedules, plan their daily work, and correct obvious coding errors on their own.
5. Incorrect cards were returned by the computer department to the operators who punched them, and the operators corrected their own errors. Weekly computer printouts of errors and productivity were sent directly to the operator rather than the supervisor.

The above enrichment efforts led to some impressive results. Fewer keypunch operators were needed, the quantity of output increased, error rates and absenteeism were reduced, and job attitudes improved. The changes reportedly saved Travelers over $90,000 a year.

Where jobs have been enriched, employee satisfaction tends to increase and there is usually lower absenteeism and reduced turnover. But the impact of job enrichment on productivity is unclear. In some situations, job enrichment has increased productivity; in others, productivity has decreased. However, when it decreases, there does appear to be more consistent, conscientious use of resources and a higher quality of product or service. In other words, in terms of efficiency, for the same input a higher quality of output is obtained.

GROUP REDESIGN OPTIONS　　During the last ten to fifteen years, the main focus of attention on redesign options has shifted from the individual to the group. The following approaches—integrated work teams, autonomous work teams, and quality circles—are each designed around group tasks.

2. J. Richard Hackman, G. R. Oldham, R. Janson, and K. Purdy, "A New Strategy for Job Enrichment," *California Management Review*, Summer 1975, pp. 57–71.

Integrated Work Teams If job enlargement is practiced at the group level rather than the individual level, you have integrated work teams. For jobs that require teamwork and cooperation, this approach can increase diversity for team members.

What would an integrated work team look like? Basically, instead of performing a single task, a large number of tasks would be assigned to a group. The group would then decide the specific assignments for members, and be responsible for rotating jobs among the members as the tasks required. The team would still have a supervisor who would oversee the group's activities. You see the frequent use of integrated work teams in such activities as building maintenance and construction. In the cleaning of a sizeable office building, it is not unusual for the foreman to identify the tasks to be completed and then let the maintenance workers, as a group, choose how the tasks will be allocated. Similarly, a road construction crew frequently decides, as a group, how its various tasks are to be completed.

Antonomous Work Teams Autonomous work teams represent job enrichment at the group level. The work that the team does is deepened through vertical integration. The team is given a goal to achieve and then is free to determine work assignments, rest breaks, inspection procedures, and the like. Fully autonomous work teams even select their own members and have the members evaluate each other's performance. As a result, supervisory positions take on decreased importance and may even be eliminated. The autonomous work team concept is a reality at the Oklahoma plant of Shaklee Corporation, where nutritional products, vitamins, and other pills are made.

About 190 of the Oklahoma plant's production employees were organized into teams with three to fifteen members. The team members set their own production schedules, decided what hours to work, selected new team members from a pool approved by the personnel department, and even initiated discharges if necessary. The results were impressive. The company reported that units produced per hour of labor went up nearly 200 percent over levels at other plants. Two-thirds of this increase was attributed to the autonomous work team concept (the rest was explained by better equipment). Management stated that the Oklahoma plant could produce the same volume as the more traditional facilities at 40 percent of the labor costs.

The improvement at Shaklee is not isolated. There are other reports of favorable improvements in worker attitudes and performance when autonomous work teams have been implemented. For instance, a three-year study of coal mining crews found that creation of autonomous teams resulted in more positive attitudes toward work and a slight positive increase in performance.

51

Quality Circles   One of the most recent additions to group job redesign is the quality circle. Originally begun in the U.S. and exported to Japan in the 1950s, it has recently been imported back to the U.S.

The quality circle is a work group of eight to ten employees and supervisors who have a shared area of responsibility. They meet regularly—typically once a week, on company time and on company premises—to discuss their quality problems, investigate causes, recommend solutions, and take corrective actions. They take over the responsibility for solving quality problems, and they generate and evaluate their own feedback. Of course, it is not presumed that employees inherently have this ability. Therefore, part of the quality circle concept includes teaching participating employees group communication skills, various quality strategies, and measurement and problem-analysis techniques.

There has been rapid growth in the use of quality circles in the U.S. since 1980. It is too early to determine whether it is a fad or truly a meaningful job redesign concept. But employees seem to welcome the idea of participating in, and generating solutions for, product-quality and production problems. Pragmatically, this enthusiasm and cooperation by workers goes beyond the mere opportunity to collaborate with management on production decisions. It can mean increased job security. Workers recognize that by improving quality and productivity, their organization's products will be more competitive, the product's market share will expand, and their jobs will be more secure.

THE JOB CHARACTERISTICS MODEL   If you want to redesign a job or set of jobs, are there any guidelines available to help you? The answer is "Yes!" The most complete framework available for analyzing a job's design is the job characteristics model (JCM). It identifies five key job characteristics, their interrelationships, and their predicted impact on employee productivity, motivation, and satisfaction. Let's review the model and show you how you can use it in analyzing and designing jobs.

Core Dimensions   According to the JCM, any job can be described in terms of the following five core job dimensions:

> **Skill variety**—the degree to which a job requires a variety of different activities so the worker can use a number of different skills and talents.
> **Task identity**—the degree to which the job requires completion of a whole and identifiable piece of work.

Task significance—the degree to which the job has a substantial impact on the lives or work of other people.

Autonomy—the degree to which the job provides substantial freedom, independence, and discretion to the individuals in scheduling the work and in determining the procedures to be used in carrying it out.

Feedback—the degree to which carrying out the work activities required by the job results in the individual obtaining direct and clear information about the effectiveness of his performance.

Interrelationships and Predictions   Figure 4-1 presents the model. Notice how the first three dimensions— skill variety, task identity, and task significance—combine to create meaningful work. That is, if these three characteristics exist in a job, we can predict that the person will view that job as being important, valuable, and worthwhile. Notice, too, that a job that possesses autonomy gives the worker a feeling of personal responsibility for the results; and that if a job provides feedback, the employee will know how effectively he or she is performing. From a motivational standpoint, the model says that internal rewards are obtained by an employee when that person *learns* (knowledge

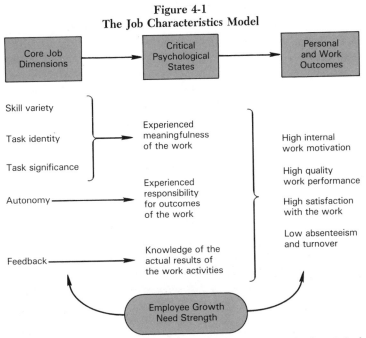

Figure 4-1
The Job Characteristics Model

Source: J. Richard Hackman, "Work Design," in *Improving Life at Work*, eds. J. Richard Hackman and J. Lloyd Suttle (Santa Monica, Calif.: Goodyear Publishing Co., 1977), p. 129.

of results) that he or she *personally* (experienced responsibility) has performed well on a task that he or she *cares about* (experienced significance). The more that these three psychological states are present, the greater will be the employee's motivation, performance, and satisfaction; and the lower his absenteeism and likelihood of leaving the job. As the model shows, the links between the job dimensions and the outcomes are moderated by the strength of the individual's growth need; that is, the employee's desire for self-esteem and self-actualization. This means that individuals with a high growth need are more likely to experience the three psychological states when their jobs are enriched than are their low-growth-need counterparts; that is, they will respond more positively to the psychological states, when they are present, than will low-growth-need individuals.

The core job dimensions can be combined into a single predictive index, called the motivating potential score (MPS). Its computation is shown in Figure 4-2.

Jobs that are high in motivating potential must be high in at least one of the three factors leading to experiencing meaningfulness, plus they must be high on both autonomy and feedback. If jobs score high on motivating potential, the model predicts that motivation, performance, and satisfaction will be positively affected, while the likelihood of absence and turnover is lessened.

Tests of the job characteristics model have generally produced encouraging results. At this point in time, we can draw the following conclusions with relative confidence:

1. People who work on jobs with high core job dimensions are more motivated, satisfied, and productive than those who do not.
2. People with strong growth needs respond more positively to jobs that are high in motivating potential than do those with weak growth needs.
3. Job dimensions operate through the psychological states in influenc-

Figure 4-2
Computing a Motivating Potential Score

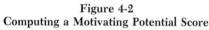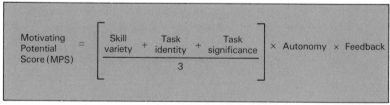

$$\begin{matrix} \text{Motivating} \\ \text{Potential} \\ \text{Score (MPS)} \end{matrix} = \left[\dfrac{\text{Skill variety} + \text{Task identity} + \text{Task significance}}{3} \right] \times \text{Autonomy} \times \text{Feedback}$$

Source: J. Richard Hackman, "Work Design," in *Improving Life at Work*, eds. J. Richard Hackman and J. Lloyd Suttle (Santa Monica, Calif.: Goodyear Publishing Co., 1977), p. 130.

ing personal and work outcome variables, rather than influencing them directly.

IMPLICATIONS FOR MANAGERS
The JCM offers some specific suggestions to managers for job redesign. The following suggestions specify what types of changes in jobs are most likely to lead to improvements in each of the five core dimensions:

1. **Combine tasks.** Managers should seek to take existing, fractionalized tasks and put them back together to form a new, larger module of work. This will increase skill variety and task identity.

2. **Create natural work units.** The creation of natural work units means that the tasks an employee does form an identifiable and meaningful whole. This increases employee "ownership" of the work and improves the likelihood that employees will view their work as meaningful and important rather than as irrelevant and boring.

3. **Establish client relationships.** The client is the user of the product or service that the employee works on. Wherever possible, managers should try to establish direct relationships between workers and their clients. This will increase skill variety, autonomy, and feedback for the employee.

4. **Expand jobs vertically.** Vertical expansion gives employees responsibilities and controls that were formerly reserved for management. It seeks to partially close the gap between the "doing" and the "controlling" aspects of the job and increases employee autonomy.

5. **Open feedback channels.** By increasing feedback, employees not only learn how well they are performing their jobs but also whether their performance is improving, deteriorating, or remaining at a constant level. Ideally, this feedback about performance should be received directly as the employee does the job, rather than from management on an occasional basis.

Table 4-1 summarizes the redesign options we have discussed in terms of their ability to meet the criteria identified in the JCM. All of the options increase skill variety. However, whether or not each increases task significance is often difficult to assess without knowing more about the work content in question. Beyond these two criteria, the various options begin to differ.

A review of Table 4-1 indicates that three options—job enrichment, autonomous work teams, and quality circles—are superior to the other options *in terms of the job characteristics model.* Of course, we have said nothing about the cost of implementing these changes. The benefits that each offers must be analyzed in relation to the cost of each approach. For

Table 4-1
Job Redesign Options Assessed in Terms
of Job Characteristics

	Job Characteristics				
Options	Skill Variety	Task Identity	Task Significance	Autonomy	Feedback
Job rotation	X		?		
Work modules	X		?	X	
Job enlargement	X		?		
Job enrichment	X	X	?	X	X
Integrated work teams	X		?		
Autonomous work teams	X	X	?	X	X
Quality circles	X	X	?	X	X

example, common sense tells us that the more complex changes—such as autonomous work teams—would have to generate significantly more benefits than a simple change—such as job rotation—to justify the greater time and effort required for implementation by management. Nevertheless, the JCM tells us that for employees who possess a high growth need, their motivation, performance, and satisfaction should be high when working in enriched jobs, on autonomous work teams, or participating in quality circles.

SELECTED REFERENCES

GLICK, WILLIAM H., G. DOUGLAS JENKINS JR., AND NINA GUPTA, "Method vs. Substance: How Strong Are Underlying Relationships Between Job Characteristics and Attitudinal Outcomes?," *Academy of Management Journal*, September 1986, pp. 441–64.

HACKMAN, J. RICHARD, AND GREG R. OLDHAM, *Work Redesign*. Reading, Mass.: Addison-Wesley, 1980.

KELLY, J.E., *Scientific Management, Job Redesign and Work Performance*. New York: Academic Press, 1982.

MEYER, GORDON W., AND RANDALL G. STOTT, "Quality Circles: Panacea or Pandora's Box?," *Organizational Dynamics*, Spring 1985, pp. 34–50.

NADLER, DAVID A., AND EDWARD E. LAWLER, III, "Quality of Work Life: Perspectives and Directions," *Organizational Dynamics*, Winter 1983, pp. 20–30.

WALL, TOBY D., NIGEL J. KEMP, PAUL R. JACKSON, AND CHRIS W. CLEGG, "Outcomes of Autonomous Workgroups: A Long-Term Field Experiment," *Academy of Management Journal*, June 1986, pp. 280–304.

5

INDIVIDUAL DECISION MAKING

Individuals in organizations make decisions. Top managers, for instance, determine their organization's goals, what products or services to offer, how best to organize corporate headquarters, or where to locate a new manufacturing plant. Middle- and lower-level managers determine production schedules, select new employees, and decide how pay raises are to be allocated. However, the making of decisions is not the sole province of managers. Nonmanagerial employees also make decisions that affect their jobs and the organizations they work for. The more obvious of these decisions might include whether to come to work or not on any given day, how much effort to put forward once at work, and whether to comply with a request made by the boss.

So every individual in every organization regularly engages in decision making; that is, they make choices from among two or more alternatives. Undoubtedly, many of these choices are almost reflex actions, undertaken with little conscious thought. The boss asks you to complete a certain report by the end of the day and you comply, assuming that the request is reasonable. In such instances, choices are still being made though they

58

don't require much contemplation. But when individuals confront new or important decisions, they can be expected to reason them out thoughtfully. Alternatives will be developed. Pros and cons will be weighed. The result is that what people do on their jobs is influenced by their decision processes. This chapter will review how individuals make decisions and will consider how this has an impact on their work behavior.

THE OPTIMIZING MODEL   Let's begin by describing how individuals should behave in order to maximize some outcome. We will call this the optimizing model of decision making.

Steps in the Optimizing Model   Table 5-1 outlines the six steps an individual should follow, either explicitly or implicitly, when making a decision.

Step 1. Ascertain the Need for a   The first step requires recognition
Decision.   that a decision needs to be made. What brings about this recognition? The existence of a problem or, more specifically, a disparity between some desired state and the actual condition. If you calculate your monthly expenses and find that you're spending $50 more than you allocated in your budget, you have ascertained the need for a decision. There is a disparity between your desired expenditure level and what you're actually spending.

Step 2: Identify the Decision   Once an individual has determined
Criteria.   the need for a decision, the criteria that will be important in making the decision must be identified. For illustration purposes, let's consider the case of a high school senior confronting the problem of choosing a college. The concepts derived from this example may be generalized to any decision a person might confront.

Table 5-1
Steps in the Optimizing
Decision Model

1. Ascertain the need for a decision
2. Identify the decision criteria
3. Allocate weights to the criteria
4. Develop the alternatives
5. Evaluate the alternatives
6. Select the best alternative

For the sake of simplicity, let's assume that our high school senior has already chosen to attend college (versus other noncollege options). We know that the need for a decision is precipitated by graduation. Once she has recognized this need for a decision, the student should begin to list the criteria or factors that will be relevant to her decision. For our example, let's assume she has identified the following criteria about the school: annual cost, availability of financial aid, admission requirements, status or reputation, size, geographic location, curricula offering, male:female ratio, quality of social life, and the physical attractiveness of the campus. These criteria represent what the decision maker thinks is relevant to her decision. Note that, in this step, what is *not* listed is as important as what *is*. For example, our high school senior did not consider factors such as where her friends were going to school, drinking age in the state in which the school is located, availability of part-time employment, or whether freshmen are required to reside on campus. To someone else making a college selection decision, the criteria used might be considerably different.

This second step is important because it identifies only those criteria that the decision maker considers relevant. If a criterion is omitted from this list, we treat it as irrelevant to the decision maker.

Step 3: Allocate Weights to the Criteria.   The criteria listed in the previous step are not all equally important. It's necessary, therefore, to weight the factors listed in Step 2 in order to prioritize their importance in the decision. All the criteria are relevant, but some are more relevant than others.

How does the decision maker weight criteria? A simple approach would merely be to give *the* most important criterion a number—say 10—and then assign weights to the rest of the criteria against this standard. So the result of Steps 2 and 3 is to allow decision makers to use their personal preferences both to prioritize the relevant criteria and to indicate their relative degree of importance by assigning a weight to each. Table 5-2 lists the criteria and weights our high school senior is using in her college decision.

Step 4: Develop the Alternatives.   The fourth step requires the decision maker to list all the viable alternatives that could possibly succeed in resolving the problem. No attempt is made in this step to appraise the alternatives; only to list them. To return to our example, let us assume that our high schooler has identified eight potential colleges—Alpha, Beta, Delta, Gamma, Iota, Omega, Phi, and Sigma.

Step 5: Evaluate the Alternatives.   Once the alternatives have been identified, the decision maker must critically evaluate each one. The strengths and weaknesses of each alternative will become evident when they are compared against the criteria and weights established in Steps 2 and 3.

Table 5-2
Criteria and Weights
in Selection of a College

Criteria	Weights
• Availability of financial aid	10
• School's reputation	10
• Annual cost	8
• Curricula offering	7
• Geographic location	6
• Admission requirements	5
• Quality of social life	4
• School size	3
• Male:female ratio	2
• Physical attractiveness of the campus	2

The evaluation of each alternative is done by appraising it against the weighted criteria. In our example, the high school senior would evaluate each college using every one of the criteria. To keep our example simple, we'll assume that a 10 means that the college is rated as "most favorable" on that criterion. The results from evaluating the various alternative colleges are shown in Table 5-3.

Keep in mind that the ratings given the eight colleges shown in Table 5-3 are based on the assessment made by the decision maker. Some assessments can be made in a relatively objective fashion. If our decision maker prefers a small school, one with an enrollment of 1,000 is obviously superior to one with 10,000 students. Similarly, if a high male:female ratio is sought, 3:1 is clearly higher than 1.2:1. But the assessment of criteria such as reputation, quality of social life, or the physical attractiveness of the campus reflects the decision maker's values. The point is that most decisions contain judgments. They are reflected in the criteria chosen in Step 2, the weights given to these criteria, and the evaluation of alternatives. This explains why two people faced with a similar problem—such as selecting a college—may look at two totally different sets of alternatives or even look at the same alternatives but rate them very differently.

Table 5-3 only represents an evaluation of the eight alternatives against the decision criteria. It does not reflect the weighting done in Step 3. If one choice had scored 10 on every criterion, there would be no need to consider the weights. Similarly, if the weights were all equal, you could evaluate each alternative merely by summing up the appropriate column in Table 5-3. For instance, Omega College would be highest, with a total score of 84. But our high school senior needs to multiply each alternative against its weight. The result of this process is shown in Table 5-4. The

Table 5-3
Evaluation of Eight Alternatives Against the Decision Criteria*

Criteria	Alpha College	Beta College	Delta College	Gamma College	Iota College	Omega College	Phi College	Sigma College
Availability of financial aid	5	4	10	7	7	8	3	7
School's reputation	10	6	6	6	9	5	9	6
Annual cost (low cost preferred)	5	7	8	8	5	10	5	8
Curricula offering	6	10	8	9	8	8	9	8
Geographic location	6	7	10	10	6	9	10	7
Admission requirements (in terms of likelihood of acceptance)	7	10	10	10	8	10	8	10
Quality of social life	10	5	7	7	3	7	10	8
School size	10	7	7	7	9	7	9	4
Male:female ratio	2	2	8	8	8	10	2	8
Physical attractiveness of the campus	8	10	6	3	4	10	5	9

*The colleges that achieved the highest rating for a criterion are given 10 points.

Table 5-4
Evaluation of College Alternatives

	Alternatives							
Criteria (and weight)	Alpha College	Beta College	Delta College	Gamma College	Iota College	Omega College	Phi College	Sigma College
Availability of financial aid (10)	50	40	100	70	70	80	30	70
School's reputation (10)	100	60	60	60	90	50	90	60
Annual cost (8)	40	56	64	64	40	80	40	64
Curricula offering (7)	42	70	56	63	56	56	63	56
Geographic location (6)	36	42	60	60	36	54	60	42
Admission requirements (5)	35	50	50	50	40	50	40	50
Quality of social life (4)	40	20	28	28	12	28	40	32
School size (3)	30	21	21	21	27	21	27	12
Male:female ratio (2)	4	4	16	16	16	20	4	16
Physical attractiveness of the campus (2)	16	20	12	6	8	20	10	18
Totals	393	373	467	438	395	459	404	420

summation of these scores represents an evaluation of each college against the previously established criteria and weights.

Step 6: Select the Best Alternative. The final step in the optimizing decision model is the selection of the best alternative from among those enumerated and evaluated. Since best is defined in terms of highest total score, the selection is quite simple. The decision maker merely chooses the alternative that generated the largest total score in Step 5. For our high school senior, that means Delta College. Based on the criteria identified, the weights given to the criteria, and the decision maker's evaluation of each college on each of the criteria, Delta College scored highest and thus becomes the best.

Assumptions of the Optimizing Model

The steps in the optimizing model contain a number of assumptions. It is important to understand these assumptions if we are to determine how accurately the optimizing model describes actual individual decision making.

The assumptions of the optimizing model are the same as those that underlie the concept of *rationality*. Rationality refers to choices that are consistent and value maximizing. Rational decision making, therefore, implies that the decision maker can be fully objective and logical. The individual is assumed to have a clear goal, and all of the six steps in the optimizing model are assumed to lead toward the selection of the alternative that will maximize that goal. Let's take a closer look at the assumptions inherent in rationality and, hence, the optimizing model.

Goal-Oriented. The optimizing model assumes that there is no conflict over the goal. Whether the decision involves selecting a college to attend, determining whether or not to go to work today, or choosing the right applicant to fill a job vacancy, it is assumed that the decision maker has a single, well-defined goal that he or she is trying to maximize.

All Options Are Known. It is assumed that the decision maker can identify *all* the relevant criteria and can list *all* viable alternatives. The optimizing model portrays the decision maker as fully comprehensive in his or her ability to assess criteria and alternatives.

Preferences Are Clear. Rationality assumes that the criteria and alternatives can be assigned numerical values and ranked in a preferential order.

Preferences Are Constant. The same criteria and alternatives should be obtained every time because, in addition to the goal and preferences being clear, it is assumed that the specific decision criteria are constant and the weights assigned to them are stable over time.

Final Choice Will Maximize the Outcome. The rational decision maker following the optimizing model will choose the alternative that rates highest. This most preferred solution will, based on Step 5 of the process, give the maximum benefits.

Predictions from the Optimizing Model Using the above assumptions, we would predict that the individual decision maker would have a clear and specific goal; a fully comprehensive set of criteria that determine the relevant factors in the decision; a precise ranking of the criteria, which will be stable over time; and that the decision maker will select the alternative that scores highest after all options have been evaluated.

In terms of the college selection decision introduced earlier, the optimizing model would predict that the high school student could identify every factor that might be important in her decision. Each of these factors would be weighted in terms of importance. All of the colleges that could possibly be viable options would be identified and evaluated against the criteria. Remember, because all alternatives are assumed to be considered, our decision maker might be looking at hundreds of colleges. Also, even if this activity took six months to complete, the criteria and weights would not vary over time. If the college's reputation was most important in September, it would still be so in March. Further, if Beta College was given a score of 6 on this criterion in September, six months later the assessment would be the same. Finally, since every factor that is important in the decision has been considered and given its proper weight, and since every alternative has been identified and evaluated against the criteria, the decision maker can be assured that the college that scores highest in the evaluation is the best choice. There are no regrets because all information has been obtained and evaluated in a logical and consistent manner.

THE SATISFICING MODEL Do individuals actually make their decisions the way the optimizing model predicts? The evidence doesn't indicate that this is so. The reason is probably obvious: The assumptions underlying the model aren't very realistic.

The optimizing model assumes that decision makers can identify all relevant criteria and all viable alternatives. Even if this were somehow possible, it further implies that the decision maker could somehow assimilate and understand all of this information. These assumptions are just not consistent with the limits that we know to exist in the information processing capacity of human beings.

It isn't feasible for a person to search for each and every alternative. Decisions aren't made in an environment of certainty, where all alternatives are known to the decision maker. Individuals cannot always objectively state their decision criteria, nor list their preferences in a rank order from most preferred to least preferred. Any list and its assigned weights will also fluctuate over time. To test this last point, ask yourself if your taste in food, reading material, or companions has changed over the years. For most of us, they have. Why? Because our decision criteria are neither fixed nor stable. As Nobel laureate Herbert Simon has aptly concluded, the assumptions of the optimizing model require decision makers to have the foresight and capacities "resembling those we usually attribute to God."[1] Our understanding of human information processing tells us that individuals have a limited capacity for comprehending the inherent complexity in decision making.

Since individuals can't optimize in the sense that is consistent with complete rationality, and given the fact that individuals obviously do make decisions, how do they do it? They engage in a decision process that *satisfices;* that is, one that provides satisfactory and sufficient solutions. Rather than optimize, they seek solutions to their problems that are "good enough." The satisficing model is characterized by bounded rationality and incrementalism.

Bounded Rationality

Decision makers respond to the complexity of their task by reducing problems to a level at which they can be readily understood. Since the capacity of the human mind for formulating and solving complex problems is far too small to meet all the requirements for full rationality, individuals operate within the confines of bounded rationality. They construct simplified models that extract the essential features from problems without capturing all their complexity. The individual can then behave rationally within the limits of the simple model.

How does bounded rationality work for the typical individual? Once a problem is identified, the search for criteria and alternatives begins. But the list of criteria is likely to be far from exhaustive. The decision maker will identify a limited list made up of the more conspicuous choices. These are the choices that are easy to find and which tend to be highly visible. In most cases, they will represent familiar criteria and the tried and true solutions.

1. Herbert A. Simon, *Models of Man* (New York: John Wiley and Sons, 1957), p. 3.

Incrementalism   If what has worked in the past proves unsatisfactory, the satisficer will resort to incrementalism. This means that the search for alternatives will be confined to the area closest to the problem. Instead of thoroughly examining a wide and cumbersome range of alternatives, as is required for optimizing, the satisficer will consider only those alternatives that differ in relatively small degree from the choice currently in effect.

Summary of Satisficing Model   An alternative satisfices if (1) there exists a set of criteria that describes minimally satisfactory alternatives and (2) the alternative in question meets or exceeds all these criteria. The satisficing decison maker, then, compares alternatives, in sequential order, against the decision criteria. If an alternative fails to satisfy the criteria, the individual will continue to the next alternative. The first alternative to meet the criteria ends the search, and the decision maker can then proceed toward implementing this acceptable course of action.

Keep in mind that, in contrast to the optimizing model, the order in which alternatives are considered when one is satisficing becomes critical in determining which alternative is selected. If the decision maker were optimizing, all alternatives would eventually be listed in a hierarchy of preferred order. Since all the alternatives would be considered, the initial order in which they would be evaluated is irrelevant. Every potential solution would get a full and complete evaluation. But this is not the case with satisficing. Assuming that a problem has more than one potential solution, the satisficing choice will be the first acceptable one the decision maker encounters. Since decision makers use simple and limited models, they typically begin by identifying alternatives that are obvious, ones with which they are familiar, and those not too far from the status quo. Those solutions that depart least from the status quo and meet the decision criteria are most likely to be selected. This may help to explain why the decisions people make are not likely to result in the selection of extremely different or radical solutions from those they have made before. A unique alternative may present an optimizing solution to the problem; however, it will rarely be chosen. An acceptable solution will be identified well before the decision maker is required to search very far beyond the status quo.

Using the satisficing model, how might we predict that the high school senior, introduced earlier in the chapter, would make her college choice? Obviously, she will not consider all of the more than 2000 colleges in the U.S. or the multitude of others in foreign countries. Based on schools that she's heard about from friends and relatives plus possibly a quick look through a guide to colleges, she would typically select a half-a-dozen or a dozen colleges to which she will send for catalogs, brochures,

67

and applications. Based on a cursory appraisal of the materials she receives from the colleges, and using her set of rough decision criteria, she will probably select an early favorite. If this selection meets her minimal requirements, she is likely to make this her choice and discontinue further search. She may continue to look at other alternatives even though she has found a satisficing choice, but this tends to be a decision confirmation activity; it is intended to rationalize and support the alternative already selected. Rather than objectively appraising alternatives after this favorite has been implicitly selected, decision makers frequently attempt to justify their favored alternative. This effort becomes self-fulfilling, in that it ensures that the implicit favorite turns out to be their "best" choice. Regardless, the decision process is characterized by creating a simplified and limited model of the real problem; the recognition of a limited number of decision criteria; consideration of only a limited number of alternatives; and the selection of an alternative that is satisfactory and sufficient.

IMPLICATIONS FOR MANAGERS

As stated at the beginning of this chapter, individuals think and reason before they act. It is because of this that an understanding of how people make decisions can be helpful if we are to explain and predict their behavior. This is best illustrated by looking at a few of the more obvious decisions that managers frequently have to make.

Selecting Among Job Applicants

Managers interview applicants for vacancies in their units. Deciding whom to hire from among the applicants can be an important decision; it may have great impact on the unit's performance.

Studies of employment interviews indicate several patterns that are consistent with the satisficing model. From among the final applicants (those selected for interviews) a person is likely to be evaluated more favorably if he or she follows weak candidates and if the interviewer perceives an absence of negative qualities in the early minutes of the interview. Interviewers use other applicants as a standard. The appraisal of a candidate may therefore be unjustly raised if he or she were directly preceded by several poor candidates, or it may be lowered if he or she were preceded by very strong candidates. Most interviewers' decisions have also been found to change very little after the first four or five minutes of the interview. As a result, a good applicant is typically characterized more by the absence of unfavorable characteristics than by the presence of favorable characteristics. In a half-hour interview, the decision maker tends to make a decision about the suitability of the candidate in the first few minutes and then uses the rest of the interview time to select information that supports the early decision.

Evaluating an Employee's Performance

Managers are regularly required to evaluate the performance of their employees. Performance evaluation, however, is far from an objective and rational decision process. Two individuals can perform at comparable levels, yet achieve very different evaluations.

Most evaluations of performance focus on visible and easy-to-measure criteria. This may explain why factors such as neatness, promptness, enthusiasm, and a positive attitude are often related to good evaluations. It also explains why quantity measures typically override quality measures. The former category is easier to appraise.

The satisficing model may also give us insights into the reason employee performance in an organization tends to follow a normal curve—a few employees are excellent, a few are poor, and the majority perform near the middle—but actual evaluations tend to be more homogeneous and skewed toward the upper ranges of the performance scale. For instance, in the U.S. Army, average performance is considered in the scoring range of 70 to 79, yet the average rating of captains is 92! Officers in the U.S. Army and managers in both private and public organizations simplify the complex task of evaluating their subordinates by inflating their appraisals and reduce pressures to explain differences by minimizing those differences.

Problem Solving

Managers, particularly those in the higher echelons of organizations, frequently confront new or novel problems for which there are no established, routine procedures available. In such cases, managers must search for alternative solutions. The satisficing model provides us with insights into this type of search. First, a manager will reflect on his experience, trying to recall similar problems and how they were solved. If this proves fruitless, he or she will look for solutions that deviate least from previous solutions. In an iterative fashion, a manager will begin with the familiar and only move to more novel or unique solutions if the iterative process continually fails to produce an acceptable solution. As soon as a satisfactory alternative is found, the search process will be discontinued.

The above problem-solving approach minimizes the need for creativity, while emphasizing previous experience. In the optimizing model, creativity could uncover novel alternatives no one else had discovered. Satisficing, on the other hand, leads to solutions that are unlikely to stray very far from the status quo. Past experience becomes a major determinant of alternatives; hence, the decision maker tends to emphasize approaches that are relatively familiar.

SELECTED REFERENCES

FORESTER, JOHN, "Bounded Rationality and the Politics of Muddling Through," *Public Administration Review*, January–February 1984, pp. 23–31.

HARRISON, E. FRANK, *The Managerial Decision-Making Process* (2nd ed.). Boston: Houghton Mifflin, 1981.

JANIS, IRVING L., AND LEON MANN, *Decision Making: A Psychological Analysis of Conflict, Choice and Commitment*. New York: The Free Press, 1977.

McK. AGNEW, NEIL, AND JOHN L. BROWN, "Bounded Rationality: Fallible Decisions in Unbounded Decision Space," *Behavioral Science*, July 1986, pp. 148–61.

ROWE, ALAN J., JAMES D. BOULGARIDES, AND MICHAEL R. McGRATH, *Managerial Decision Making*. Chicago: Science Research Associates, Inc., 1984.

SIMON, HERBERT A., *Administrative Behavior* (3rd ed.). New York: The Free Press, 1976.

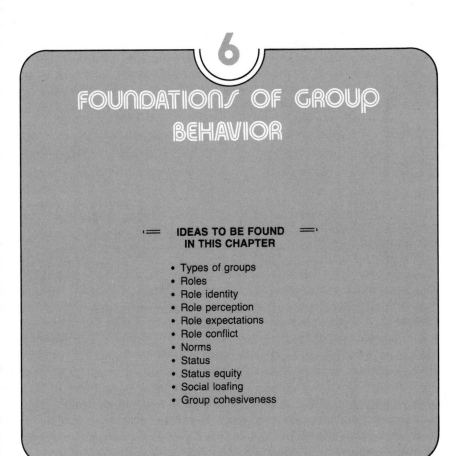

FOUNDATIONƧ OF GROUP BEHAVIOR

6

The behavior of individuals in groups is something more than the sum total of each acting in his or her own way. When individuals are in groups they act differently from when they are alone. This chapter introduces some basic concepts about groups and demonstrates how an understanding of groups can help to explain the larger phenomenon of organizational behavior.

DEFINING AND CLASSIFYING GROUPS   A group is defined as two or more individuals, interacting and inter-dependent, who come together to achieve particular objectives. Groups can be either formal or informal. By formal, we mean defined by the organization's structure, with designated work assignments establishing tasks and work groups. In formal groups, the behaviors that one should engage in are stipulated by and directed toward organizational goals. In contrast, informal groups are alliances that are

71

neither structured nor organizationally determined. In the work environment, these groups form naturally as responses to the need for social contact.

It is possible to further subclassify groups into command, task, interest, or friendship categories. Command and task groups are dictated by the formal organization, whereas interest and friendship groups are informal alliances.

The *command group* is determined by the organization chart. It is composed of the subordinates who report directly to a given manager. An elementary school principal and her twelve teachers form a command group, as do the director of postal audits and his five inspectors.

Task groups, also organizationally determined, represent those working together to complete a job. However, a task group's boundaries are not limited to its immediate hierarchical superior. It can cross command relationships. For instance, if a college student is accused of a campus crime, it may require communication and coordination among the Dean of Academic Affairs, the Dean of Students, the Registrar, the Director of Security, and the student's advisor. Such a formation would constitute a task group. It should be noted that all command groups are also task groups, but because task groups can cut across the organization, the reverse need not be true.

People who may or may not be aligned into common command or task groups may affiliate to attain a specific objective with which each is concerned. This is an *interest group*. Employees who band together to have their vacation schedule altered, to support a peer who has been fired, or to seek increased fringe benefits represent the formation of a united body to further their common interest.

Groups often develop because the individual members have one or more common characteristics. We call these formations *friendship groups*. Social allegiances, which frequently extend outside the work situation, can be based on, for example, similar age, support for "Big Red" Nebraska football, having attended the same college, or holding similar political views.

Informal groups provide a very important function by satisfying their members' social needs. Because of interactions that result from the close proximity of work stations or tasks, we find workers playing golf together, riding to and from work together, lunching together, and spending their breaks around the water cooler together. We must recognize that these types of interactions among individuals, even though informal, deeply affect their behavior and performance.

WHY DO PEOPLE JOIN GROUPS?

There is no single reason why individuals join groups. Because most people belong to a number of groups, it's obvious that different groups provide different benefits to their members. The most popular reasons for joining a group are related to our needs for security, status, self-esteem, affiliation, power, and goal achievement.

Security

"There's strength in numbers." By joining a group, we can reduce the insecurity of standing alone—we feel stronger, have fewer self-doubts, and are more resistant to threats. New employees are particularly vulnerable to a sense of isolation and turn to the group for guidance and support. However, whether we are talking about new employees or those with years on the job, we can state that few individuals like to stand alone. We get reassurances from interacting with others and being part of a group. This often explains the appeal of unions—if management creates an environment in which employees feel insecure, they are likely to turn to unionization to reduce their feelings of insecurity.

Status

"I'm a member of our company's running team. Last month, at the National Corporate Relays, we won the national championship. Didn't you see our picture in the company newsletter?" These comments demonstrate the role that a group can play in giving prestige. Inclusion in a group viewed as important by others provides recognition and status for its members.

Self-Esteem

"Before I was asked to pledge Phi Omega Chi, I felt like a nobody. Being in a fraternity makes me feel much more important." This quote demonstrates that groups can provide people with feelings of self-worth. That is, in addition to conveying status to those outside the group, membership can also give increased feelings of worth to the group members themselves. Our self-esteem is bolstered, for example, when we are accepted by a highly valued group. Being assigned to a task force whose purpose is to review and make recommendations for the location of the company's new corporate headquarters can fulfill one's needs for competence and growth, as well as for status.

Affiliation

"I'm independently wealthy, but I wouldn't give up my job. Why? Because I really like the people I work with!" This quote, from a $45,000-a year purchasing agent who inherited several million dollars' worth of real estate, verifies that groups can fulfill our social needs. People enjoy the regular interaction that comes with group membership. For many people, these on-the-job interactions are their primary source for fulfilling their needs for affiliation. For almost all people, work groups significantly contribute to fulfilling their needs for friendship and social relations.

Power   "I tried for two years to get the plant
                                       management to increase the number
of female restrooms on the production floor to the same number as the men
have. It was like talking to a wall. But I got about fifteen other women who
were production employees together and we jointly presented our demands to management. The construction crews were in here adding female
restrooms within ten days!"

This episode demonstrates that one of the appealing aspects of groups
is that they represent power. What often cannot be achieved individually
becomes possible through group action. Of course, this power may not be
sought only to make demands on others. It may be desired merely as a
countermeasure. In order to protect themselves from unreasonable demands by management, individuals may align with others.

Informal groups additionally provide opportunities for individuals to
exercise power over others. For individuals who desire to influence others,
groups can offer power without a formal position of authority in the organization. As a group leader, you may be able to make requests of group
members and obtain compliance without any of the responsibilities that
traditionally go with formal managerial positions. So, for people with a high
power need, groups can be a vehicle for fulfillment.

Goal Achievement   "I'm part of a three-person team
                                       studying how we can cut our com-
pany's transportation costs. They've been going up at over 30 percent a
year for several years now so the corporate controller assigned representatives from cost accounting, shipping, and marketing to study the problem
and make recommendations."

This task group was created to achieve a goal that would be considerably more difficult if pursued by a single person. There are times when it
takes more than one person to accomplish a particular task—there is a need
to pool talents, knowledge, or power in order to get a job completed. In
such instances, management will rely on the use of a formal group.

STAGES OF GROUP   Group development is a dynamic
DEVELOPMENT   process. Most groups are in a contin-
                                       ual state of change. But just because
groups probably never reach complete stability doesn't mean that there
isn't some general pattern that describes how most groups evolve. There is
strong evidence that groups pass through a standard sequence of four
stages. As shown in Figure 6-1, these four stages have been labeled *forming, storming, norming,* and *performing*.

The first stage—*forming*—is characterized by a great deal of uncer-

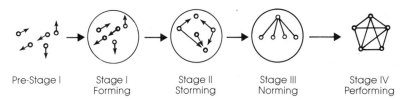

Pre-Stage I	Stage I	Stage II	Stage III	Stage IV
	Forming	Storming	Norming	Performing

Figure 6-1
Stages of Group Development

tainty about the group's purpose, structure, and leadership. Members are testing the waters to determine what types of behavior are acceptable. This stage is complete when members have begun to think of themselves as part of a group.

The *storming* stage is one of intragroup conflict. Members accept the existence of the group, but there is resistance to the control that the group imposes on individuality. There is also conflict over who will control the group. When Stage II is complete, there will be a relatively clear hierarchy of leadership within the group.

The third stage is one in which close relationships develop and the group demonstrates cohesiveness. There is now a strong sense of group identity and camaraderie. This *norming* stage is complete when there is a continuing structure for the group and the group has assimilated a common set of expectations of what defines correct member behavior.

The final stage is *performing*. The structure at this point is fully functional and accepted. Group energy has moved from getting to know and understand each other to the job of task performance.

Most of you have probably encountered each of these stages when you have had to do a group project for a class. Group members are selected and then you meet for the first time. There is a period of feeling out to assess what the group is going to do and how it is going to do it. This is usually followed rapidly by the battle for control. Who is going to lead us? Once this is resolved and a hierarchy is agreed upon, the group moves to identify specific activities of what needs to be done, who is going to do it, and dates by which the parts need to be completed. General expectations become set and agreed upon by and for each member. This forms the foundation for what you hope will be a coordinated group effort culminating in a project that group members and the instructor agree is a job well done. Of course, groups occasionally don't get much beyond the first or second stage, which frequently results in projects and grades that are disappointing.

Should one assume from the foregoing that group effectiveness improves as progression is made through the four stages? While some have argued that effectiveness of work units increases at advanced stages, it is not that simple. Although this assumption may be generally true, what makes a group effective is a complex issue. Under some conditions, high levels of conflict are conducive to high group performance. So we might expect to find situations where groups in Stage II outperform those in Stages III or IV. Similarly, movement through stages is not always clear. Sometimes, in fact, several stages are going on simultaneously—as when groups are storming and performing at the same time. Groups even occasionally regress to previous stages. Therefore, to assume that this developmental process is followed precisely by all groups or that Stage IV is always the most preferable is likely to prove incorrect. It is better to think of this four-stage model as a general framework. It reminds you that groups are dynamic entities and can help you toward a better understanding of the problems and issues that are most likely to surface during a group's life.

GROUP STRUCTURE Three concepts underlie a basic understanding of group structure—roles, norms, and status. These seem, on the surface, everyday terms. But in order to understand and analyze group behavior, a thorough understanding of the theory upon which these concepts are built is fundamental. This section provides a clear explanation and definition of each concept.

Roles

Shakespeare said, "All the world's a stage, and all the men and women merely players." Using the same metaphor, all group members are actors, each playing a *role*. A role is a set of expected behavior patterns attributed to someone occupying a given position in a social unit. The understanding of role behavior would be dramatically simplified if each of us chose one role and played it regularly and consistently. Unfortunately, we are required to play a number of diverse roles, both on and off our jobs. As we shall see, one of the tasks in understanding behavior is grasping the role that a person is currently playing.

For example, on his job, Bill Patterson is a plant manager with Electrical Industries, a large electrical equipment manufacturer in Phoenix. He has a number of roles that he fulfills on that job: Electrical Industries employee, member of middle management, electrical engineer, and the primary company spokesman in the community. Off the job, Bill Patterson finds himself in still more roles: husband, father, Catholic, Rotarian, tennis player, member of the Thunderbird Country Club, and president of his homeowner's association. Many of these roles are compatible; some create conflicts. For instance, how does his religious involvement influence his managerial decisions regarding layoffs, expense account padding, or providing accurate information to government agencies? A recent offer of promotion requires Bill to relocate, yet his family very much wants to stay in Phoenix. Can the role demands of his job be reconciled with the demands of husband and father roles?

The issue should be clear: Like Bill Patterson, we all are required to play a number of roles, and our behavior varies with the role we are playing. Bill's behavior when he attends church on Sunday morning is different from his behavior on the golf course later that same day. We act differently in the role of student than when we play husband or wife, or boyfriend or girlfriend.

Role Identity. There are certain attitudes and actual behaviors consistent with a role, and they create the role identity. People have the ability to shift roles rapidly when they recognize that the situation and its demands clearly require major changes. For instance, when union stewards were promoted to foreman positions, it was found that their attitudes changed from pro-union to pro-management within a few months of their promotion. When these promotions had to be rescinded later because of economic difficulties in the firm, it was found that the demoted foremen had once again adopted their pro-union attitudes.

When the situation is more vague and the role one is to play less clear, people often revert to old role identities. An investigation of high school reunions verified this view. At the reunions studied, even though participants had been away from high school and their peers for five, ten, or twenty or more years, they reverted to their old roles. The "ins" replayed their former roles, as did the "outs." Even though entirely new criteria were being used in the real world for success, the former jocks, student officers, and the cheerleaders acted as "ins" and the others expected them to. In spite of the fact that some of the former losers were now winners by society's standards, they found it very difficult to deal with the winner's role when placed in an environment in which they had always been losers. With the role requirements ill-defined, identities became clouded, and individuals reverted back to old patterns of behavior.

Role Perception. One's view of how one is supposed to act in a given situation is a role perception. Based on an interpretation of how we believe we are supposed to behave, we engage in certain types of behavior.

Where do we get these perceptions? From stimuli all around us—friends, books, movies, television. Undoubtedly many of today's young surgeons formed their role identities from their perception of Hawkeye on "M.A.S.H.," while college instructors may be emulating the character of Professor Kingsfield in *The Paper Chase*. It also seems reasonable to conclude that many future police officers will have been influenced by "Hill

Street Blues." Of course, the primary reason that apprenticeship programs exist in many trades and professions is to allow individuals to watch an expert so they can learn to act as they are supposed to.

Role Expectations. Role expectations are defined as how others believe you should act in a given situation. How you behave is determined, to a large part, by the role defined in the context in which you are acting. The role of a U.S. Senator is viewed as having propriety and dignity, whereas a football coach is seen as aggressive, dynamic, and inspirational to his players. In the same context, we might be surprised to learn that the neighborhood priest moonlights during the week as a bartender. Why? Because our role expectations of priests and bartenders tend to be considerably different. Role stereotypes are role expectations concentrated into generalized categories.

During the last several decades we have seen a major change in the general population's role stereotypes of females. In the 1950s, a woman's role was to stay home, take care of the house, raise children, and generally care for her husband. Today, most of us no longer hold this stereotype. Girls can aspire to be doctors, lawyers, and astronauts as well as the more traditional positions as nurse, school teacher, secretary, or housewife. In other words, many of us have changed role expectations of women and, similarly, many women carry new role perceptions.

In the workplace, it can be helpful to look at the topic of role expectations through the perspective of the *psychological contract*. There is an unwritten agreement that exists between employees and their employer. This psychological contract sets out mutual expectations—what management expects from workers and vice versa. In effect, this contract defines the behavioral expectations that accompany every role. Management is expected to treat employees justly, provide acceptable working conditions, clearly communicate what is a fair day's work and give feedback on how well the employee is doing. Employees are expected to respond by demonstrating a good attitude, following directions, and showing loyalty to the organization.

What happens when role expectations as implied in the psychological contract are not met? If management is derelict in keeping up its part of the bargain, we can expect negative repercussions on employee performance and satisfaction. When employees fail to live up to expectations, the result is usually some form of disciplinary action up to and including firing.

The psychological contract should be recognized as a powerful determiner of behavior in organizations. It points out the importance of communicating accurately role expectations.

Role Conflict. When an individual is confronted by divergent role expectations, the result is *role conflict*. It exists when an individual finds that compliance with one role requirement may make more difficult the compliance with another. At the extreme it would include situations where two or more role expectations are mutually contradictory.

Many believe that the topic of role conflict is the most critical role concept in attempting to explain behavior. This, for example, is one of the classic problems of college presidents, a fact which became highly evident in the late 1960s. The college president is forced to reconcile diverse role expectations by faculty, students, board members, alumni, and other administrators. The behavior expectations that are perceived as acceptable by one group are often totally in disagreement with the expectations of other groups.

Our previous discussion of the many roles Bill Patterson had to deal with included several role conflicts—for instance, Bill's attempt to reconcile the expectations placed on him as head of his family and as an executive with Electrical Industries. The former emphasizes stability and concern for the desire of his wife and children to remain in Phoenix. Electrical Industries, on the other hand, expects its employees to be responsive to the needs and requirements of the company. Although it might be in Bill's financial and career interests to accept a relocation, the conflict is the choice between family and career role expectations.

All of us have faced and will continue to face role conflicts. The critical issue, from our standpoint, is how conflicts, imposed by divergent expectations within the organization, have an impact on behavior. Certainly they increase internal tension and frustration. There are a number of behavioral responses one may engage in. For example, one can give a formalized bureaucratic response. The conflict is then resolved by relying on the rules, regulations, and procedures that govern organizational activities. For example, a worker, faced with the conflicting requirements imposed by the corporate controller's office and his own plant manager, decides in favor of his immediate boss, the plant manager. Similarly, many college professors create a formal environment in class by calling their students Mr. and Ms., and expecting to be called Professor in order to avoid allowing friendships to interfere with the objective requirements of the professorial role. Other behavioral responses may include withdrawal, stalling, negotiation or, as we found in our discussion of dissonance in Chapter 2, redefining the facts or the situation to make them appear congruent.

Norms

On the first Friday of every month, the six men and two women who make up the executive board of Consolidated Foods meet to review the company's prior month's performance. Upon arriving at the meeting, the executives exchange handshakes. At the meeting's conclusion, and again before departing, they shake hands. But at a recent dinner party given by one of the executives and at which the other seven were in attendance, the male and female executives greeted each other with kisses. Similarly, upon saying goodnight at the end of the evening, they again exchanged kisses. Why handshakes on one occasion and kisses on another? Norms!

All groups have established norms; that is, acceptable standards of behavior that are shared by the group's members. Norms tell members what they ought or ought not to do under certain circumstances. From an individual's standpoint, they tell what is expected in certain situations. When agreed to and accepted by the group, norms act as a means of influencing the behavior of group members with a minimum of external controls. Norms may differ among groups, communities, and societies, but each has it own set of them.

Formalized norms are written up in organizational manuals, which set out rules and procedures for employees to follow. However, the majority of norms are informal. We do not need someone to tell us that throwing paper airplanes or engaging in prolonged bull sessions at the water cooler is unacceptable behavior when the "big boss from New York" is touring the office. Similarly, we all know that when we are in an employment interview discussing what we did not like about our previous job, there are certain things we should not talk about (difficulty in getting along with co-workers or our supervisor), while it is very appropriate to talk about other things (inadequate opportunities for advancement, or unimportant and meaningless work). Evidence indicates that even high school students recognize that in such interviews certain answers are more socially desirable than others.

Students are very good at quickly assimilating classroom norms. Depending on the environment created by the instructor, the norms may support unequivocal acceptance of the material suggested by the instructor, or, at the other extreme, students may be expected to question and challenge the instructor on any point that is unclear. For example, in most classroom situations, the norms dictate that one not engage in loud, boisterous discussion that makes it impossible to hear the lecturer, nor humiliate the instructor by pushing him or her too far, even if one has obviously located a weakness in something the instructor has said. Should some individuals in the classroom group behave in such a way as to violate these norms, we can expect pressure to be applied against the deviant members to bring their behavior into conformity with group standards.

The Hawthorne Studies.   Behavioral scientists generally agree that the role that norms play in influencing worker behavior was not fully recognized until the early 1930s. This enlightenment grew out of a study undertaken at Western Electric Company's Hawthorne Works in Chicago between 1927 and 1932. Conducted under the direction of Harvard professor Elton Mayo, the Hawthorne studies concluded that a worker's behavior and sentiments were closely related, that group influences were significant in affecting individual behavior, that group standards were highly effective in establishing individual worker output, and that money was less a factor in determining worker output than group standards, sentiments, and security. Let us briefly review the Hawthorne investigations and demonstrate the importance of these findings in explaining group behavior.

The Hawthorne researchers began by examining the relationship between the physical environment and productivity. Illumination, temperature, and other working conditions were selected to represent this physical environment. The researchers' initial findings contradicted their anticipated results.

They began with illumination experiments with various groups of workers. The researchers manipulated the intensity of illumination upward and downward, while at the same time noting changes in group output. Results varied, but one thing was clear: In no case was the increase or decrease in output in proportion to the increase or decrease in illumination. So the researchers introduced a control group: An experimental group was presented with varying intensity of illumination, while the controlled unit worked under a constant illumination intensity. Again, the results were bewildering to the Hawthorne researchers. As the light level was increased in the experimental unit, output rose for each group. But to the surprise of the researchers, as the light level was dropped in the experimental group, productivity continued to increase in both. In fact, a productivity decrease was observed in the experimental group only when the light intensity had been reduced to that of moonlight. Mayo and his associates concluded that illumination intensity was only a minor factor among the many influences that affected an employee's productivity, but they could not explain the behavior they had witnessed.

As a follow-up to the illumination experiments, the researchers began a second set of experiments in the relay-assembly test room at Western Electric. A small group of women were isolated away from the main work group so that their behavior could be more carefully observed. They went about their job of assembling small telephone relays in a room laid out much like their normal department. The only difference was the placement in the room of a research assistant who acted as an observer by keeping records of output, rejects, working conditions, and a daily log sheet describing everything that happened. Over a two-and-a-half-year period, this small group's output increased steadily, as did its morale. The number of personal absences and those due to sickness were approximately one-third of those recorded by women in the regular production department. What became evident was that this group's performance was significantly influenced by its status of being special. The women in the test room thought being in the experimental group was fun, that they were in some sort of an elite group, and that management was concerned with their interest by engaging in such experimentation.

A third experiment in the bank wiring observation room was similar in design to the experiment in the relay test room, except male workers were used. In addition, a sophisticated wage incentive plan was introduced on the assumption that individual workers would maximize their productivity when they saw that it was directly related to economic rewards. The most important finding from this experiment was that employees did not individually maximize their outputs. Rather, their output became controlled by a group norm that determined what was a proper day's work. Output was not only being restricted, but individual workers were giving erroneous reports. The total for a week would check with the total week's output, but the daily reports showed a steady, level output regardless of actual daily production. What was going on?

Interviews determined that the group was operating well below its capability and was leveling output in order to protect itself. Members were afraid that if they significantly increased their output the unit incentive rate would be cut, the expected daily output would be increased, layoffs might occur, or that slower men would be reprimanded. So the group established its idea of a fair output—neither too much nor too little. They helped each other out to ensure that their reports were nearly level.

The norms that the group established included a number of "don'ts." *Don't* be a rate-buster, turning out too much work. *Don't* be a chiseler, turning out too little work. *Don't* be a squealer on any of your peers.

How did the group enforce these norms? Their methods were neither gentle nor subtle. They included sarcasm, name-calling, ridicule, and even physical punches to the upper arms of members who violated the group's norms. Members would also ostracize individuals whose behavior was against the group's interest.

The Hawthorne studies made an important contribution to our understanding of group behavior, particularly the significant place that norms have in determining an individual's work behavior.

Common Norms in Organizations. An organization's norms are like an individual's fingerprints—each is unique. Yet there are still common classes of norms that appear in most organizations.

Probably the most widespread norms, as demonstrated in the Hawthorne studies, relate to levels of *effort* and *performance*. Work groups typically provide their members with very explicit cues on how hard they should work, their level of output, when to look busy, when it's acceptable to goof off, and the like. These norms are extremely powerful in affecting an individual employee's performance—capable of modifying significantly a performance prediction based solely on the employee's ability and level of personal motivation.

Some organizations have formal *dress* codes. However, even in their absence, norms frequently develop to dictate the kind of clothing that should be worn to work. College seniors, interviewing for their first postgraduate job, pick up this norm quickly. Every spring on college campuses throughout the country, those interviewing for jobs can usually be spotted—they're the ones walking around in the dark gray or blue pinstriped suits. They are enacting the dress norms they have learned are expected in professional positions. Of course, what connotes acceptable dress in one organization may be very different from another. Faculty members in the Graduate Schools of Business at Harvard and U.C.L.A. may teach the same subject matter, but the social norms at Harvard dictate a much more formal dress attire than exists at the West Coast school.

Few managers appreciate employees who disparage the organization. Similarly, professional employees and those in the executive ranks recognize that most employers view with a great deal of disfavor those who actively look for another job. If such people are unhappy, they know to keep their job search secret. These examples demonstrate that *loyalty* norms are widespread in organizations. This concern for demonstrating loyalty, by the way, often explains why ambitious aspirants to top management positions in an organization willingly take work home at night, come in on weekends, and accept transfers to cities where they would otherwise not prefer to live.

The "How" and "Why" of Norms. *How* do norms develop? *Why* are they enforced? The following offers answers to these two questions.

Norms typically develop gradually as group members learn what behaviors are necessary for the group to function effectively. Of course, critical events in the group might short-circuit the process and act quickly to solidify new norms. Most norms develop in one or more of the following four ways: (1) *Explicit statements made by a group member*—often the group's supervisor or a powerful member. The group leader might, for instance, specifically say that no personal phone calls are allowed during working hours or that coffee breaks are to be kept to ten minutes. (2) *Critical events in the group's history.* These set important precedents. A bystander is injured while standing too close to a machine, and, from that point on, members of the work group regularly monitor each other to ensure that no one other than the operator gets within five feet of any machine. (3) *Primacy.* The first behavior pattern that emerges in a group frequently sets group expectations. Friendship groups of students often stake out seats near each other on the first day of class and become perturbed if an outsider takes the seats they consider theirs in a later class. (4) *Carry-over behaviors from past situations.* Group members bring expectations with them from other groups of which they have been members. This can explain why work groups typically prefer to add new members who are similar to current ones in background and experience. This is likely to increase the probability that the expectations they bring are consistent with those already held by the group.

But groups do not establish or enforce norms for every conceivable situation. The norms that the group will enforce tend to be those that are important to it. A norm is important: (1) *If it facilitates the group's survival*. Groups don't like to fail, so they look to enforce those norms that increase their chances for success. This means that they will try to protect themselves from interference from other groups or individuals. (2) *If it increases the predictability of group members' behaviors*. Norms that increase predictability enable group members to anticipate each other's actions and to prepare appropriate responses. (3) *If it reduces embarrassing interpersonal problems for group members*. Norms are important that ensure the satisfaction of their members and prevent as much interpersonal discomfort as possible. (4) *If it allows members to express the central values of the group and clarify what is distinctive about the group's identity*. Norms that encourage expression of the group's values and distinctive identity help to solidify and maintain the group.

Conformity.   As a member of a group, you desire continued acceptance by the group. Because of this you are susceptible to conforming to the group's norms. There is considerable evidence that groups can place strong pressures on individual members to change their attitudes and behaviors to conform to the group's standard.

Do individuals conform to the pressures of all the groups they belong to? Obviously not, because people belong to many groups and their norms vary. In some cases, they may even have contradictory norms. So what do people do? They conform to the important groups to which they belong or hope to belong. The important groups have been referred to as *reference groups* and are characterized as ones in which the person is aware of the other members defines himself or herself as a member (or would like to be a member), and feels that the group members are significant to him or her. The implication, then, is that *all* groups do not impose equal conformity pressures on their members.

The impact that group pressures for conformity can have on an individual member's judgment and attitudes was demonstrated in the now-classic studies by Solomon Asch.[1] Asch made up groups of seven or eight people, who sat in a classroom and were asked to compare two cards held by the experimenter. One card had one line, the other had three lines of varying length. As shown in Figure 6-2, one of the lines on the three-line

---

1. Solomon E. Asch, "Effects of Group Pressure upon the Modification and Distortion of Judgments," in *Groups, Leadership and Men*, ed. Harold Guetzkow (Pittsburgh: Carnegie Press, 1951), pp. 177–90.

 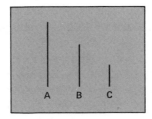

Figure 6-2
Examples of Cards Used in the Asch Study

card was identical to the line on the one-line card. Also, as shown in Figure 6-2, the difference in line length was quite obvious; under ordinary conditions, subjects made less than 1 percent errors. The object was to announce aloud which of the three lines matched the single line. But what happens if all the members in the group begin to give incorrect answers? Will the pressures to conform result in the unsuspecting subject (USS) altering his or her answer to align with the others? That was what Asch wanted to know. So he arranged the group so only the USS was unaware that the experiment was "fixed." The seating was prearranged so that the USS was the last to announce his or her decision.

The experiment began with several sets of matching exercises. All the subjects gave the right answers. On the third set, however, the first subject gave an obviously wrong answer—for example, saying "C" in Figure 6-2. The next subject gave the same wrong answer, and so did the others until it got to the unsuspecting subject. He knew "B" was the same as "X," yet everyone had said "C." The decision confronting the USS was this: Do you state a perception publicly that differs from the preannounced position of the others? Or do you give an answer that you strongly believe is incorrect in order to have your response agree with the other group members?

The results obtained by Asch demonstrated that over many experiments and many trials, subjects conformed in about 35 percent of the trials; that is, the subjects gave answers that they knew were wrong but that were consistent with the replies of other group members.

What can we conclude from this study? The results suggest that there are group norms that press us toward conformity. We desire to be one of the group and avoid being visibly different. We can generalize further to say that when an individual's opinion of objective data differs significantly from that of others in the group, he or she feels extensive pressure to align his or her opinion to conform with those of the others.

Status

While teaching a college course on adolescence a few years ago, the instructor asked the class to list things that contributed to status when they were in high school. The list was long, including such activities as being a jock, being able to cut class without getting caught, and having your own car. Then the instructor asked the students to list things that didn't contribute to status. Again, it was easy for the students to create a long list—getting straight A's, having your mother drive you to school, and so forth. Finally, the students were asked to develop a third list—those things that didn't matter one way or the other. There was a long silence. Finally, a young woman in the back row volunteered, "In high school, nothing didn't matter."

Status permeates far beyond the walls of high school. It would not be incorrect to rephrase the above quotation to read, "In the status hierarchy of life, nothing doesn't matter." In spite of the fact that most of us are quick to declare how unimportant status is, most of us are greatly concerned with acquiring status symbols. We live in a class-structured society. In spite of attempts to make our world more egalitarian, we have made little movement toward a classless society. As far back as scientists have been able to trace human groupings, we have had chiefs and Indians, noblemen and peasants, the haves and the have-nots. This continues to be the case today. Even the smallest group will develop roles, rites, and rituals to differentiate its members. Status is an important factor in understanding behavior because it is a significant motivator and has major behavioral consequences when individuals see a disparity between what they perceive their status to be and what others perceive it to be.

Status is a prestige grading, position, or rank within a group. It may be formally imposed by a group; that is, organizationally imposed, through titles or amenities like "the heavyweight champion of the world," or "most congenial." We are all familiar with the trappings that are associated with high organizational status—large offices with thick carpeting, impressive titles, high pay and fringe benefits, preferred work schedules, and so on. Whether management acknowledges the existence of a status hierarchy, organizations are filled with amenities that are not uniformly available to everyone and, hence, carry status value.

More often, we deal with status in an informal sense. Status may be informally acquired by such characteristics as education, age, sex, skill, or experience. Anything can have status value if others in the group evaluate it as such. But just because status is informal does not mean that it is less important or that there is less agreement on who has it or who does not. This was supported when individuals were asked to rank the status of their high school classmates a number of years following graduation. The respondents were able to place former classmates into a status hierarchy and the rankings were almost identical. We can and do place people into status categories, and there appears to be high agreement among members as to who is high, low, and in the middle.

In his classic restaurant study, William F. Whyte demonstrated the importance of status.[2] Whyte proposed that people work more smoothly if high-status personnel customarily originate action for lower-status personnel. He found a number of instances where, when those of lower status were initiating action, this created a conflict between formal and informal status systems. For example, he cited one instance in which waitresses passed their customers' orders directly on to countermen—and thus low-status servers were initiating action for high-status cooks. By the simple addition of an aluminum spindle to which the order could be hooked, a buffer was created, thus allowing the countermen to initiate action on orders when they felt ready.

Whyte also noted that in the kitchen, supply men secured food supplies from the chefs. This was, in effect, a case of low-skilled employees initiating action upon the high-skilled. Conflict was stimulated when several supply men explicitly and implicitly urged the chefs to "get a move on." However, Whyte observed that one supply man had little trouble. He gave the chef the order and asked that the chef call him when it was ready, thus reversing the initiating process. In Whyte's analysis, he suggested several changes in procedures, which aligned interactions more closely with the accepted status hierarchy and resulted in substantial improvements in worker relations and effectiveness.

It is important for group members to believe that the status hierarchy is equitable. When inequity is perceived, it creates disequilibrium resulting in various types of corrective behavior.

The concept of equity, presented in Chapter 3, applies to status. Individuals expect rewards to be proportionate to costs incurred in obtaining those rewards. If Sally and Betty are the two finalists for the position of head nurse in a hospital, and it is clear that Sally has more seniority and better preparation for assuming the promotion, Betty will view the selection of Sally as equitable. However, if Betty is chosen because she is the daughter-in-law of the hospital director, Sally will see there is an injustice.

The trappings that go with formal positions are also important elements in maintaining equity. If we believe there is an inequity between the perceived ranking of an individual and the status accouterments he or she is given by the organization, we are experiencing status incongruence. Some examples of incongruence are the supervisor earning less than her subordinates, the more desirable office location being held by a lower-ranking individual, or paid country club membership being provided by the company for division managers but not for vice-presidents. Employees expect the things an individual has and receives to be congruent with his or her status.

2. William F. Whyte, "The Social Structure of the Restaurant," *American Journal of Sociology*, January 1954, pp. 302–8.

In spite of our acknowledgement that groups generally agree within themselves on status criteria and hence tend to rank individuals fairly closely, individuals can find themselves in conflict when they move between groups whose status criteria are different or where groups are formed of individuals with heterogeneous backgrounds. Businessmen may use income, total wealth, or size of the companies they run as determinants. Government bureaucrats might use the size of their agencies. Academics may use the number of grants received or articles published. Blue-collar workers may use years of seniority, job assignments, or bowling scores. Where groups are made up of heterogeneous individuals or where heterogeneous groups are forced to be interdependent, there is a potential for status differences to initiate conflict as the group attempts to reconcile and align the differing hierarchies.

CONTINGENCY VARIABLES   Several contingency variables have been identified that improve our ability to explain and predict group behavior. Among these variables are individual personality characteristics, group size, and the degree of heterogeneity among members.

Personality Characteristics   There has been a great deal of research on the relationship between personality traits and group attitudes and behavior. The general conclusion is that attributes that tend to have a positive connotation in our culture tend to be positively related to group productivity, morale, and cohesiveness. These include traits such as sociability, self-reliance, and independence. In contrast, negatively evaluated characteristics such as authoritarianism, dominance, and unconventionality tend to be negatively related to the dependent variables.

Is any one personality characteristic a good predictor of group behavior? The answer is "No." The magnitude of the effect of any *single* characteristic is small, but taken *together*, the consequences for group behavior are of major significance. We can conclude, therefore, that personality characteristics of group members play an important part in determining behavior in groups.

Group Size   Does the size of a group affect the group's overall behavior? The answer to this question is a definite "Yes," but the effect depends on the group's goal.

The evidence indicates, for instance, that smaller groups are faster at completing tasks than are larger ones. However, if the group is engaged in problem solving, large groups consistently get better marks than their smaller counterparts. Translating these results into specific numbers is a bit more hazardous, but we can offer some parameters. Large groups (those with a dozen or more members) are good for gaining diverse input. So if the goal of the group is fact-finding, larger groups should be more effective. On the other hand, smaller groups are better at doing something productive with that input. Groups of approximately seven members, therefore, tend to be more effective for action taking.

One of the most important findings related to the size of a group has been labeled "social loafing." It directly challenges the logic that the productivity of the group as a whole should at least equal the sum of the productivity of each individual in that group.

A common stereotype about groups is that the sense of team spirit spurs individual effort and enhances the group's overall productivity. In the late 1920s, a German psychologist named Ringelmann compared the results of individual and group performance on a rope-pulling task. He expected that the group's effort would be equal to the sum of the efforts of individuals within the group. That is, three people pulling together should exert three times as much pull on the rope as one person, and eight people should exert eight times as much pull. Ringelmann's results, however, did not confirm his expectations. Groups of three people exerted a force only two-and-a-half times the average individual performance. Groups of eight collectively achieved less than four times the solo rate.

Replications of Ringelmann's research with similar tasks have generally supported his findings. Increases in group size are inversely related to individual performance. More may be better in the sense that the total productivity of a group of four is greater than one or two, but the individual productivity of each group member declines.

What causes this social loafing effect? It may be due to a belief that others in the group are not pulling their own weight. If you see others as lazy or inept, you can reestablish equity by reducing your effort. Another explanation is the dispersion of responsibility. Because the results of the group cannot be attributed to any single person, the relationship between an individual's input and the group's output is clouded. In such situations, individuals may be tempted to take a free ride and coast on the group's efforts. In other words, there will be a reduction in efficiency where individuals think that their contribution cannot be measured.

For OB, the implications of this effect on work groups are significant. Where managers utilize collective work situations to enhance morale and teamwork, they must also provide means by which individual efforts can be identified. If this is not done, management must weigh the potential losses in productivity against any possible gains in worker satisfaction.

The research on group size also leads us to two additional conclusions:

(1) Groups with an odd number of members tend to be preferred over those with an even number, and (2) groups composed of five or seven members do a pretty good job of extracting the best elements of both small and large groups. The preference for an odd number of members eliminates the possibility of ties. Groups made up of five or seven members are large enough to form a majority and allow for diverse input yet avoid the negative outcomes often associated with large groups such as domination by a few members, development of subgroups, inhibited participation by some members, and excessive time taken to reach a decision.

Heterogeneity of Members   Most group activities require a variety of skills and knowledge. Given this requirement, it would be reasonable to conclude that heterogeneous groups—those made up of dissimilar individuals—would be more likely to have diverse abilities and information and should be more effective than homogeneous groups. Research studies substantiate this conclusion.

When a group is heterogeneous in terms of personalities, opinions, abilities, skills, and perspectives, there is an increased probability that the group will possess the needed characteristics to complete its tasks effectively. The group may be more imbued with conflict and less expedient as diverse positions are introduced and assimilated, but the evidence generally supports the conclusion that heterogeneous groups perform more effectively than those that are homogeneous.

GROUP COHESIVENESS   This section will determine whether cohesiveness, as a group characteristic, is desirable. And, if it is, should management actively seek to create work groups that are highly cohesive?

Intuitively, it would appear that groups with a lot of internal disagreement and a lack of cooperative spirit would complete their tasks less effectively than would groups in which individuals generally agree, cooperate, and like each other. Research to test this intuition has focused on the concept of *group cohesiveness*, defined as the degree to which members are attracted to one another and share the group's goals. That is, the more that members are attracted to each other and the more that the group's goals align with their individual goals, the greater the group's cohesiveness. In the following pages, we'll review the factors that have been found to influence group cohesiveness and then look at the effect of cohesiveness on group productivity.

Determinants of Cohesiveness   What factors determine whether group members will be attracted to one another? Cohesiveness can be affected by such factors as time spent together, the severity of initiation, group size, external threats, and previous successes.

Time Spent Together. If you rarely get an opportunity to see or interact with other people, you're unlikely to be attracted to them. The amount of time that people spend together, therefore, influences cohesiveness. As people spend more time together, they become more friendly. They naturally begin to talk, respond, gesture, and engage in other interactions. These interactions typically lead to discovery of common interests and increased attraction.

The opportunity for group members to spend time together is dependent on their physical proximity. We would expect more close relationships among members who are located close to one another rather than far apart. People who live on the same block, ride in the same car pool, or share a common office are more likely to become a cohesive group because the physical distance between them is minimal. For instance, among clerical workers in one organization, it was found that the distance between their desks was the single most important determinant of the rate of interaction between any two of the clerks.

Severity of Initiation. The more difficult it is to get into a group, the more cohesive that group becomes. The hazing through which fraternities typically put their pledges is meant to screen out those who don't want to "pay the price" and to intensify the desire of those who do to become fraternity actives. But group initiation needn't be as blatant as hazing. The competition to be accepted to a good medical school results in first-year medical school classes that are highly cohesive. The common initiation rites—applications, test taking, interviews, and the long wait for a final decision—all contribute to creating this cohesiveness. Similarly, the months or often years that an apprentice trade worker must put in to develop his or her skills before being advanced to journeyman status results in union journeymen generally being a cohesive group.

Group Size. If group cohesiveness tends to increase with the time members are able to spend together, it seems logical that cohesiveness should decrease as group size increases, since it becomes more difficult for a member to interact with all the members. This is generally what the research indicates. As group size expands, interaction with all members becomes more difficult, as does the ability to maintain a common goal. Not surprisingly, too, as a single group's size increases, the likelihood of cliques forming also increases. The creation of groups within groups tends to decrease overall cohesiveness.

Evidence suggests that these size-cohesiveness conclusions may be moderated by the gender of the group members. In experiments comparing groups of four and sixteen members, some made up of males only, some of females only, and others mixed, the small groups proved to be more cohesive than large ones as long as all the members were of the same sex. But when the groups were made up of both males and females, the larger groups were more cohesive. Members of both sexes liked the mixed groups more than the single-sex groups, and apparently the opportunity to interact with a larger set of both sexes increased cohesiveness. While it is dangerous to generalize from this study, we should nevertheless be aware of the possible moderating effect of sex on the size-cohesiveness relationship, especially as more women enter the work force, and the ratio of male to female employees decreases.

External Threats. Most of the research supports the proposition that a group's cohesiveness will increase if the group comes under attack from external sources. Management threats frequently bring together an otherwise disarrayed union. Efforts by management unilaterally to redesign even one or two jobs or to discipline one or two employees occasionally grab local headlines when the entire work force walks out in support of the "abused" few. These examples illustrate a cooperative phenomenon that can develop within a group when it is attacked from outside.

While a group generally moves toward greater cohesiveness when threatened by external agents, this does not occur under all conditions. If group members perceive that their group may not meet an attack well, then the group becomes less important as a source of security, and cohesiveness will not necessarily increase. Additionally, if members believe the attack is directed at the group merely because of its existence and that it will cease if the group is abandoned or broken up, there is likely to be a decrease in cohesiveness.

Previous Successes. Everyone loves a winner! If a group has a history of previous successes, it builds an esprit de corps that attracts and unites members. Successful firms find it easier to attract and hire new employees. The same holds true for successful research groups, well-known and prestigious universities, and winning athletic teams. When Bill Bowerman was head track coach at the University of Oregon during the 1960s, he never had trouble attracting the country's top track and field athletes to his campus. The best athletes wanted to come to Oregon because of Bowerman's highly successful program. In fact, Bowerman claims never to have initiated contact with an athlete. In contrast to track coaches at other major universities, if an athlete wanted to compete at Oregon, he had to prove his interest by taking the first step. By the same token, for those readers who harbor ambitions to attend a top-quality graduate school of business, you should recognize that the success of these schools attracts large numbers of aspiring candidates—many have twenty or more applicants for every vacancy. Again, everyone loves a winner!

Effects of Cohesiveness on Group Productivity   The previous section indicates that, generally speaking, group cohesiveness is increased when members spend time together and undergo a severe initiation, when the group size is small, when external threats exist, and when the group has a history of previous successes. But is increased cohesiveness always desirable from the point of view of management? Is it related to increased productivity?

Research has generally shown that highly cohesive groups are more effective than those with less cohesiveness, but the relationship is more complex than merely allowing us to say high cohesiveness is good. First, high cohesiveness is both a cause and an outcome of high productivity. Second, the relationship is moderated by the degree to which the group's attitude aligns with its formal goals or those of the larger organization of which it is a part.

Cohesiveness influences productivity and productivity influences cohesiveness. Camaraderie reduces tension and provides a supportive environment for the successful attainment of group goals. But as already noted, the successful attainment of group goals and the members' feelings of having been a part of a successful unit can serve to enhance the commitment of members. Basketball coaches, for example, are famous for their endearment of teamwork. They believe that if the team is going to win games, members have to learn to play together. Popular coaching phrases include, "There are no individuals on this team" and "We win together, or we lose together." The other side of this view, however, is that winning reinforces camaraderie and leads to increased cohesiveness; that is, successful performance leads to increased intermember attractiveness and sharing.

More important has been the recognition that the relationship of cohesiveness and productivity depends on the alignment of the group's attitude with its formal goals, or for work groups, those of the larger organization of which it is a part. The more cohesive a group, the more its members will follow its goals. If these attitudes are favorable (i.e., high output, quality work, cooperation with individuals outside the group), a cohesive group will be more productive than a less cohesive group. But if cohesiveness is high and attitudes unfavorable, there will be decreases in productivity. If cohesiveness is low and there is support of goals, productivity increases but less than in the high cohesiveness–high support situation. Where cohesiveness is low and attitudes are not in support of the organization's goal, there seems to be no significant effect of cohesiveness upon productivity. These conclusions are summarized in Figure 6-3.

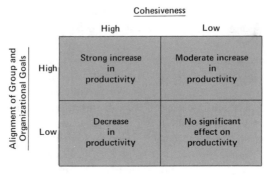

Figure 6-3
Relationship of Cohesiveness to Productivity

GROUP BEHAVIOR MODEL   Now we want to synthesize the factors that influence group performance, member satisfaction, and group cohesiveness into a group behavior model (see Figure 6-4). This model not only summarizes the key concepts that were introduced in this chapter but also demonstrates how the topics we'll discuss in the next four chapters—communication, group decision making, leadership, power, politics, and conflict—interrelate.

The core of our group behavior model is the group's structure. Every group has roles, norms, and a status hierarchy that define its structure. However, the effect of group structure on the outcome variables is moderated by the personality characteristics of the group's members, the size and composition of the group, and the stage of the group's development.

While leadership provides direction to a group, it is through collective communication and decision making that leaders and group members interact. That is, communication and decision making provide the "grease" that facilitates the potential synergistic gains from group interaction. Of course, that interaction also creates power differences and the potential for political maneuvers and conflicts. As we'll show in Chapters 9 and 10, politics and conflict are not necessarily bad. Sometimes they improve a group's performance. But they can be dysfunctional by reducing, or even completely offsetting, any of the synergistic benefits created through group interaction.

IMPLICATIONS FOR   In order to accomplish work tasks,
MANAGERS   the individuals who make up an organization are typically united into departments, committees, or other forms of work groups. In addition to these formal groups, individuals also create informal groups based on

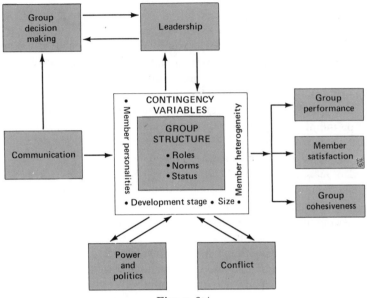

Figure 6-4
Group Behavior Model

common interests or friendships. It is important for managers to look at employees as members of a group because, in reality, group behavior is not merely the summation of the individual behavior of its members. The group itself adds an additional dimension to its members' behavior.

How is it relevant to understanding group behavior to know that a Maryland woman, for example, has to reconcile her roles of mother, Methodist, Democrat, councilwoman, and police officer with the City of Baltimore? Knowledge of the role that a person is attempting to enact can make it easier for us to deal with the person, for we have insight into her expected behavior patterns. Also, knowledge of a job incumbent's role makes it easier for others to work with her, for she should behave in ways consistent with others' expectations. In other words, when a person plays out her role as it is supposed to be played, it improves the ability of others to predict the behavior of the role incumbent. We can predict an individual's behavior in new encounters by superimposing the role requirements of the situation upon her.

Knowledge of an incumbent's role perception and others' expectations can also be beneficial in predicting role conflict and possibly explaining the behavior of the individual experiencing the conflict.

Norms control group member behavior by establishing standards of right or wrong. If we know the norms of a given group, it can help us to explain the attitudes and behaviors of its members. Where norms support high output, we can expect individual performance to be markedly higher than where group norms aim to restrict output. Similarly, acceptable standards of absence will be dictated by the group norms. Given the inverse correlation between satisfaction and turnover, it would also be reasonable to assume that if the group's norms reinforce complaining and consistent outward demonstration of job dissatisfaction, the propensity for members to terminate employment may be greater. On the other hand, members may enjoy this complaining and it may not affect turnover rates. To illustrate, it is not unusual for union members to play the role of a so-called abused and exploited worker. The group may establish such a role stereotype as part of the norm. In such cases, it may have no real influence on satisfaction or quit rates.

Can managers control group norms? Not completely, but they can influence them. By making explicit statements about desirable behaviors, by regularly reinforcing these preferred behaviors, and by linking rewards to the acceptance of preferred norms, managers can exert some degree of influence over group norms.

Status inequities within a group divert activity away from goal accomplishment and direct it toward resolving the inequities. When inequities exist, managers may find that group members reduce their work effort, attempt to undermine the activities of those members with higher status, or pursue similar dysfunctional behaviors. To the degree that a manager controls status accoutrements, he or she should insure that they are distributed carefully and consistently with status equity. Inequities are likely to have a negative motivational impact on the group.

A final point relates to cohesiveness. Should managers seek cohesive groups? Our answer is a qualified "Yes." The qualification lies in the degree of alignment between the group and the organization's goals. Managers should attempt to create work groups whose goals are consistent with those of the organization. If this is achieved, then high group cohesiveness will make a positive contribution to the group's performance.

SELECTED REFERENCES

CUMMINGS, THOMAS G., "Designing Effective Work Groups," in *Handbook of Organizational Design*, eds. P.C. Nystrom and W.H. Starbuck, Vol. 2, pp. 250–71. New York: Oxford University Press, 1981.

GLADSTEIN, DEBORAH L., "Groups in Context: A Model of Task Group Effectiveness," *Administrative Science Quarterly*, December 1984, pp. 499–517.

GOODMAN, PAUL S., AND ASSOCIATES, *Designing Effective Work Groups*. San Francisco: Jossey-Bass, 1986.

JEWELL, LINDA N., AND H. JOSEPH REITZ, *Group Effectiveness in Organizations*. Glenview, Ill.: Scott, Foresman, 1981.

MCGRATH, JOSEPH E., AND DAVID A. KAVITZ, "Group Research," in *Annual Review of Psychology*, eds. M.R. Rosenzweig and L.W. Porter, Vol. 33, pp. 195–230. Palo Alto, Calif.: Annual Reviews, 1982.

ZANDER, ALVIN, *Making Groups Effective*. San Francisco: Jossey-Bass, 1982.

7

COMMUNICATION AND GROUP DECISION MAKING

<== **IDEAS TO BE FOUND** ==>
IN THIS CHAPTER

- Communication process
- Communication networks
- Grapevine
- Barriers to communication
- Group decision making
- Nominal Group Technique
- Delphi Technique

Probably the most frequently cited source of interpersonal conflict is poor communication. Because we spend nearly 70 percent of our waking hours communicating—writing, reading, speaking, listening—it seems reasonable to conclude that one of the most inhibiting forces to successful group performance is a lack of effective communication.

No group can exist without communication: the transference of meaning among its members. It is only through transmitting meaning from one person to another that information and ideas can be conveyed. Communication, however, is more than merely imparting meaning. It must also be understood. In a group where one member speaks only German and the others do not know German, the individual speaking German will not be fully understood. Therefore, communication must include both the *transference* and *understanding* of meaning.

An idea, no matter how great, is useless until it is transmitted and understood by others. Perfect communication, if there were such a thing, would exist when a thought or idea was transmitted so that the mental picture perceived by the receiver was exactly the same as that envisioned by the sender. Although elementary in theory, perfect communication is never achieved in practice, for reasons we shall expand upon later.

Before making too many generalizations concerning communication and problems in communicating effectively, we should construct a model to depict and explain the components in the communication process.

THE COMMUNICATION PROCESS

Before communication can take place, a purpose, expressed as a message to be conveyed, is needed. It passes between a source (the sender) and a receiver. The message is encoded (converted to symbolic form) and passed by way of some medium (channel) to the receiver, who retranslates (decodes) the message initiated by the sender. The result is a transference of meaning from one person to another.

Figure 7-1 depicts the communication process. This model is made up of seven parts: (1) the communication source, (2) encoding, (3) the message, (4) the channel, (5) decoding, (6) the receiver, and (7) feedback. Unfortunately, each of these components has the potential to create distortion, and therefore, impinges upon the goal of perfect communication.

The source initiates a message by encoding a thought. Four conditions have been described that affect the encoded message: skill, attitudes, knowledge, and the social-cultural system.

My success in communicating to you is dependent upon my writing skills; in the writing of textbooks, if the authors are without the requisite skills, their message will not reach students in the form desired. One's total communicative success includes speaking, reading, listening, and reasoning skills as well as writing. As discussed in Chapter 2, attitudes influence our behavior. We hold predisposed ideas on numerous topics, and our communications are affected by these attitudes. Further, we are restricted in our communicative activity by the extent of our knowledge on a particular topic. We cannot communicate what we do not know; and should our knowledge be too extensive, it is possible that our receiver will not understand our message. Clearly, the amount of knowledge the source holds about his subject will affect the message he seeks to transfer. And finally, just as attitudes influence our behavior, so does our position in the social-

Figure 7-1
The Communication Process

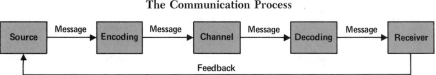

-cultural system in which we exist. Your beliefs and values, all part of your culture, act to influence you as a communicative source.

The message itself can cause distortion in the communicative process, regardless of the supporting apparatus used to convey it. Our message is the actual physical product from the source encoding. When we speak, the speech is the message. When we write, the writing is the message. When we gesture, the movements of our arms and the expressions on our faces are the message. Our message is affected by the code or group of symbols we use to transfer meaning, the content of the message itself, and the decisions that the source makes in selecting and arranging both codes and content. Each of these three segments can act to distort the message.

The channel is the medium through which the message travels. It is selected by the source, who must determine whether to use a formal or informal channel. Formal channels are established by the organization and transmit messages that relate to the professional activities of members. They traditionally follow the authority chain within the organization. Other forms of messages, such as personal or social, follow the informal channels in the organization.

The receiver is the object to whom the message is directed. But before the message can be received, the symbols in it must be translated into a form that can be understood by the receiver. This is the decoding of the message. Just as the encoder was limited by his skills, attitudes, knowledge, and social-cultural system, so is the receiver equally restricted. Just as the source must be skillful in writing or speaking, the receiver must be skillful in reading or listening; and both must be able to reason. One's level of knowledge influences the ability to receive, just as it does the ability to send. Additionally, the receiver's predisposed attitudes and cultural background can distort the message being transferred.

The final link in the communicative process is a feedback loop. Feedback is the check on how successful we have been in transferring our messages as originally intended. It determines whether understanding has been achieved.

POPULAR WAYS TO COMMUNICATE

How do group members transfer meaning between and among each other? There are three basic methods. People essentially rely on oral, written, and nonverbal communication.

The Obvious: Oral and Written Communication

The chief means of conveying messages is oral communication. Speeches, formal one-on-one and group discussions, and the informal rumor mill or grapevine are popular forms of oral communication.

The advantages of oral communication are speed and feedback. A verbal message can be conveyed and a response received in a minimal amount of time. If the receiver is unsure of the message, rapid feedback allows for early detection by the sender and, hence, allows for early correction.

The major disadvantage of oral communication surfaces in organizations, or whenever the message has to be passed through a number of people. The more people a message must pass through, the greater the potential distortion. If you ever played the game "telephone" at a party, you know the problem. Each person interprets the message in his or her own way. The message's content, when it reaches its destination, is often very different from the original. In an organization, where decisions and other communiqués are verbally passed up and down the authority hierarchy, there exists considerable opportunity for messages to become distorted.

Written communications include memos, letters, organizational periodicals, notices placed on bulletin boards, or any other device that is transmitted via written words or symbols.

Why would a sender choose to use written communications? They're permanent, tangible, and verifiable. Typically, both the sender and receiver have a record of the communication. The message can be stored for an indefinite period of time. If there are questions concerning the content of the message, it is physically available for later reference. This is particularly important for complex and lengthy communications. The marketing plan for a new product is likely to contain a number of tasks spread out over several months. By putting it in writing, those who have to initiate the plan can readily refer to it over the life of the plan. A final benefit of written communication comes from the process itself. Except in rare instances, such as when you're presenting a formal speech, you're more careful with the written word than the oral word. You're forced to think more thoroughly about what you want to convey in a written message. Thus, written communications are more likely to be well thought out, logical, and clear.

Of course, written messages have their drawbacks. They're time consuming. You could convey far more information to a college instructor in a one-hour oral exam than in a one-hour written exam. In fact, you could probably say the same thing in ten to fifteen minutes that it would take you an hour to write. So while writing may be more precise, it also consumes a great deal of time. The other major disadvantage is feedback, or lack of it. Oral communication allows the receiver to respond rapidly to what he thinks he hears. However, written communication does not have a built-in feedback mechanism. The result is that the mailing of a memo is no assurance that it has been received and, if received, there is no guarantee that the recipient will interpret it as the sender intended. The latter point is also relevant in oral communiqués, except that it's easy in such cases merely to ask the receiver to summarize what you've said. An accurate summary presents feedback evidence that the message has been received and understood.

The Not-So-Obvious: Nonverbal Communication

Some of the most meaningful communications are not conveyed verbally or in writing. These are the "not-so-obvious" nonverbal communications.

Every time we verbally give a message to someone, we also impart a nonverbal message. In some instances, the nonverbal component may stand alone. For example, in a singles bar, a glance, a stare, a smile, a frown, or a provocative body movement all convey meaning. Obviously, no discussion of communication would be complete without consideration of this not-so-obvious dimension of communication. For our purposes, we'll define nonverbal communication to include body movements, the intonations or emphasis we give to words, facial expressions, and the physical distance between the sender and receiver.

The academic study of body motions has been labeled *kinesics*. It refers to gestures, facial configurations, and other movements of the body. But it is a relatively new field, and it has been subject to far more conjecture and popularizing than the research findings support. Hence, while we acknowledge the fact that body movement is an important segment of the study of communication and behavior, conclusions must, of necessity, be guarded. Recognizing this qualification, let us briefly consider the ways body motions convey meaning.

It can be argued that every *body movement* has a meaning and that no movement is accidental. For example, through body language we say "Help me, I'm lonely"; "Take me, I'm available"; "Leave me alone, I'm depressed." And rarely do we send our messages consciously. We act out our state of being with nonverbal body language. We lift one eyebrow for disbelief. We rub our noses for puzzlement. We clasp our arms to isolate ourselves or to protect ourselves. We shrug our shoulders for indifference, wink one eye for intimacy, tap our fingers for impatience, slap our forehead for forgetfulness.

While we may disagree with the specific meanings of the above movements, body language adds to, and often complicates, verbal communication. A body position or movement does not by itself have a precise or universal meaning, but when it is linked with spoken language, it gives fuller meaning to a sender's message.

If you read the verbatim minutes of a meeting, you could not grasp the impact of what was said in the same way you could if you had been there or saw the meeting on film. Why? There is no record of nonverbal communication. The emphasis given to words or phrases is missing. To illustrate how *intonations* can change the meaning of a message, consider the student in class who asks the instructor a question. The instructor replies, "What do you mean by that?" The student's reaction will be different depending on the tone of the instructor's response. A soft, smooth tone creates a different meaning than an intonation that is abrasive with strong emphasis placed on the last word.

The *facial expression* of the instructor in the above illustration will also convey meaning. A snarling face says something different than a smile. Facial expressions, along with intonations, can show arrogance, aggressiveness, fear, shyness, and other characteristics that would never be communicated if you read a transcript of what had been said.

The way individuals space themselves in terms of *physical distance* also has meaning. What is considered proper spacing is largely dependent on cultural norms. For example, what is considered a businesslike distance in some European countries would be viewed as intimate in many parts of North America. If someone stands closer to you than is considered appropriate, it may indicate aggressiveness or sexual interest; if farther away than usual, it may mean disinterest or displeasure with what is being said.

It is important for the receiver to be alert to these nonverbal aspects of communication. You should look for nonverbal cues as well as listen to the literal meaning of a sender's words. You should particularly be aware of contradictions between the messages. Your boss may say that she is free to talk to you about a pressing budget problem, but you may see nonverbal signals that suggest that this is *not* the time to discuss the subject. Regardless of what is being said, an individual who frequently glances at her wristwatch is giving the message that she would prefer to terminate the conversation. We misinform others when we express one emotion verbally, such as trust, but nonverbally communicate a contradictory message that reads, "I don't have confidence in you." These contradictions often suggest that "actions speak louder (and more accurately) than words."

COMMUNICATION NETWORKS The channels by which information flows are critical once we move beyond groups of two or three individuals. The way a group structures itself will determine the ease and availability with which members can transmit information.

Most studies of communication networks have taken place in groups created in a laboratory setting. As a result, the research conclusions tend to be constrained by the artificial setting and limited to small groups. Five common networks are shown in Figure 7-2; these are the chain, all-channel, wheel, "Y," and circle. For our discussion purposes, let us think in an organizational context, and assume that the organization has only five members. We can then translate the networks in Figure 7-2 into their organizational equivalents.

103

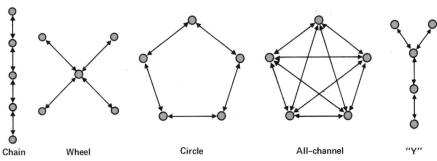

Figure 7-2
Common Communication Networks

The Five Common Networks   In a five-member organization, the chain would represent a five-level hierarchy where communications cannot move laterally, only upward and downward. In a formal organization, this type of network would be found in direct-line authority relations with no deviations. For example, the payroll clerk reports to the payroll supervisor, who in turn reports to the general accounting manager, who reports to the plant controller, who reports to the plant manager. These five individuals would represent a chain network.

If we turn the "Y" network upside down, we can see two subordinates reporting to a supervisor, with two levels of hierarchy still above the supervisor. This is, in effect, a four-level hierarchy.

If we look at the wheel diagram in Figure 7-2 as if we were standing above the network, it becomes obvious that the wheel represents a supervisor with four subordinates. However, there is no interaction among the subordinates. All communications are channeled through the supervisor.

The circle network allows members to interact with adjoining members, but no further. It represents a three-level hierarchy in which there is communication between superiors and subordinates, and cross communication at the lowest level.

Finally, the all-channel network allows each of the subjects to communicate freely with the other four. Of the networks discussed, it is the least structured. While it is like the circle in some respects, the all-channel network has no central position. However, there are no restrictions; all members are equal. A committee best illustrates this network, where no one member either formally or informally assumes a dominant or take-charge position. All members are free to share their viewpoints.

The Five Networks and Group
Effectiveness   Certain communication networks foster speed of decision making. Some are more effective in ensuring that directions are followed and for control purposes. Others have demon-

strated success in maintaining high levels of morale. No single network will be best for all group efforts; rather, the network used should reflect the goals of the group.

Laboratory experiments have found that the circle is considerably slower than either the chain or the wheel for transmitting information among all members, and that the circle rates poorest in accuracy of communication flows. As a result, the wheel and chain are rated as the most effective in terms of high job performance. However, morale is significantly higher in the circle, and, for complex problems, the circle and all-channel networks are faster and more effective. The "Y" shares advantages and disadvantages of the wheel and chain. It is fast and generates higher performance, but with lower satisfaction.

The Informal Group Communication Network The previous discussion of networks emphasized formal communication patterns, but the formal system is not the only communication system in a group or organization. Let us, therefore, now turn our attention to the informal system—where information flows along the well-known grapevine, and rumors can flourish.

A classic study of the grapevine was reported thirty years ago.[1] The researcher investigated the communication pattern among sixty-seven managerial personnel in a small manufacturing firm. The basic approach used was to learn from each communication recipient how he first received a given piece of information and then trace it back to its source. It was found that, while the grapevine was an important source of information, only 10 percent of the executives acted as liaison individuals; that is, passed the information on to more than one other person. For example, when one executive decided to resign to enter the insurance business, 81 percent of the executives knew about it, but only 11 percent transmitted this information on to others.

Two other conclusions from this study are also worth noting. Information on events of general interest tended to flow between the major functional groups (production, sales) rather than within them. Also, no evidence surfaced to suggest that any one group consistently acted as liaisons; rather, different types of information passed through different liaison persons.

An attempt to replicate this study among employees in a small state government office also found that only 10 percent act as liaison individuals.[2] This is interesting since the replication contained a wider spectrum of employees, including rank and file as well as managerial personnel. However, the flow of information in the government office took place within, rather

1. Keith Davis, "Management Communication and the Grapevine," *Harvard Business Review*, September–October 1953, pp. 43–49.
2. Harold Sutton and Lyman W. Porter, "A Study of the Grapevine in a Governmental Organization," *Personnel Psychology*, Summer 1968, pp. 223–30.

than between, functional groups. It was proposed that this discrepancy might be due to comparing an executive-only sample against one which also included rank-and-file workers. Managers, for example, might feel greater pressure to stay informed and thus cultivate others outside their immediate functional group. Also, in contrast to the findings of the original study, the replication found that a consistent group of individuals acted as liaisons by transmitting information in the government office.

Is the information that flows along the grapevine accurate? The evidence indicates that about 75 percent of what is carried is accurate. But what conditions foster an active grapevine? What gets the rumor mill rolling?

It is frequently assumed that rumors start because they make titillating gossip. This is rarely the case. Rumors emerge as a response to situations that are *important* to us, where there is *ambiguity*, and under conditions that arouse *anxiety*. Work situations frequently contain these three elements, which explains why rumors flourish in organizations. The secrecy and competition that typically prevail in large organizations—around such issues as the appointment of new bosses, the relocation of offices, and the realignment of work assignments—create conditions that encourage and sustain rumors on the grapevine. A rumor will persist either until the wants and expectations creating the uncertainty underlying the rumor are fulfilled, or until the anxiety is reduced.

What can we conclude from the above discussion? Certainly the grapevine is an important part of any group or organization's communication network and is well worth understanding. It identifies for managers those confusing issues that employees consider important and that create anxiety. It acts, therefore, as both a filter and a feedback mechanism, picking up the issues that employees consider relevant. For employees, the grapevine is particularly valuable for translating formal communications into their group's own jargon. Maybe more importantly, again from a managerial perspective, it seems possible to analyze grapevine information and to predict its flow, given that only a small set of individuals (around 10 percent) actively pass on information to more than one other person. By assessing which liaison individuals will consider a given piece of information to be relevant, we can improve our ability to explain and predict the pattern of the grapevine.

BARRIERS TO EFFECTIVE COMMUNICATION In our discussion of the communication process, we noted the consistent potential for distortion. As illustrated in Table 7-1, what managers say can be different from what they mean and still different from a subordinate's interpretation. What causes such com-

Table 7-1
How Communications Break Down

What the Manager Said	What the Manager Meant	What the Subordinate Heard
I'll look into hiring another person for your department as soon as I complete my budget review.	We'll start interviewing for that job in about three weeks.	I'm tied up with more important things. Let's forget about hiring for the indefinite future.
Your performance was below par last quarter. I really expected more out of you.	You're going to have to try harder, but I know you can do it.	If you screw up one more time, you're out.
I'd like that report as soon as you can get to it.	I need that report within the week.	Drop that rush order you're working on and fill out that report today.
I talked to the boss but at the present time, due to budget problems, we'll be unable to fully match your competitive salary offer.	We can give you 95 percent of that offer and I know we'll be able to do even more for you next year.	If I were you, I'd take that competitive offer. We're certainly not going to pay that kind of salary to a person with your credentials.
We have a job opening in Los Angeles that we think would be just your cup of tea. We'd like you to go out there and look it over.	If you'd like that job, it's yours. If not, of course, you can stay here in Denver. You be the judge.	You don't have to go out to L.A. if you don't want to. However, if you don't, you can kiss good-bye to your career with this firm.
Your people seem to be having some problems getting their work out on time. I want you to look into this situation and straighten it out.	Talk to your people and find out what the problem is. Then get with them and jointly solve it.	I don't care how many heads you bust, just get me that output. I've got enough problems around here without you screwing things up too.

Source: *Organizational Behavior: Theory and Practice* by Steven Altman, Enzo Valenzi, and Richard M. Hodgetts, copyright © 1985 by Harcourt Brace Jovanovich, Inc. Reproduced by permission of the publisher.

munication breakdown? In addition to the general distortions identified in the communication process, there are a number of other barriers to effective communication.

Filtering

Filtering refers to a sender's purposely manipulating information so that it will be seen more favorably by the receiver. For example, when a manager tells his boss what he feels his boss wants to hear, he is filtering information.

The major determinant of filtering is the number of levels in an organization's structure. The more vertical levels in the organization's hierarchy, the more opportunities there are for filtering.

Selective Perception

We have mentioned selective perception before in this book. It appears again because the receiver, in the communication process, sees and hears things in a selective way, based on his needs, motivations, experience, background, and other personal characteristics. The receiver also projects his interests and expectations into communications as he decodes them. The employment interviewer who expects a female job candidate to put family before career is likely to *see* that in female candidates, regardless of whether the candidates feel that way or not. As we said in Chapter 2, we don't see reality but rather we interpret what we see and call it reality.

Emotions

How the receiver feels at the time of receipt of a communication message will influence how he or she interprets it. The same message received when you're angry or distraught is often interpreted differently than when you're happy. Extreme emotions such as jubilation or depression are most likely to hinder effective communication. In such instances, we are most prone to disregard our rational and objective thinking processes, and substitute emotional judgments. The old adage about avoiding decisions when you're upset because you're not likely to be thinking clearly developed as a result of this fact.

Language

Words mean different things to different people. Age, education, and cultural background are three of the more obvious variables that influence the language a person uses and the definitions he gives to words. The language of William F. Buckley, Jr. is clearly different from that of a factory worker who has earned only a high school diploma. The latter, in fact, would undoubtedly have trouble understanding much of Buckley's vocabulary. In an organization, employees usually come from diverse backgrounds. Further, the grouping of employees into departments creates specialists who develop their own jargon or technical language. In large organizations, members are also frequently widely dispersed geographically—even operating in different countries—and individuals in each locale will use terms and phrases that are unique to their area. The existence of vertical levels can also cause language problems. For instance, differences in meaning with regard to words such as *incentives* and *quotas* have been found at different levels in management. Top managers often speak about the need for incentives and quotas, yet these terms imply manipulation and create resentment among many lower managers.

The point is that while you and I both speak a common language—English—our usage of that language is far from uniform. If we knew how each of us modified the language, communication difficulties would be minimized. The problem is that members in an organization usually don't know how those with whom they interact have modified the language. Senders tend to assume that the words and terms they use mean the same to the receiver as they do to them. This is often incorrect, thus creating communication difficulties.

Nonverbal Cues

Earlier, we noted that nonverbal communication is an important way in which people convey messages to others. But nonverbal communication is almost always accompanied by oral communication. As long as the two are in agreement, they act to reinforce each other. My boss's words tell me he is angry, his tone and body movements indicate anger; so I can conclude, probably correctly, that he is angry. When nonverbal cues are inconsistent with the oral message, however, the receiver becomes confused and the clarity of the message suffers.

IMPLICATIONS FOR MANAGERS

Given that there are barriers to communication, what can managers do to minimize problems and attempt to overcome these barriers? The following suggestions should be helpful in making communication more effective.

Use Feedback

Many communication problems can be attributed directly to misunderstandings and inaccuracies. These are less likely to occur if the manager ensures that the feedback loop is utilized in the communication process. This feedback can be verbal, written, or nonverbal.

If a manager asks a receiver, "Did you understand what I said?", the response to this question represents feedback. But the "yes"- or -"no" type of feedback can definitely be improved upon. The manager can ask a set of questions relating to a message in order to determine whether or not the message was received as intended. Better yet, the manager can ask the receiver to restate the message, in his or her own words. If the manager then hears what was intended, understanding and accuracy should be enhanced. Feedback can also be more subtle than the direct asking of questions or the summarizing of the message by the receiver. General comments can give the manager a sense of a receiver's reaction to a message. Additionally, performance appraisals, salary reviews, and promotion decisions represent important, but more subtle, forms of feedback.

Feedback, of course, does not have to be conveyed in words. Actions *can* speak louder than words. For instance, a sales manager sends out a directive to her staff describing a new monthly sales report that all sales personnel will need to complete. If some of the salespeople fail to turn in the new report, this is a type of feedback. It should suggest to her that she needs to clarify further her initial directive. Similarly, when you give a speech to a group of people, you watch their eyes and look for other nonverbal clues to tell you whether group members are getting your message or not. This may explain why television performers on situation-comedy shows prefer to tape their programs in front of a live audience. Immediate laughter and applause, or their absence, convey to the performers whether they are getting their message across.

Simplify Language

Since language can be a barrier, a manager should seek to structure messages in ways that will make them clear and understandable. Words should be chosen carefully. The manager needs to simplify his or her language and consider the audience to whom a message is directed, so that the language will be compatible with the receiver. Remember, effective communication is achieved when a message is both received and *understood*. Understanding is improved by simplifying the language used in relation to the audience intended. This means, for example, that a hospital administrator should always try to communicate in clear and easily understood terms and that the language used for conveying messages to the surgical staff should be purposely different from that used with employees in the admissions office. Jargon can facilitate understanding when it is used with other group members who speak that language, but it can cause innumerable problems when used outside that group.

Listen Actively

When someone talks, we hear. But, too often, we don't listen. Listening is an active search for meaning, while hearing is passive. When you listen, two people, the receiver and the sender, are thinking.

Many of us are poor listeners. Why? Because it's difficult and because it's usually more satisfying to be on the offensive. Listening, in fact, is often more tiring than talking. It demands intellectual effort. Unlike hearing, active listening demands total concentration. The average person speaks at a rate of about 150 words per minute, whereas we have the capacity to listen at the rate of over 1,000 words per minute. The difference obviously leaves idle brain time and opportunities for mind wandering.

Active listening is enhanced when the receiver develops empathy with the sender; that is, when the receiver tries to place himself in the sender's position. Since senders differ in attitudes, interests, needs, and expectations, empathy makes it easier to understand the actual content of a message. An empathetic listener reserves judgment on the message's content and carefully listens to what is being said. The goal is to improve one's ability to receive the full meaning of a communication, without having it distorted by premature judgments or interpretations. Other suggestions for active listening include demonstrating to a sender that you want to listen, removing distractions, showing patience by not interrupting, and asking questions.

Constrain Emotions

It would be naive to assume that a manager always communicates in a fully rational manner. Yet we know that emotions can severely cloud and distort the transference of meaning. If we're emotionally upset over an issue, we're more likely to misconstrue incoming messages, and we may fail to express clearly and accurately our outgoing messages. What can the manager do? The best approach is to defer further communication until one's composure is regained.

Watch Your Nonverbal Cues

Assuming that actions speak louder than words, it's important to watch your actions to make sure they align with, and reinforce, the words that go along with them. We noted that nonverbal messages carry a great deal of weight. Given this fact, the effective communicator watches his or her nonverbal cues to ensure that they, too, convey the message desired.

Use the Grapevine

You can't eliminate the grapevine. What managers should do, therefore, is use it and make it work for them.

Managers can use the grapevine to transmit information rapidly, to test the reaction to various decisions prior to their final consummation, and as a valuable source of feedback when the managers themselves are grapevine members. Of course, the grapevine can carry damaging rumors that reduce the effectiveness of formal communication. To lessen this potentially destructive force, managers should make good use of formal channels by ensuring that they regularly carry the relevant and accurate information that employees seek.

GROUP DECISION MAKING   One of the more obvious applications of communication concepts is in the area of group decision making. We know that, today, many decisions in organizations are made by groups or committees. The communicative interaction in a group decision can either increase or decrease the quality of the decision over that made by an individual alone. In the following pages, we will review both the advantages and disadvantages of group decisions in contrast to individual decisions. In addition, we will compare their effectiveness and efficiency, and offer two techniques for improving group decision making.

Advantages   Individual and group decisions each have their own set of strengths. Neither is ideal for all situations. The following list identifies the major advantages that groups offer over individuals in the making of decisions:

1. **More complete information and knowledge.** Two heads can be better than one. There is more information in a group than typically resides with one individual. So groups can provide more diverse input into the decision.

2. **Increases acceptance of a solution.** Many decisions fail after the final choice has been made because people do not accept the solution. However, if people who will be affected by a decision and who will be instrumental in implementing it are able to participate in the decision itself, they will be more likely to accept it and encourage others to accept it. Participation in the process increases the commitment and motivation of those who will carry out the decision. Since members are reluctant to fight or undermine a decision that they helped to develop, group decisions increase acceptance of the final solution and facilitate its implementation.

3. **Increases legitimacy.** Our society fosters democratic methods. The group decision-making process is consistent with democratic ideals and, therefore, may be perceived as more legitimate than decisions made by a single person. When an individual decision maker fails to consult with others before making a decision, the fact that the decision maker has complete power can create the perception that the decision was made autocratically and arbitrarily.

Disadvantages   Of course, group decisions are not without drawbacks. The following lists the major *disadvantages* to group decision making:

112

1. **Time consuming.** It takes time to assemble a group. The interaction that takes place once the group is in place is frequently inefficient. The result is that groups take more time to reach a solution than would be the case if an individual were making the decision.

2. **Pressures to conform.** There are social pressures in groups. The desire by group members to be accepted and considered as an asset to the group can result in squashing any overt disagreement, thus encouraging conformity among viewpoints.

3. **Ambiguous responsibility.** Group members share responsibility, but who is actually responsible for the final outcome? In an individual decision, it is clear who is responsible. In a group decision, the responsibility of any single member is watered down and less clearly defined.

Effectiveness and Efficiency   Whether groups are more effective than individuals depends on the criteria you use for defining effectiveness. In terms of *accuracy,* group decisions will tend to be correct more often. The evidence indicates that, on the average, groups make better decisions than individuals. This doesn't mean, of course, that *all* groups will outperform *every* individual. Rather, group decisions have been found to be better than those that would be reached by the average individual in the group. However, they are seldom better than the performance of the best individual.

If decision effectiveness is defined in terms of *speed,* individuals are superior. Group decision processes are characterized by give and take, which consumes time.

Effectiveness may mean the degree to which a solution demonstrates *creativity.* If creativity is important, groups tend to be more effective than individuals. In spite of pressures to conform, certain group methods have proven successful for stimulating novel alternatives. For instance, in *brainstorming,* a half dozen to a dozen people sit around a table. The group leader states the problem in a clear manner so that it is understood by all participants. Members then "free wheel" as many alternatives as they can in a given length of time. No criticism is allowed, and all the alternatives are recorded for later discussion and analysis. The fact that one idea stimulates others and that judgment of even the most bizarre suggestions is withheld until later, encourages group members to "think the unusual."

A final criterion for effectiveness is the degree of *acceptance* the final solution achieves. As noted previously, group decisions, because they have input from more people, are likely to develop solutions that will be more widely accepted.

The effectiveness of group decision making has also been shown to be influenced by the size of the group. The larger the group, the greater the opportunity for heterogeneous representation. On the other hand, increased size requires more coordination and increased time to allow all members to contribute. What this means is that groups probably should not be too large—a minimum of five, a maximum of about fifteen. In fact, as noted in the previous chapter, groups of five and, to a lesser extent, seven appear to be the most effective. Because they are odd numbers, strict deadlocks are avoided. Such groups are large enough for members to shift roles and withdraw from embarrassing positions, but still small enough for quieter members to participate actively in discussions.

Effectiveness should not be considered without also assessing efficiency. In terms of efficiency, groups almost always stack up a poor second to the individual decision maker. With few exceptions, group decision making consumes more work hours than if an individual were to tackle the same problem alone. The exception tends to be those instances where, to achieve comparable quantities of diverse input, the single decision maker must spend a great deal of time reviewing files and talking to people. Because groups can include members from diverse areas, the time spent searching for information can be reduced. However, as we noted, these advantages in efficiency tend to be the exception. Groups are generally less efficient than individuals. In deciding whether to use groups, then, primary consideration must be given to assessing whether increases in effectiveness are more than enough to offset the losses in efficiency.

Improving Group Decision Making When members of a group physically confront and interact with one another, they can censor themselves and pressure individuals toward conformity of opinion. Two techniques have been suggested as ways to make the group decision-making process realize its potential more fully. These two approaches are the Nominal Group Technique and the Delphi Technique.

Nominal Group Technique. The nominal group restricts discussion or interpersonal communication during the decision-making process; hence the term *Nominal* Group Technique. Group members are all physically present, as in a traditional committee meeting, but the members are required to operate independently. Specifically, the following steps take place:

1. Members meet as a group but, before any discussion takes place, each member independently writes down his or her ideas on the problem.
2. This silent period is followed by each member presenting one idea to the group. Each member takes his or her turn, going around the table, presenting a single idea until all ideas have been presented

and recorded (typically on a flip chart or chalkboard). No discussion takes place until all ideas have been recorded.

3. The group then discusses the ideas for clarity and evaluates them.

4. Each group member silently and independently ranks the ideas. The final decision is determined by the idea with the highest aggregate ranking.

The chief advantage of this technique is that it permits the group to meet formally but does not restrict independent thinking, as so often happens in the traditional interacting group.

Delphi Technique. A more complex and time-consuming alternative is the Delphi Technique. It is similar to the nominal group except that it does not require the physical presence of the group members. This is because the Delphi Technique never allows the group members to meet face-to-face. The following steps characterize the Delphi Technique:

1. The problem is identified and members are asked to provide potential solutions through a series of carefully designed questionnaires.

2. Each member anonymously and independently completes the first questionnaire.

3. Results of the first questionnaire are compiled at a central location, transcribed, and reproduced.

4. Each member receives a copy of the results.

5. After viewing the results, members are again asked for their solutions. The results typically trigger new solutions or cause changes in the original position.

6. Steps 4 and 5 are repeated as often as necessary until consensus is reached.

Like the Nominal Group Technique, the Delphi Technique insulates group members from the undue influence of others. Because it does not require the physical presence of the participants it has some interesting applications. For instance, Boeing can use the technique to query its sales managers in Tokyo, Paris, London, New York, Toronto, Mexico City, and Melbourne about what equipment should be offered as standard on the new 787. The cost of bringing the executives together at a central location is avoided, yet input is obtained from Boeing's major markets. Of course, the Delphi Technique has its drawbacks. The method is extremely time consuming. It is frequently inapplicable where a speedy decision is necessary. Additionally, the method may not develop the rich array of alternatives that the interacting or nominal groups do. The ideas that can surface from the heat of face-to-face interaction may never arise.

Implications for Managers In contrast to decisions made by individuals alone, group decisions are more time consuming, more prone to conformity pressures, and more likely to cloud responsibility. However, group solutions are often more accurate, creative, and acceptable than those reached by a single individual. So whether managers choose to make a decision themselves or use a group depends on factors such as accountability, the importance of the decision, and how quickly it needs to be made. If a manager chooses to use a group, he or she may want to consider either the Nominal Group Technique or the Delphi Technique as a means to lessen conformity pressures.

SELECTED REFERENCES

GUZZO, RICHARD A., ed., *Improving Group Decision Making in Organizations: Approaches from Theory and Research*. New York: Academic Press, 1982.

MINER, FREDERICK C., JR., "Group Versus Individual Decision Making: An Investigation of Performance Measures, Decision Strategies, and Process Losses/Gains," *Organizational Behavior and Human Performance*, February 1984, pp. 112–24.

PENLEY, LARRY E., AND BRIAN HAWKINS, "Studying Interpersonal Communication in Organizations: A Leadership Application," *Academy of Management Journal*, June 1985, pp. 309–26.

ROBERTS, KARLENE H., *Communicating In Organizations*. Chicago: Science Research Associates, Inc., 1984.

SNYDER, ROBERT A., AND JAMES H. MORRIS, "Organizational Communication and Performance," *Journal of Applied Psychology*, August 1984, pp. 461–65.

WEICK, KARL E., AND LARRY D. BROWNING, "Argument and Narration in Organizational Communication," *Journal of Management*, Summer 1986, pp. 243–59.

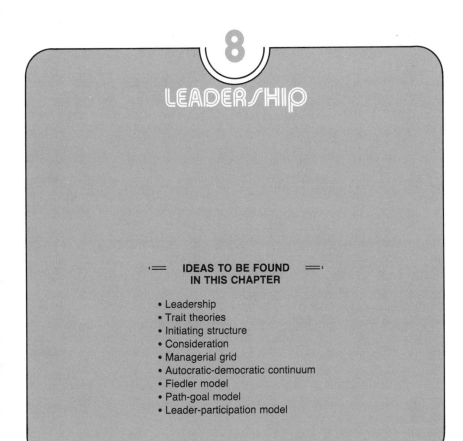

8
LEADERSHIP

IDEAS TO BE FOUND IN THIS CHAPTER

- Leadership
- Trait theories
- Initiating structure
- Consideration
- Managerial grid
- Autocratic-democratic continuum
- Fiedler model
- Path-goal model
- Leader-participation model

It has been accepted as a truism that good leadership is essential to business, to government, and to the countless groups and organizations that shape the way we live, work, and play. If leadership is such an important factor, the critical issue is: What makes a great leader? The tempting answer to give is: Great followers! While there is some truth to this response, the issue is far more complex.

WHAT IS LEADERSHIP? Leadership is the ability to influence a group toward the achievement of goals. The source of this influence may be formal, such as that provided by the possession of managerial rank in an organization. Since management positions come with some degree of formally designated authority, an individual may assume a leadership role as a result of the position he or she holds in the organization. But not all leaders are managers nor, for that matter, are all managers leaders. Just because an organization provides its managers with certain rights is no assurance that they will be able to lead effectively.

We find that nonsanctioned leadership, that is, the ability to influence that arises outside of the formal structure of the organization, is as important or more important than formal influence. In other words, leaders can emerge from within a group as well as being formally appointed.

TRANSITIONS IN LEADERSHIP THEORIES The leadership literature is voluminous, and much of it is confusing and contradictory. In order to make our way through this "forest," we shall consider three basic approaches to explaining what makes an effective leader. The first sought to find universal personality traits that leaders had to some greater degree than nonleaders. The second approach tried to explain leadership in terms of the behavior that a person engaged in. Both of these approaches proved to be false starts, based on their erroneous and oversimplified conception of leadership. Most recently, we have looked to contingency models to explain the inadequacies of previous leadership theories in reconciling and bringing together the diversity of research findings. In this chapter, we shall present the contributions and limitations of each of the three approaches and conclude by attempting to ascertain the value of the leadership literature in explaining and predicting behavior.

TRAIT THEORIES If one were to describe a leader based on the general connotations presented in today's media, one might list qualities such as intelligence, charisma, decisiveness, enthusiasm, strength, bravery, integrity, self-confidence, and so on—possibly eliciting the conclusion that effective leaders must be one part Boy Scout and two parts Jesus Christ. The search for characteristics such as those listed that would differentiate leaders from nonleaders occupied the early psychologists who studied leadership.

Is it possible to isolate one or more personality traits in individuals we generally acknowledge as leaders—Adolph Hitler, Susan B. Anthony, Cezar Chavez, Martin Luther King, Jr., John F. Kennedy, Mahatma Gandhi—that nonleaders do not possess? We may agree that these individuals meet our definition of a leader, but they represent individuals with utterly different characteristics. If the concept of traits were to be proved valid, specific characteristics had to be found that all leaders possess.

Research efforts at isolating these traits resulted in a number of dead ends. If the search was to identify a set of traits that would always differentiate leaders from followers and effective from ineffective leaders, the search failed. Perhaps it was a bit optimistic to believe that there could be consistent and unique personality traits that would apply across the board to all effective leaders no matter whether they were in charge of the Hell's Angels, the Mormon Tabernacle Choir, General Electric, the CIA, the Ku Klux Klan, or the Congress of Racial Equality.

If, however, the search was to identify traits that were consistently associated with leadership, the results could be interpreted in a more impressive light. For example, intelligence, dominance, self-confidence, high energy level, and task-relevant knowledge are five traits that show consistently positive correlations with leadership. But *positive correlations* should not be interpreted to mean *definitive predictors*. The correlations between these traits and leadership have generally been in the range of +.25 to +.35; interesting results, but not earth shattering!

The above results represent the conclusions based on seventy years of trait research. These modest correlations coupled with the inherent limitations of the trait approach—which ignores the needs of followers, generally fails to clarify the relative importance of various traits, and ignores situational factors—naturally led researchers in other directions. Although there has been some resurgent interest in traits during the past decade, a major movement away from traits began as early as the 1940s. Leadership research from the late 1940s through the mid-1960s emphasized the preferred behavioral styles that leaders demonstrated.

BEHAVIORAL THEORIES   The inability to strike gold in the trait mines led researchers to look at the behaviors that specific leaders exhibited. They wondered if there was something unique in the way that effective leaders behave. For example, do they tend to be more democratic than autocratic?

Not only, it was hoped, would the behavioral approach provide more definitive answers about the nature of leadership but, if successful, it would have practical implications quite different from those of the trait approach. If trait research had been successful, it would have provided a basis for selecting the right person to assume formal positions in groups and organizations requiring leadership. In contrast, if behavioral studies were to turn up critical behavioral determinants of leadership, we could *train* people to be leaders. The difference between trait and behavioral theories, in terms of application, lies in their underlying assumptions. If trait theories were valid, then leaders are basically born: You either have it or you don't. On the other hand, if there were specific behaviors that identified leaders, then we could teach leadership—we could design programs that implanted these behavioral patterns in individuals who desired to be effective leaders. This was surely a more exciting avenue, for it would mean that the supply of leaders could be expanded. If training worked, we could have an infinite supply of effective leaders.

There were a number of studies that looked at behavioral styles. We shall briefly review the two most popular studies: the Ohio State group and the University of Michigan group. Then we shall see how the concepts that these studies developed could be used to create a grid for looking at and appraising leadership styles.

Ohio State Studies

The most comprehensive and replicated of the behavioral theories resulted from research that began at Ohio State University in the late 1940s. These studies sought to identify independent dimensions of leader behavior. Beginning with over a thousand dimensions, they eventually narrowed the list into two categories that substantially accounted for most of the leadership behavior described by subordinates. They called these two dimensions initiating structure and consideration.

Initiating structure refers to the extent to which a leader is likely to define and structure his or her role and those of subordinates in the search for goal attainment. It includes behavior that attempts to organize work, work relationships, and goals. The leader characterized as high in initiating structure could be described in terms such as: assigns group members to particular tasks; expects workers to maintain definite standards of performance; and emphasizes the meeting of deadlines.

Consideration is described as the extent to which a person is likely to have job relationships that are characterized by mutual trust, respect for subordinates' ideas, and regard for their feelings. This type of leader shows concern for his followers' comfort, well-being, status, and satisfaction. A leader high in consideration could be described as one who helps subordinates with personal problems, is friendly and approachable, and treats all subordinates as equals.

Extensive research, based on these definitions, found that leaders high in initiating structure *and* consideration (a "high-high" leader) tended to achieve high subordinate performance and satisfaction more frequently than those who rated low on either initiating structure, consideration, or on both. However, the "high-high" style did not *always* result in positive consequences. For example, leader behavior characterized as high on initiating structure led to greater rates of grievances, absenteeism and turnover, and lower levels of job satisfaction for workers performing routine tasks. Other studies found that high consideration was negatively related to performance ratings of the leader by his superior. In conclusion, the Ohio State studies suggested that the "high-high" style generally resulted in positive outcomes, but enough exceptions were found to indicate that situational factors needed to be integrated into the theory.

University of Michigan
Studies

Leadership studies undertaken at the University of Michigan's Survey Research Center, at about the same time as those being done at Ohio State, had similar research objectives: to locate behavioral characteristics of leaders that appeared to be related to measures of performance effectiveness.

The Michigan group also came up with two dimensions of leadership behavior, which they labeled *employee-oriented* and *production-oriented*. Leaders who were employee-oriented were described as emphasizing interpersonal relations; they took a personal interest in the needs of their subordinates and accepted individual differences among members. The production-oriented leaders, in contrast, tended to emphasize the technical or task aspects of the job—their main concern was in accomplishing their group's tasks, and the group members were a means to that end.

The conclusions arrived at by the Michigan researchers strongly favored the leaders who were employee-oriented in their behavior. Employee-oriented leaders were associated with higher group productivity and higher job satisfaction. Production-oriented leaders tended to be associated with low group productivity and lower worker satisfaction.

The Managerial Grid

A graphic portrayal of a two-dimensional view of leadership style has been developed by Blake and Mouton. They propose a managerial grid based on the styles of "concern for people" and "concern for production," which essentially represent the Ohio State dimensions of consideration and initiating structure or the Michigan dimensions of employee-oriented and production-oriented.

The grid, depicted in Figure 8-1, has nine possible positions along each axis, creating eighty-one different positions in which the leader's style may fall. The grid does not show results produced, but rather the dominating factors in a leader's thinking in regard to getting results.

Based on the findings from the research Blake and Mouton conducted, they concluded that managers perform best under a 9,9 style, as contrasted, for example, with a 9,1 (task-oriented) or the 1,9 (country-club type) leader. Unfortunately, the grid offers a better framework for conceptualizing leadership style than for presenting any tangible new information in clarifying the leadership quandary, since there is little substantive evidence to support the conclusion that a 9,9 style is most effective in all situations.

Summary of Behavioral Theories

We have described the most popular and important of the attempts to explain leadership in terms of the behavior exhibited by the leader. Unfortunately, there was very little success in identifying consistent relationships

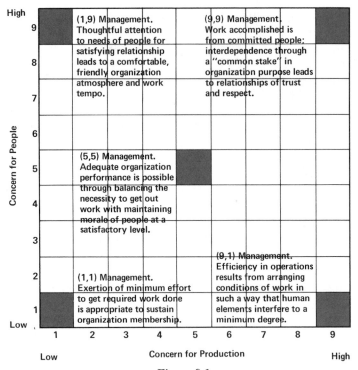

Figure 8-1
The Managerial Grid

Source: Robert R. Blake, Jane S. Mouton, Louis B. Barnes, and Larry E. Greiner, "Breakthrough in Organization Development," *Harvard Business Review*, November-December 1964, p. 136. Copyright © 1964 by the President and Fellows of Harvard College; all rights reserved.

between patterns of leadership behavior and group performance. General statements could not be made because results would vary over different ranges of circumstances. What was missing was consideration of the situational factors that influence success or failure. For example, it seems unlikely that Martin Luther King, Jr., would have been a great leader of his people at the turn of the century, yet he was in the 1950s and 1960s. Would Ralph Nader have risen to lead a consumer activist group had he been born in 1834 rather than 1934, or in Costa Rica rather than Connecticut? It seems quite unlikely, yet the behavioral approaches we have described could not clarify these situational factors.

CONTINGENCY THEORIES   It became increasingly clear to those who were studying the leadership phenomenon that predicting leadership success was more complex than isolating a few traits or preferable behaviors. The failure to obtain consistent results led to a new focus on situational influences. The relationship between leadership style and effectiveness suggested that under condition *a*, style *x* would be appropriate, while style *y* would be more suitable for condition *b*, and style *z* for condition *c*. But what were the conditions *a*, *b*, *c*, and so forth? It was one thing to say that leadership effectiveness was dependent on the situation, and another to be able to isolate those situational conditions.

There have been many studies attempting to isolate the critical situational factors that affect leadership effectiveness. To illustrate, some of the more popular variables have included the type of task being performed, the style of the leader's immediate supervisor, group norms, time demands, and the organization's culture.

Several approaches to isolating key situational variables have proven more successful than others, and, as a result, have gained wider recognition. We shall consider four of these: the autocratic-democratic continuum, the Fiedler, the path-goal, and the Vroom-Yetton models.

Autocratic-Democratic Continuum   If autocratic and democratic behavior
                Model   were viewed only as two extreme po-
                                        sitions, this model would be correctly labeled as a behavioral theory. However, they are merely two of many positions along a continuum. At one extreme the leader makes the decision, tells his subordinates, and expects them to carry out that decision. At the other extreme, the leader fully shares his decision-making power with his subordinates, allowing each member of the group to carry an equal voice—one person, one vote. Between these two extremes fall a number of leadership styles, with the style selected dependent upon forces in the leader himself, his operating group, and the situation. Although this represents a contingency theory, we shall find, upon investigating other contingency approaches, that it is quite primitive.

As depicted in Figure 8-2, there is a relationship between the degree of authority used and the amount of freedom available to subordinates in reaching decisions. This continuum is seen as a zero-sum game; as one gains, the other loses, and vice versa. However, most of the research using this model has been concentrated on the extreme positions.

A review of the research indicates that participative or democratic leadership is associated with greater subordinate satisfaction than is autocratic leadership. The relationship between democratic leadership and employee productivity, however, is unclear. Some studies find participative groups to be more productive; some studies find autocratically led groups to be more productive; while still other studies demonstrate no appreciable differences. We are left to conclude that employees like democracy but that it may not necessarily result in higher productivity.

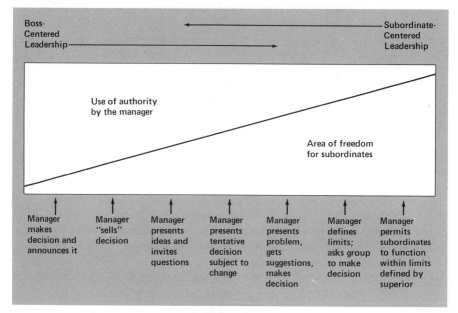

Figure 8-2
Leadership-Behavior Continuum

Source: Robert Tannenbaum and Warren H. Schmidt, "How to Choose a Leadership Pattern," *Harvard Business Review*, March-April 1958, p. 96. With permission. Copyright © 1958 by the President and Fellows of Harvard College; all rights reserved.

A contingency approach would recognize that neither the democratic nor autocratic extreme is effective in all situations. The following models more comprehensively appraise these situational characteristics.

Fiedler Model   The first comprehensive contingency model for leadership was developed by Fred Fiedler. His model proposes that effective group performance depends upon the proper match between the leader's style of interacting with his or her subordinates and the degree to which the situation gives control and influence to the leader. Fiedler developed an instrument, which he called the least-preferred co-worker (LPC) questionnaire, that purports to measure whether a person is task- or relationship-oriented. Further, he isolated three situational criteria—leader-member relations, task structure, and position power—that he believes can be manipulated so as to create the proper match with the behavioral orientation of the leader. In a sense, the Fiedler model is an outgrowth of trait theory, since the LPC questionnaire is a simple psychological test. However, Fiedler goes significantly beyond trait and behavioral approaches by attempting to isolate situations, relating his personality measure to his situational classification, and then predicting leadership effectiveness as a function of the two.

The above description of the Fiedler model is somewhat abstract. Let us now look at the model more closely.

Fiedler believes that an individual's basic leadership style is a key factor in leadership success. So he began by trying to find out what that basic style is. Fiedler created the LPC questionnaire for this purpose. It contains sixteen contrasting adjectives (such as pleasant-unpleasant, efficient-inefficient, open-guarded, supportive-hostile). The questionnaire then asks the respondent to think of all the co-workers he has ever had and to describe the one person he *least enjoyed* working with by rating him or her on a scale of 1 to 8 for each of the sixteen sets of contrasting adjectives. Fiedler believes that based on the respondents' answers to this LPC questionnaire, he can determine their basic leadership style. If the least-preferred co-worker is described in relatively positive terms (a high LPC score), then the respondent is primarily interested in good personal relations with this co-worker. That is, if you essentially describe the person you are least able to work with in favorable terms, Fiedler would label you relationship oriented. In contrast, if the least-preferred co-worker is seen in relatively unfavorable terms (a low LPC score), the respondent is primarily interested in productivity and thus would be labeled task oriented. Notice that Fiedler assumes that an individual's leadership style is fixed; that is, either relationship- or task-oriented. As we'll show in a moment, this is important because it means that if a situation requires a task-oriented leader and the person in that leadership position is relationship oriented, either the situation has to be modified or the leader removed and replaced if optimum effectiveness is to be achieved. Fiedler argues that leadership style is innate to a person—you *can't* change your style to fit changing situations!

After an individual's basic leadership style has been assessed through the LPC, it is necessary to match the leader with the situation. The three situational factors or contingency dimensions identified by Fiedler are defined as follows:

1. **Leader-member relations**—the degree of confidence, trust, and respect subordinates have in their leader
2. **Task structure**—the degree to which the job assignments are structured or unstructured
3. **Position power**—the degree of influence a leader has over power variables such as hiring, firing, discipline, promotions, and salary increases

So the next step in the Fiedler model is to evaluate the situation in terms of these three contingency variables. Leader-member relations are either good or poor, task structure either high or low, and position power either strong or weak.

Fiedler states the better the leader-member relations, the more highly structured the job, and the stronger the position power, the more control or influence the leader has. For example, a very favorable situation (where the leader would have a great deal of control) might involve a payroll manager who is well respected and whose subordinates have confidence in her (good leader-member relations), where the activities to be done—such as wage computation, check writing, report filing—are specific and clear (high task structure), and the job provides considerable freedom for her to reward and punish her subordinates (strong position power). On the other hand, an unfavorable situation might be the disliked chairman of a voluntary United Way fund-raising team. In this job, the leader has very little control. Altogether, by mixing the three contingency variables, there are potentially eight different situations or categories in which a leader could find himself or herself.

With knowledge of an individual's LPC and an assessment of the three contingency variables, the Fiedler model proposes matching them up to achieve maximum leadership effectiveness. Based on Fiedler's study of over twelve hundred groups, where he compared relationship versus task-oriented leadership styles in each of the eight situational categories, he concluded that task-oriented leaders tend to perform better in situations that are *very favorable* to them and in situations that are *very unfavorable* (see Figure 8-3). So Fiedler would predict that when faced with a category I, II, III, VII, or VIII situation, task-oriented leaders perform better. Relationship-oriented leaders, however, perform better in moderately favorable situations—categories IV through VI.

Given Fiedler's findings, how would you apply them? You would seek to match leaders and situations. Individuals' LPC scores would determine the type of situation for which they were best suited. That situation would be defined by evaluating the three contingency factors of leader-member relations, task structure, and position power. But remember that Fiedler views an individual's leadership style as being fixed. Therefore, there are really only two ways in which to improve leader effectiveness. First, you can change the leader to fit the situation. Analogous to a baseball game, management can reach into its bullpen and put in a right-handed pitcher or a left-handed pitcher, depending on the situational characteristics of the hitter. So, for example, if a group situation rates as highly unfavorable but is currently led by a relationship-oriented manager, the group's performance could be improved by replacing that manager with one who is task oriented. The second alternative would be to change the situation to fit the leader. That could be done by restructuring tasks or increasing or decreasing the power that the leader has to control factors such as salary increases, promo-

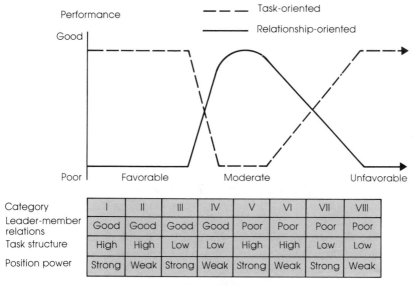

Figure 8-3
Findings from the Fiedler Model

tions, and disciplinary actions. To illustrate, assume a task-oriented leader were in a category IV situation. If this leader could increase his or her position power, then the leader would be operating in category III and the leader-situation match would be compatible for high group performance.

One should not surmise that Fiedler has closed all the gaps and put to rest all the questions underlying leadership effectiveness. Continued research strongly confirms that the Fiedler model predicts categories I and IV with relatively high consistency. Predictions for categories V and VIII are confirming, but at a more moderate level. Most pertinent, the model's predictions appear irrelevant to categories II, III, VI, and VII.

The ability of the model to predict in several categories may mean that Fiedler has made some important insights into leadership. On the other hand, the model has a number of weaknesses. First, the contingency variables are complex and difficult to assess. It's often difficult in practice to determine how good the leader-member relations are, how structured the task is, and how much position power the leader has. Second, the model gives little attention to the characteristics of the subordinates. Third, no attention is given to varying technical competencies of the leader or the subordinates. The model assumes that both the leader and subordinates have adequate technical competence. Fourth, the correlations Fiedler presents in defense of the model are relatively weak. Though generally in the right direction, they are often low and statistically nonsignificant. Finally, the LPC instrument is open to question. The logic underlying the LPC is not well understood, and studies have shown that respondents' LPC scores are not stable.

In spite of these criticisms, the Fiedler model continues to be a dominant input in the development of a contingency explanation of leadership effectiveness. Its greatest contribution, however, may be in the direction it has taken leadership research, rather than in any definitive answers that it provides.

Path-Goal Model   Robert House has proposed a contingency model for leadership that integrates the expectancy model of motivation with the Ohio State leadership research. The model considers the effort-performance and performance-goal satisfaction linkages, and the leadership dimensions of initiating structure and consideration. The model describes the leader as responsible for helping subordinates to achieve their work goals by clarifying the paths to these goals, reducing roadblocks and pitfalls, all the while increasing the opportunities for personal satisfaction en route.

Since the theory is described in terms of path clarification and goal attainment, it is referred to as the path-goal model of leadership. That is, initiating structure acts to clarify the path and consideration makes the path easier to travel.

You will remember that the Ohio State group concluded that effective leaders would score high on both initiating structure and consideration. Yet, there were exceptions. What House has done, therefore, is to reconcile the apparent contradictions in the findings of the Ohio State group. The "high-high" leader is not always the most effective, so House asks: In what situations is initiating structure desirable? In what situations is consideration desirable?

The model has two general propositions: (1) Leader behavior is acceptable and satisfying to subordinates to the extent that the subordinates see such behavior as either an immediate source of satisfaction or as instrumental to future satisfaction. (2) Leader behavior will be motivational to the extent that (a) it makes satisfaction of subordinate needs contingent on effective performance, and (b) it complements the environment of subordinates by providing the coaching, guidance, support, and rewards necessary for effective performance and that may otherwise be lacking in subordinates or in their environment.

In addition, two sets of contingency variables moderate the relationship between the leader's behavior and the subordinate's output. These are

(1) personal characteristics of the subordinates, and (2) environmental pressures and task demands. The model's relationships are summarized in Figure 8-4. Given these two general propositions and two sets of moderating variables, the model would make hypotheses such as the following regarding the behavioral dimensions a leader should use:

Consideration with subordinates who score low on the Locus of Control Scale (those who believe that their rewards are contingent on their own behavior) and initiating structure with subordinates who score high on the Locus of Control Scale (those who believe their rewards are the result of luck or another's behavior)

Initiating structure with highly authoritarian subordinates

Less initiating structure as the subordinate's perception of his or her abilities relative to task demands increases

Less initiating structure where the routine nature of the task, clear group norms, or objective controls of the formal authority system already make goals and paths apparent

Less initiating structure and more consideration with subordinates who find their work tasks dissatisfying, fatiguing, frustrating, or stress-inducing.

Figure 8-4
Summary of Path-Goal Relationships

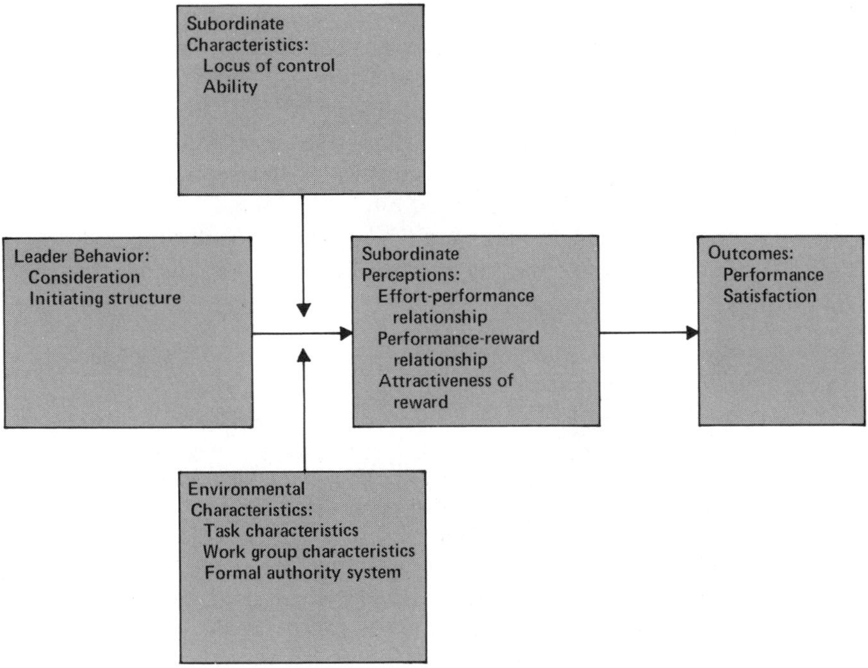

In summary, the path-goal model proposes that consideration is most helpful to subordinates in structured situations and less helpful in unstructured ones; and that initiating structure will lead to greater satisfaction when the tasks are ambiguous or stressful than when they are highly structured and well laid out. Where the tasks to be done are not clear, subordinates appreciate the leader's clarifying the path to goal achievement. High consideration, on the other hand, results in high employee satisfaction when subordinates are performing structured or routine tasks. In clearly defined and structured tasks, efforts by the leader to explain tasks that are already clear will be seen by the subordinate as redundant or even insulting.

Does research confirm the path-goal model? Because the model has undergone a number of modifications, it's difficult to draw any definitive conclusions. Overall, the findings are stronger for the consideration hypothesis than the initiating structure hypothesis, and stronger for predicting satisfaction as a criterion than for performance. Yet, given the criticisms of Fiedler's model and the support for an expectancy theory of motivation, it appears that the direction the path-goal model is taking holds promise.

Leader-Participation Model   The most recent addition to the contingency approach is the leadership-participation model proposed by Victor Vroom and Phillip Yetton. It relates leadership behavior and participation to decision making. Recognizing that task structures have varying demands for routine or nonroutine activities, these researchers suggest that leader behavior must adjust to reflect the task structure. Vroom and Yetton's model is normative; it provides a sequential set of rules that should be followed in determining the form and amount of participation in decision making, as determined by different types of situations. As shown in Figure 8-5, the model is a decision tree incorporating eight contingencies and five alternative leadership styles.

The model assumes that any of five behaviors may be feasible in a given situation:

AI. You solve the problem or make a decision yourself using information available to you at that time.

AII. You obtain the necessary information from subordinates, then decide on a solution to the problem yourself. You may or may not tell subordinates what the problem is in getting the information from them. The role played by your subordinates in making the decision is clearly one of providing the necessary information to you, rather than generating or evaluating alternative solutions.

CI. You share the problem with relevant subordinates individually, getting their ideas and suggestions without bringing them together as a group. Then *you* make the decision which may or may not reflect your subordinates' influence.

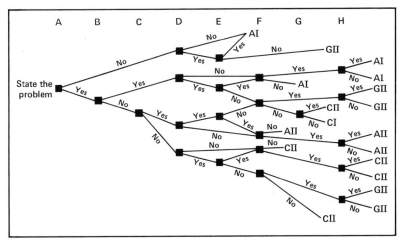

Figure 8-5
Leader-Participation Model

CII. You share the problem with your subordinates as a group, collectively obtaining their ideas and suggestions. Then, you make the decision which may or may not reflect your subordinates' influence.

GII. You share the problem with your subordinates as a group. Together you generate and evaluate alternatives and attempt to reach consensus on a solution.

Although these five decision behaviors closely parallel the autocratic-democratic continuum depicted in Figure 8-2, the Vroom-Yetton model goes beyond that model by suggesting a specific way of analyzing problems by means of eight contingency questions. By answering "Yes" or "No" to these questions, the leader can arrive at which of the five decision behaviors is preferred—that is, how much participation should be used.

The eight questions must be answered in order from A to H:

A. If the decision were accepted, would it make a difference which course of action were adopted?

B. Do I have sufficient information to make a high-quality decision?

C. Do subordinates have sufficient additional information to result in a high-quality decision?

D. Do I know exactly what information is needed, who possesses it, and how to collect it?

E. Is acceptance of the decision by subordinates critical to effective implementation?

F. If I were to make the decision by myself, is it certain that it would be accepted by my subordinates?

G. Can subordinates be trusted to base solutions on organizational considerations?

H. Is conflict among subordinates likely in the preferred solution?

Again, referring to Figure 8-5, based on the answers to questions A through H, the leader follows the decision tree until reaching its end. The designation at the end of the branch (either AI, AII, CI, CII, or GII) tells the leader what to do.

To date, the research testing the leader-participation model has been encouraging, but considerably more investigations are needed to test the model's normative propositions against effectiveness data. It does, however, confirm existing empirical evidence that leaders use participatory methods (1) when the quality of the decision is important; (2) when it is important that subordinates accept the decision and it is unlikely that they will do so unless they are allowed to take part in it; and (3) when subordinates can be trusted to pay attention to the goals of the group rather than simply to their own preferences.

This model has also confirmed that leadership research should be directed at the situation rather than the person. It probably makes more sense to talk about autocratic and participative *situations*, rather than autocratic and participative *leaders*. This, importantly, is a fundamental deviation from Fiedler's viewpoint. The Fiedler model emphasizes changing the situation to match the inherent characteristics of the leader. The leader's style is basically assumed to be inflexible. Vroom and Yetton would disagree. They demonstrate that leaders are not rigid, but adjust their style to different situations. Only through further research will we learn whether leaders are, in actuality, rigid or flexible in terms of their leadership style.

Sometimes Leadership Is Irrelevant! In keeping with the contingency spirit, we want to conclude this section by offering this notion: The belief that some leadership style *will always* be effective *regardless* of the situation may not be true. Leadership may not always be important. Data from numerous studies collectively demonstrate that, in many situations, whatever behaviors leaders exhibit are irrelevant. Certain individual, job, and organizational variables can act as substitutes for leadership, negating the formal leader's ability to exert either positive or negative influence over subordinate attitudes and effectiveness.

For instance, characteristics of subordinates such as their experience, training, professional orientation, or need for independence can neutralize the effect of leadership. These characteristics can replace the need for a leader's support or ability to create structure and reduce task ambiguity. Similarly, jobs that are inherently unambiguous and routine or that are intrinsically satisfying may place less demands on the leadership variable.

Finally, organizational characteristics like explicit formalized goals, rigid rules and procedures, or cohesive work groups can act in the place of formal leadership.

The above comments should not be surprising. After all, in Chapter 2 and subsequent chapters, we have introduced independent variables that have been documented to impact on employee performance and satisfaction. Yet supporters of the leadership concept have tended to place an undue burden on this variable for explaining and predicting behavior. It is too simplistic to consider subordinates as guided to goal accomplishments based solely on the behavior of their leader. It is important, therefore, to recognize explicitly that leadership is merely another independent variable in explaining organizational behavior. In some situations it may contribute a lot toward explaining employee productivity, absence, turnover, and satisfaction; but in other situations, it may contribute little toward that end.

IMPLICATIONS FOR MANAGERS

The topic of leadership certainly doesn't lack for theories. But from an overview perspective, what does it all mean? Let's try to identify commonalities among the leadership theories and attempt to determine what, if any, practical value the theories hold for managers.

Careful examination discloses that the concepts of "task" and "people"—often expressed in more elaborate terms that hold substantially the same meaning—permeate most of the theories. The task dimension is called just that by Fiedler, but it goes by the name of "initiating structure" for the Ohio State group and the path-goal supporters, "production-orientation" by the Michigan researchers, and "concern for production" by Blake and Mouton. The people dimension gets similar treatment, going under such aliases as "consideration" and "employee-oriented" or "relationship-oriented" leadership. It seems clear that leadership behavior can be shrunk down to two dimensions—task and people—but researchers continue to differ as to whether the orientations are two ends of a single continuum (you could be high on one or the other but not both) or two independent dimensions (you could be high or low on both).

How should we interpret the findings presented in this chapter? Some traits have shown, over time, to be modest predictors of leadership effectiveness. But the fact that a manager possessed intelligence, dominance, self-confidence, or the like would by no means assure us that his or her subordinates would be productive and satisfied employees. The ability of these traits to predict leadership success is just not that strong.

The early task-people approaches (the Ohio State, Michigan, and managerial grid theories) also offer us little substance. The strongest statement one can make based on these theories is that leaders who rate high in people orientation should end up with satisfied employees. The research is too mixed to make predictions regarding employee productivity or the effect of a task orientation on productivity and satisfaction.

The wealth of research on the Fiedler model has failed to confirm the theory in its entirety, but parts of it are supported. When category I, IV, V, or VIII situations exist, the utilization of the LPC instrument to assess whether there is a leader-situation match and the use of that information to predict employee productivity and satisfaction outcomes seem warranted.

The path-goal model represents an up-to-date task-people approach. Its use of individual and task characteristics as moderating variables has met with reasonable success, especially in predicting satisfaction. Yet the theory itself is relatively new to the field of organizational behavior. As such, the path-goal model is probably better considered as a tool for directing research and stimulating insight than as a proven guide for managerial action.

The autocratic-participative continuum and its modern-day equivalent, the Vroom-Yetton leadership-participation model, offer a diversity of leadership styles. Although studies to validate the Vroom-Yetton model are still scarce, the early results are encouraging. One investigation, for example, found that leaders who were high in agreement with the model had subordinates with higher productivity and higher satisfaction than those leaders who were in low agreement with the model. A major reservation, in addition to the need for more confirming studies, is the complexity of the model itself. With five styles, eight contingency variables, and eighteen possible outcomes, it would be difficult to use as a guide for practicing managers. One might additionally question whether, under the stress of day-to-day activities, managers could be expected to follow the rational, conscious process the model requires. Of course, from our descriptive perspective, we might answer, "It doesn't matter." What does matter is that where we find leaders who follow the model, we should expect also to find productive and satisfied employees.

SELECTED REFERENCES

BLAKE, ROBERT R., AND JANE S. MOUTON, *The Versatile Manager: A Grid Profile*. Homewood, Ill.: Richard D. Irwin, 1982.

FIEDLER, FRED E., *A Theory of Leadership Effectiveness*. New York: McGraw-Hill, 1967.

HOUSE, ROBERT J., AND TERENCE R. MITCHELL, "Path-Goal Theory of Leadership," *Journal of Contemporary Business*, Autumn 1974, pp. 81–97.

HOWELL, JON P., AND PETER W. DORFMAN, "Leadership and Substitutes for Leadership Among Professional and Nonprofessional Workers," *Journal of Applied Behavioral Science*, 22, No. 1 (1986), pp. 29–46.

JAGO, ARTHUR G., "Leadership: Perspectives in Theory and Research," *Management Science*, March 1982, pp. 315–36.

VROOM, VICTOR H., AND PHILLIP W. YETTON, *Leadership and Decision-Making*. Pittsburgh: University of Pittsburgh Press, 1973.

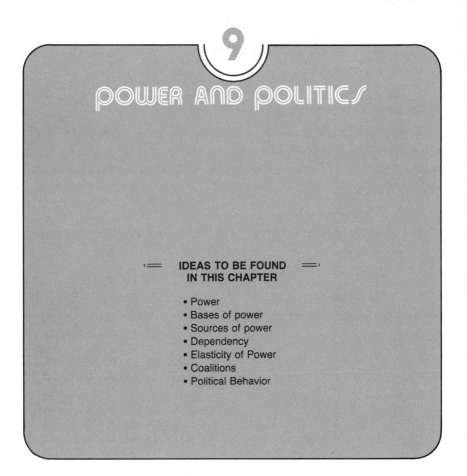

ꝔOꟺꝪ Ꝇꝺ ꝔOꝈITICꟻ

**IDEAS TO BE FOUND
IN THIS CHAPTER**

- Power
- Bases of power
- Sources of power
- Dependency
- Elasticity of Power
- Coalitions
- Political Behavior

Power may be the last dirty word. It is easier for most of us to talk about money or even sex than it is to talk about power. People who have it, deny it; people who want it, try not to appear to be seeking it; and those who are good at getting it, are secretive about how they got it.

In this chapter, we'll show that power determines what goals a group will pursue and how the group's resources will be distributed among its members. Further, we'll show how group members with good political skills use their power to influence the distribution of resources in their favor.

A DEFINITION OF POWER   Power refers to a capacity that A has to influence the behavior of B, so that B does something he or she would not otherwise do. This definition implies (1) a *potential* that need not be actualized to be effective, (2) a *dependence* relationship, and (3) that B has some *discretion* over his or her own behavior. Let's look at each of these points more closely.

Power may exist but not be used. It is, therefore, a capacity or potential. Arthur Fonzarelli, appearing nightly in reruns of "Happy Days," has power. Everyone is afraid of "The Fonz," yet he has never actually had to use his power to get others to comply with his wishes. They respond in fear that he *might* use his physical force but, as long as no one calls his bluff, his capacity to influence others is as effective as if he actually used physical force. Our point again is that one can have power but not impose it.

Probably the most important aspect of power is that it is a function of dependence. The greater B's dependence on A, the greater is A's power in the relationship. Dependence, in turn, is based on alternatives that B perceives and the importance that B places on the alternative(s) that A controls. A person can have power over you only if he or she controls something you desire. If you want a college degree, have to pass a certain course to get that degree, and your current instructor is the only faculty member in the college that teaches that course, he or she has power over you. Your alternatives are definitely limited and you place a high degree of importance on obtaining a passing grade. Similarly, if you're attending college on funds provided entirely by your parents, you probably recognize the power that they hold over you. You are dependent on them for financial support. But once you're out of school, have a job, and are making a solid income, your parents' power is reduced significantly. Who among us, though, has not known or heard of the rich relative who is able to control a large number of family members merely through the implicit or explicit threat of writing them out of the will?

For A to get B to do something he or she otherwise would not do means that B must have the discretion to make choices. At the extreme, if B's job behavior is so programmed that he is allowed no room to make choices, he obviously is constrained in his ability to do something other than what he is doing. For instance, job descriptions, group norms, organizational rules and regulations, as well as community laws and standards constrain people's choices. As a nurse, you may be dependent on your supervisor for continued employment. But in spite of this dependence, you're unlikely to comply with her request to perform heart surgery on a patient or steal several thousand dollars from petty cash. Your job description and laws against stealing constrain your ability to make these choices.

CONTRASTING LEADERSHIP AND POWER A careful comparison of our description of power with our description of leadership in the previous chapter should bring the recognition that the two concepts are closely intertwined. Leaders use power as a means of attaining group goals. Leaders achieve goals, and power is a means for facilitating their achievement.

What differences are there between the two terms? One difference relates to goal compatibility. Power does not require goal compatibility, merely dependence. Leadership, on the other hand, requires some congruence between the goals of the leader and the led. The other difference deals with the direction that research on the two concepts has taken. Leadership research, for the most part, emphasizes style. It seeks answers to questions like: How supportive should a leader be? How much decision making should be shared with subordinates? In contrast, the research on power has tended to encompass a broader area and focus on tactics for gaining compliance. It has gone beyond the individual as exerciser because power can be used by groups as well as individuals to control other individuals or groups.

BASES AND SOURCES OF POWER

Where does power come from? What is it that gives an individual or group influence over others? The early answer to these questions was a five-category classification scheme identified by French and Raven.[1] They proposed that there were five bases or sources of power which they termed coercive, reward, expert, legitimate, and referent power. Coercive power depends on fear; reward power is derived from the ability to distribute anything of value (typically money, favorable performance appraisals, interesting work assignments, friendly colleagues, and preferred work shifts or sales territories); expert power refers to influence that is derived from special skills or knowledge; legitimate power is based on the formal rights one receives as a result of holding an authoritative position or role in an organization; and referent power develops out of others' admiration for an individual and their desire to model their behavior and attitudes after that person. While French and Raven's classification scheme provided an extensive repertoire of possible bases of power, their categories created ambiguity because they confused bases of power with sources of power. The result was much overlapping. We can improve our understanding of the power concept by separating bases and sources to develop clearer and more independent categories.

The term *bases* of power refers to what the powerholder has that gives him or her power. Assuming you're the powerholder, your bases are what you control that enables you to manipulate the behavior of others. There are four power bases—coercive power, reward power, persuasive power, and knowledge power. We'll amplify on each in a moment.

1. J.R.P. French, Jr. and Bertram Raven, "The Bases of Social Power," in *Studies in Social Power*, ed. D. Cartwright (Ann Arbor: University of Michigan, Institute for Social Research, 1959), pp. 150–67.

How are *sources* of power different from bases of power? The answer is that sources tell us where the powerholder gets his or her power bases. That is, sources refer to how you come to control the bases of power. There are four sources—the position you hold, your personal characteristics, your expertise, and the opportunity you have to receive and obstruct information. Each of these will also be discussed in a moment.

Let us now turn back to the four bases of power and define them.

Bases of Power

Coercive Power. The coercive base depends on fear. One reacts to this power out of fear of the negative ramifications that might result if one fails to comply. It rests on the application, or the threat of application, of physical sanctions such as infliction of pain, deformity, or death; the generation of frustration through restriction of movement; or the controlling through force of basic physiological or safety needs.

In the 1930s, when John Dillinger went into a bank, held a gun to the teller's head, and asked for the money, he was incredibly successful at getting compliance to his request. His power base? Coercive. A loaded gun gives its holder power because others are fearful that they will lose something that they hold dear—their lives.

At the organizational level, A has coercive power over B if A can dismiss, suspend, or demote B, assuming that B values his or her job. Similarly, if A can assign B work activities that B finds unpleasant or can treat B in a manner that B finds embarrassing, A possesses coercive power over B.

Reward Power. The opposite of coercive power is the power to reward. People comply with the wishes of another because it will result in positive benefits; therefore, one who can distribute rewards that others view as valuable will have power over them. Our definition of rewards is here limited only to material rewards. These would include salaries and wages, commissions, fringe benefits, and the like.

Persuasive Power. Persuasive power rests on the allocation and manipulation of symbolic rewards. If you can decide who is hired, manipulate the mass media, control the allocation of status symbols, or influence a group's norms, you have persuasive power. For instance, when a teacher uses the class climate to control a deviant student, or when a union steward arouses the members to use their informal power to bring a deviant member into line, you are observing examples of persuasive power.

Knowledge Power. Knowledge, or access to information, is the final base of power. We can say that when an individual in a group or organization controls unique information, and when that information is needed to make a decision, that individual has knowledge-based power.

To summarize the above, the bases of power refer to what the power-holder controls that enables him or her to manipulate the behavior of others. The coercive base of power is the control of punishment; the reward base is the control of material rewards; the persuasive base is the control of symbolic rewards; and the knowledge base is the control of information.

Sources of Power

Position Power. In formal groups and organizations, probably the most frequent access to one or more of the power bases is one's structural position. A teacher's position includes significant control over symbols, a secretary frequently is privy to important information, and the head coach of an NFL team has substantial coercive resources at his disposal. All of these bases of power are achieved as a result of the formal position each holds within a structural hierarchy.

Personal Power. Personality traits were discussed in Chapter 2 and again in the previous chapter on leadership. They reappear within the topic of power when we acknowledge the fact that one's personal characteristics can be a source of power. If you are articulate, domineering, physically imposing, or possessed of that mystical quality called charisma, you hold personal characteristics that may be used to get others to do what you want.

Expert Power. Expertise is a means by which the powerholder comes to control specialized information (rather than the control itself, which we have discussed as the knowledge base of power). Those who have expertise in terms of specialized information can use it to manipulate others. Expertise is one of the most powerful sources of influence, especially in a technologically oriented society. As jobs become more specialized, we become increasingly dependent on experts to achieve goals. So, while it is generally acknowledged that physicians have expertise and hence expert power—when your doctor talks, you listen—you should also recognize that computer specialists, tax accountants, solar engineers, industrial psychologists and other specialists are able to wield power as a result of their expertise.

Opportunity Power. Finally, being in the right place at the right time can give a person the opportunity to exert power. One need not hold a formal position in a group or organization to have access to information that is important to others or be able to exert coercive influence. An example of how one can use an opportunity to create a power base is the story of Lyndon Johnson, when he was a student at Southwestern Texas State Teachers College. He had a job as special assistant to the college president's personal secretary.

As special assistant, Johnson's assigned job was simply to carry messages from the president to the department heads and occasionally to other faculty members. Johnson saw that the rather limited function of messenger had possibilities for expansion, for example, encouraging recipients of the messages to transmit their own communications through him. He occupied a desk in the president's outer office, where he took it upon himself to announce the arrival of visitors. These added services evolved from a helpful convenience into an aspect of the normal process of presidential business. The messenger had become an appointments secretary, and, in time, faculty members came to think of Johnson as a funnel to the president. Using a technique which was later to serve him in achieving mastery over the Congress, Johnson turned a rather insubstantial service into a process through which power was exercised.[2]

Johnson eventually broadened his informal duties to include handling the president's political correspondence and preparing his reports for state agencies. Regularly, he accompanied the college president on his trips to the state capital with the president eventually relying on his young apprentice for political counsel. Certainly this represents an example of someone using an opportunity to redefine his job and to give himself power.

Summary The foundation for understanding power begins by identifying where power comes from (sources) and, given that one has the means to exert influence, what it is that one manipulates (bases). Figure 9-1 depicts the relationship between sources and bases. Sources are the means. Individuals can use their position in the structure, rely on personal characteristics, develop expertise, or take advantage of opportunities to control information. Control of one or more of these sources allows the powerholder to manipulate the behavior of others via coercion, reward, persuasion, or knowledge bases. To reiterate, sources are *where* you get power. Bases are *what* you manipulate. Those who seek power must develop a source of power. Then, and only then, can they acquire a power base.

DEPENDENCY: THE KEY TO POWER

Earlier in this chapter we noted the important relationship between power and dependence. In this section, we'll show how an understanding of dependency is central to furthering our understanding of power itself.

2. Doris Kearns, "Lyndon Johnson and the American Dream," *The Atlantic Monthly*, May 1976, p. 41.

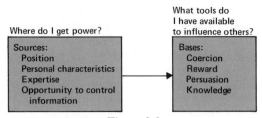

Figure 9-1
Sources and Bases of Power

The General Dependency Postulate Let's begin with a general postulate: *The greater B's dependency on A, the greater power A has over B.* When you possess anything that others require but that you alone control, you make them dependent upon you and, therefore, you gain power over them. Dependency, then, is inversely proportional to the alternative sources of supply. If something is plentiful, possession of it will not increase your power. If everyone is intelligent, intelligence gives no special advantage. Similarly, among the superrich, money is no longer power. But as the old saying goes, "in the land of the blind, the one-eyed man is king!" If you can create a monopoly by controlling information, prestige, or anything that others crave, they become dependent on you. Conversely, the more that you can expand your options, the less power you place in the hands of others. This explains, for example, why most organizations use many suppliers rather than give their business to only one. It also explains why so many of us aspire to financial independence. Financial independence reduces the power that others can have over us.

Michael Milken provides an example of the role that dependency plays in a work force or an organization. He is the incredibly successful head of the corporate bond department at the New York brokerage firm of Drexel Burnham Lambert. A native Californian, Milken grew disenchanted with New York and decided to return to southern California and a warmer climate. But Milken made so much money for his employer that the firm was not about to let him go. The solution: Rather than lose his skills to a competitor with West Coast connections, the company agreed to move its entire bond department to California. Milken and his staff were all moved to Los Angeles. The cost of setting up the office, moving employees and their families, and absorbing housing subsidies were all part of the price Drexel Burnham Lambert was willing to pay to keep Milken's skills.

Another example took place in professional basketball during the fall of 1981. Earvin "Magic" Johnson, the then twenty-two-year-old superstar on the Los Angeles Laker team, chose one Wednesday evening to blast his coach's system. He told the press that he could not continue to play under his coach, Paul Westhead, and demanded to be traded. Within twenty-four hours, the Lakers' owner fired Westhead.

Westhead's record was not in question. He had led the Lakers to the NBA championship during the 1979–80 season. At the time of his firing, the team was only half-a-game behind its conference leader with a 7–4 win-loss record. The issue really was: Who was dispensable? In the summer of 1981, Johnson had signed a twenty-five-year, $25 million contract with the Laker organization. Westhead, on the other hand, was operating under a far less lucrative four-year pact. Johnson was a major asset to the Laker team and his twenty-five-year contract made it almost impossible for him to be traded. No other team was willing to assume such a contractual obligation. The Laker owner had little choice but to fire the coach. Regardless of the fact that a professional coach is the formal boss over the team members, this example dramatizes that a player or any employee (who has no legitimate position power) can still be extremely influential if the "team's" options are severely restricted.

What Creates Dependency? Dependency is increased when the resource you control is *important*, *scarce*, and *nonsubstitutable*.

Importance. If nobody wants what you've got, it's not going to create dependency. To create dependency, therefore, the thing(s) you control must be perceived as important. It's been found, for instance, that organizations seek to avoid uncertainty. We should, therefore, expect that those individuals or groups who can absorb an organization's uncertainty will be understood to control an important resource. For instance, a study of industrial organizations found that the marketing departments in these firms were consistently rated as the most powerful. It was concluded by the researcher that the most critical uncertainty facing these firms was selling their products. This might suggest that during a labor strike, the organization's negotiating representatives have increased power or that engineers, as a group, would be more powerful at Apple Computer than at Procter & Gamble. These inferences appear to be generally valid. Labor negotiators do become more powerful within the personnel area and the organization as a whole during periods of labor strife. An organization such as Apple Computer, which is a technological company, is dependent on its engineers to maintain its product quality. And, at Apple, engineers are clearly the most powerful group. At Procter & Gamble, marketing is the name of the game, and marketers are the most powerful group. These examples support not only the view that the ability to reduce uncertainty increases a group's importance and, hence, its power but also that what's important is situational. It varies among organizations and undoubtedly also varies over time within any given organization.

Scarcity.　　　　　　　　As noted previously, if something is plentiful, possession of it will not increase your power. A resource needs to be perceived as scarce to create dependency.

This can help to explain how low-ranking members in an organization, who have important knowledge not available to high-ranking members, gain power over the high-ranking members. Possession of a scarce resource—in this case, important knowledge—makes the high-ranking member dependent on the low-ranking member. This also helps to make sense out of behaviors of low-ranking members that, otherwise, might seem illogical, such as destroying the procedure manuals that describe how a job is done, refusing to train people in their job or even to show others exactly what they do, creating specialized language and terminology that inhibit others from understanding their jobs, or operating in secrecy so that the activity will appear more complex and difficult than it really is.

The scarcity-dependency relationship can further be seen in the power of different occupations. Individuals in occupations in which the supply of personnel is low relative to demand can negotiate compensation and benefit packages far more attractive than those in occupations where there is an abundance of candidates. College administrators have no problem today finding English instructors. The market for business teachers, in contrast, is extremely tight—with demand high and the supply limited. The result is that the bargaining power of business faculty allows them to negotiate higher salaries, lighter teaching loads, and other benefits. Similarly, petroleum engineers were able to negotiate attractive deals with employers in the late 1970s. But by 1982, when the demand for oil dropped and exploration projects were shelved, those same petroleum engineers found their bargaining power greatly reduced. There is nothing inherently magic about the skills of petroleum engineers that allowed new college graduates in the field to earn 30 percent more than other engineering graduates in 1979—scarcity had temporarily created dependency, which, in turn, increased the bargaining power of petroleum engineers.

Nonsubstitutability.　　　　　　　　The more a resource has no viable substitutes, the more power that control over that resource provides. This is illustrated in a concept we'll call the elasticity of power.

In economics, considerable attention is focused on the elasticity of demand, which is defined as the relative responsiveness of quantity demanded to change in price. This concept can be modified to explain the strength of power.

Elasticity of power is defined as the relative responsiveness of power to change in available alternatives. One's ability to influence others is viewed as being dependent on how these others perceive their alternatives.

As shown in Figure 9-2, assume that there are two individuals. A's

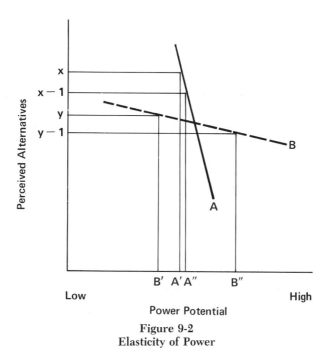

Figure 9-2
Elasticity of Power

power elasticity curve is relatively inelastic. This would describe, for example, an employee who believed that she had a large number of employment opportunities outside her current organization. Fear of being fired would have only a moderate impact on A, for she perceives that she has a number of other alternatives. A's boss finds that threatening A with termination has only a minimal impact on influencing A's behavior. A reduction in alternatives (from X to $X-1$) only increases the power of A's boss slightly (A' to A''). However, B's curve is relatively elastic. He sees few other job opportunities. His age, education, present salary, or lack of contacts may severely limit his ability to find a job somewhere else. As a result, B is dependent on his present organization and boss. If B loses his job (Y to $Y-1$), he may face prolonged unemployment, and it shows itself in the increased power of B's boss. As long as B perceives his options as limited and B's boss holds the power to terminate his employment, B's boss will hold considerable power over him. In such a situation, it is obviously important for B to get his boss to believe that his options are considerably greater than they really are. If this is not achieved, B places his fate in the hands of his boss and makes him captive to almost any demands the boss devises.

Higher education provides an excellent example of how this elasticity concept operates. In universities where there are strong pressures for the faculty to publish, we can say that a department head's power over a faculty member is inversely related to that member's publication record. The more recognition the faculty member receives through publication, the more mobile he or she is. That is, since other universities want faculty who are widely published and visible, there is an increased demand for his or her services. Although the concept of tenure can act to alter this relationship by restricting the department head's alternatives, those faculty members with little or no publications have the least mobility and are subject to the greatest influence from their superiors.

POWER IN GROUPS: COALITIONS

Those "out of power" and seeking to be "in" will first try to increase their power individually. Why spread the spoils if one doesn't have to? But if this proves ineffective, the alternative is to form a coalition. There *is* strength in numbers.

The natural way to gain influence is to become a powerholder. Therefore, those who want power will attempt to build a personal power base. But in many instances, this may be difficult, risky, costly, or impossible. In such cases, efforts will be made to form a coalition of two or more "outs" who, by joining together, can each better themselves at the expense of those outside the coalition.

In the late 1960s, college students found that by joining together to form a student power group they could achieve ends that had been impossible individually. Historically, employees in organizations who were unsuccessful in bargaining on their own behalf with management resorted to labor unions to bargain for them. In recent years, even some managers have joined unions after finding it difficult individually to exert power to attain higher wages and greater job security.

What predictions can we make about coalition formation? First, coalitions in organizations often seek to maximize their size. In political science theory, coalitions move the other way—they try to minimize their size. They tend to be just large enough to exert the power necessary to achieve their objectives. But legislatures are different from organizations in that legislators make the policy decisions which are then carried out by separate administrators or managers. Decision making in organizations does not end with merely selecting from among a set of alternatives. The decision must also be implemented. In organizations, the implementation of and commitment to the decision is at least as important as the decision itself. It's necessary, therefore, for coalitions in organizations to seek a broad constituency to support the coalition's objectives. This means expanding the coalition to encompass as many interests as possible. This coalition expansion to facilitate consensus building, of course, is more likely to occur in organizational cultures where cooperation, commitment, and shared decision making are highly valued. In autocratic and hierarchically controlled organizations, the maximization of the coalition's size is less likely to be sought.

Another prediction about coalitions relates to the degree of interdependence within the organization. More coalitions will likely be created where there is a great deal of task and resource interdependence. In contrast, there will be less interdependence among subunits and less coalition formation activity where subunits are largely self-contained or resources are abundant.

Finally, coalition formation will be influenced by the actual tasks that workers perform. The more routine the task of a group, the greater the likelihood that coalitions will form. The more that the work that people do is routine, the greater their substitutability for each other and, thus, the greater their dependence. To offset this dependence, they can be expected to resort to a coalition. We see, therefore, that unions appeal more to low-skill and nonprofessional workers than to skilled and professional types. Of course, where the supply of skilled and professional employees is high relative to their demand or where organizations have standardized traditionally unique jobs, we would expect even these incumbents to find unionization attractive.

POLITICS: POWER IN ACTION When people get together, power will be exerted. People want to carve out a niche from which to exert influence, to earn rewards, and to advance their careers. When employees in organizations convert their power into action, they are engaged in politics. Those with good political skills have the ability to use their bases of power effectively.

A Definition of Political Behavior There have been no shortages of definitions for organizational politics. Essentially, however, they have focused on the use of power to affect decision making in the organization or on behaviors by members that are self-serving and organizationally nonsanctioned. For our purposes, we shall define *political behavior* in organizations as *those activities that are not required as part of one's formal role in the organization, but that influence, or attempt to influence, the distribution of advantages and disadvantages within the organization.*

This definition encompasses key elements from what most people mean when they talk about organizational politics. Political behavior is *outside* one's specified job requirements. The behavior requires some

147

attempt to use one's *power* bases. Our definition encompasses efforts to influence the goals, criteria, or processes used for *decision making* when we state that politics is concerned with the distribution of advantages and disadvantages within the organization. Our definition is broad enough to include such varied political behaviors as withholding key information from decision makers, whistleblowing, filing of grievances, spreading rumors, leaking confidential information about organizational activities to the media, exchanging favors with others in the organization for mutual benefit, or lobbying on behalf of or against a particular individual or decision.

A final comment relates to what has been referred to as the "legitimate-illegitimate" dimension in political behavior. Legitimate political behavior refers to normal everyday politics—complaining to your supervisor, bypassing the chain of command, forming coalitions, obstructing organizational policies or decisions through inaction or excessive adherence to rules, and developing contacts outside the organization through one's professional activities. On the other hand, there are also illegitimate or extreme political behaviors that violate the implied rules of the game. Those who pursue such activities are often described as individuals who "play hardball." Illegitimate activities include sabotage, whistleblowing, and symbolic protests such as unorthodox dress, wearing protest buttons, or groups of employees concurrently calling in sick.

The vast majority of all organizational political actions are of the legitimate variety. The reasons are pragmatic: the extreme illegitimate forms of political behavior pose a very real risk of loss of organizational membership or extreme sanctions against those who use them and then fall short in having enough power to insure they work.

The Importance of a Political Perspective

Those who fail to acknowledge political behavior ignore the reality that organizations are political systems. It would be nice if all organizations or formal groups within organizations could be described as supportive, harmonious, trusting, collaborative, or cooperative. A nonpolitical perspective can lead one to believe that employees will always behave in ways consistent with the interests of the organization. In contrast, a political view can explain much of what may seem to be irrational behavior in organizations. It can help to explain, for instance, why employees withhold information, restrict output, attempt to "build empires," publicize their successes, hide their failures, distort performance figures to make themselves look better, and engage in similar activities that appear to be at odds with the organization's desire for effectiveness and efficiency.

Factors Contributing to Political Behavior   Recent research and observation have identified a number of factors that appear to be associated with political behavior. Some are individual characteristics, derived from the unique qualities of the people whom the organization employs; others are a result of the organization's culture or internal environment.

Individual Factors.   At the individual level, researchers have identified certain personality characteristics, needs, and other individual factors that are likely to be related to political behavior. Employees who are authoritarian, have a high-risk propensity, or possess an external locus of control act politically with less regard for the consequences to the organization. A high need for power, autonomy, security, or status is also a major contributor to an employee's tendency to engage in political behavior.

In addition, an individual's investment in the organization, perceived alternatives, and expectations of success will influence the degree to which he or she will pursue illegitimate means of political action. The more that a person has invested in the organization in terms of expectations of increased future benefits, the more a person has to lose if forced out, and the less likely he or she is to use illegitimate means. The more alternative job opportunities an individual has due to a favorable job market, scarce skills or knowledge, prominent reputation, or influential contacts outside the organization, the more likely he or she is to risk illegitimate political actions. Last, if an individual places a low expectation of success in using illegitimate means, it is unlikely that he or she will attempt them. Conversely, high expectations of success—and use of illegitimate means—are most likely to be the province of experienced and powerful individuals with polished political skills and inexperienced and naive employees who misjudge their probabilities of success.

Organizational Factors.   Political activity is probably more a function of the organization's culture than of individual differences. Why? Because most organizations have a large number of employees with the characteristics we listed, yet the presence of political behavior varies widely.

While we acknowledge the role that individual differences can play in fostering politicking, the evidence more strongly supports that certain cultures promote politics. Cultures characterized by low trust, role ambiguity, unclear performance evaluation systems, zero-sum reward allocation practices, and democratic decision making will create opportunities for political activities to be nurtured.

The less trust there is within the organization, the higher the level of political behavior and the more likely that the political behavior will be of the illegitimate kind. So high trust should suppress the level of political behavior in general and inhibit illegitimate actions in particular.

Role ambiguity means that the prescribed behaviors of the employee are not clear. There are fewer limits, therefore, to the scope and functions of the employee's political actions. Since political activities are defined as those not required as part of one's formal role, the greater the role ambiguity, the more one can engage in political activity with little chance of its being visible.

The practice of performance evaluation is far from a perfected science. The more that organizations use subjective criteria in the appraisal, emphasize a single outcome measure, or allow significant time to pass between an action and its appraisal, the greater the likelihood that an employee can get away with politicking. Subjective performance criteria create ambiguity. The use of a single outcome measure encourages individuals to do whatever is necessary to look good on that measure, but often at the expense of performing well on other important parts of the job that are not being appraised. The amount of time that elapses between an action and its appraisal is also a relevant factor. The longer the time period, the more unlikely that the employee will be held accountable for his or her political behaviors.

The more that an organization's culture emphasizes the zero-sum or win-lose approach to reward allocations, the more employees will be motivated to engage in politicking. The zero-sum approach treats the reward "pie" as fixed so that any gain one person or group achieves has to come at the expense of another person or group. If I win, you must lose! If $10,000 in annual raises is to be distributed among five employees, then any employee who gets more than $2,000 takes money away from one or more of the others. Such a practice encourages making others look bad and increasing the visibility of what you do.

In the last twenty-five years there has been a general move in North America toward making organizations less autocratic. While much of this trend has been more in theory than in practice, it is undoubtedly true that in many organizations, managers are being asked to behave more democratically. Managers are told that they should allow subordinates to advise them on decisions and that they should rely to a greater extent on group input into the decision process. Such moves toward democracy, however, are not necessarily desired by individual managers. Many managers sought their positions in order to have legitimate power to make unilateral decisions. They fought hard and often paid high personal costs to achieve their influential positions. Sharing their power with others rubs directly against their desires. The result is that managers may use the required committees, conferences, and group meetings in a superficial way—as arenas for maneuvering and manipulating.

IMPLICATIONS FOR MANAGERS

If you want to get things done in a group or organization, it helps to have power. As a manager who wants to maximize your power, you will want to increase others' dependence on you. You can, for instance, increase your power in relation to your boss by developing knowledge or a skill that he needs and for which he perceives no ready substitute. But power is a two-way street. You will not be alone in attempting to build your power sources. Others, particularly subordinates, will be seeking to make you dependent on them. The result is a continual battle. While you seek to maximize others' dependence on you, you will be seeking to minimize your dependence on others. And, of course, others you work with will be trying to do the same.

The effective manager accepts the political nature of organizations. By assessing behavior in a political framework, you can better predict the actions of others and use this information to formulate political strategies that will gain advantages for you and your work unit.

SELECTED REFERENCES

BACHARACH, SAMUEL B., AND EDWARD J. LAWLER, *Power and Politics in Organizations*. San Francisco: Jossey-Bass, 1980.

KOTTER, JOHN P., "Power, Dependence, and Effective Management," *Harvard Business Review*, July-August 1977, pp. 125–36.

PFEFFER, JEFFREY, *Power in Organizations*. Marshfield, Mass.: Pitman, 1981.

PODSAKOFF, PHILIP M., AND CHESTER A. SCHRIESHEIM, "Field Studies of French and Raven's Bases of Power: Critique, Reanalysis, and Suggestions for Future Research," *Psychological Bulletin*, May 1985, pp. 387–411.

VREDENBURGH, DONALD J., AND JOHN G. MAURER, "A Process Framework of Organizational Politics," *Human Relations*, January 1984, pp. 47–66.

YUKL, GARY, AND TOM TABER, "The Effective Use of Power," *Personnel*, March–April 1983, pp. 37–44.

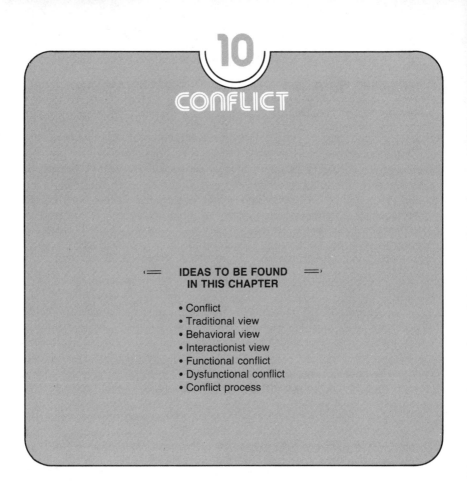

10

CONFLICT

It has been said that conflict is a theme that has occupied the thinking of man more than any other—with the exception of God and love. It has been only recently, though, that conflict has become a major area of interest and research for students of organizational behavior. The evidence suggests that this interest has been well-placed: the type and intensity of conflict *does* affect group behavior.

A DEFINITION OF CONFLICT   There has been no shortage of definitions for conflict. In spite of the divergent meanings the term has acquired, several common themes underlie most definitions. Conflict must be *perceived* by the parties to it. Whether conflict exists or not is a perception issue. If no one is aware of a conflict, it is generally agreed that no conflict exists. Of course, conflicts perceived may not be real while many situations that otherwise could be described as conflictive are not because the group members involved do not perceive the conflict. For a conflict to exist, therefore, it must be perceived. Additional commonalities among most conflict definitions are the concepts of *opposition, scarcity,* and *blockage,* and the assumption that there are two or more parties whose interests or goals appear to be incompatible. Resources—money, jobs, prestige, power, for example—are not unlimited, and their scarcity encourages blocking behavior. The parties are therefore in opposition. When one party blocks the means to a goal of another, a conflict state exists.

Differences between definitions tend to center around *intent* and whether conflict is a term limited only to *overt* acts. The intent issue is a debate over whether blockage behavior must be a determined action or whether it could occur as a result of fortuitous circumstances. As to whether conflict can only refer to overt acts, some definitions, for example, require signs of manifest fighting or open struggle as criteria for the existence of conflict.

Our definition of conflict acknowledges awareness (perception), opposition, scarcity, and blockage. Further, we assume it to be a determined action, which can exist at either the latent or overt level. We define conflict as *a process in which an effort is purposely made by A to offset the efforts of B by some form of blocking that will result in frustrating B in attaining his goals or furthering his interests.*

TRANSITIONS IN CONFLICT THOUGHT

It is entirely appropriate to say that there has been conflict over the role of conflict in groups and organizations. One school of thought has argued that conflict must be avoided, that it indicates a malfunction within the group. We call this the *traditional* view. Another school of thought, the *behavioral* view, argues that conflict is a natural and inevitable outcome in any group. It need not be evil, but rather has the potential to be a positive force in determining group performance. The third, and most recent, perspective proposes not only that conflict *can* be a positive force in a group, but explicitly argues that some conflict is *absolutely necessary* for a group to perform effectively. We label this third school the *interactionist* approach. Let us take a closer look at each of these views.

The Traditional View

The early approach to conflict assumed that conflict was bad. Conflict was viewed negatively, and it was used synonymously with terms like violence, destruction, and irrationality in order to reinforce its negative connotation. Conflict, then, was to be avoided.

The traditional view was consistent with the attitudes that prevailed about group behavior in the 1930s and 1940s. From findings provided by studies like those done at Hawthorne, it was argued that conflict was a dysfunctional outcome resulting from poor communication, a lack of openness and trust between people, and the failure of managers to be responsive to the needs and aspirations of their employees.

The view that all conflict is bad certainly offers a simple approach to looking at the behavior of people who create conflict. Since all conflict is to be avoided, we need merely direct our attention to the causes of conflict and correct these malfunctionings in order to improve group and organizational performance. Although research studies now provide strong evidence to dispute that this approach to conflict reduction results in high group performance, most of us still evaluate conflict situations utilizing this outmoded standard.

The Behavioral View   The behavioral position argued that conflict was a natural occurrence in all groups and organizations. Since conflict was inevitable, the behavioral school advocated acceptance of conflict. They rationalized its existence: It cannot be eliminated, and there are even times when conflict may benefit a group's performance. The behavioral view dominated conflict theory from the late 1940s through the mid-1970s.

The Interactionist View   The current view toward conflict is the interactionist perspective. While the behavioral approach *accepted* conflict, the interactionist approach *encourages* conflict on the grounds that a harmonious, peaceful, tranquil, and cooperative group is likely to become static, apathetic, and nonresponsive to needs for change and innovation. The major contribution of the interactionist approach, therefore, is encouraging group leaders to maintain an ongoing minimal level of conflict—enough to keep the group alive, self-critical, and creative.

Given the interactionist view, and it is the one we shall take in this chapter, it becomes evident that to say conflict is all good or all bad is inappropriate and naïve. Whether a conflict is good or bad depends on the type of conflict. Specifically, it's necessary to differentiate between functional and dysfunctional conflicts.

DIFFERENTIATING   The interactionist view does not pro-
FUNCTIONAL FROM   pose that *all* conflicts are good.
DYSFUNCTIONAL CONFLICTS   Rather, some conflicts support the goals of the group and improve its performance; these are functional, constructive forms of conflict. There are also conflicts that hinder group performance; these are dysfunctional or destructive forms.

154

How does one tell if a conflict is functional or dysfunctional? The demarcation between functional and dysfunctional is neither clear nor precise. No one level of conflict can be adopted as acceptable or unacceptable under all conditions. The type and level of conflict that creates healthy and positive involvement toward one group's goals may, in another group or in the same group at another time, be highly dysfunctional.

The important criterion is group performance. Since groups exist to attain a goal or goals, it is the impact that the conflict has on the group, rather than on any singular individual, that defines functionality. The impact of conflict on the individual and on the group is rarely mutually exclusive, so the ways that individuals perceive a conflict may have an important influence on its effect on the group. However, this need not be the case and when it is not, our orientation will be to the group. In appraising the impact of conflict on group behavior—to consider its functional and dysfunctional effects—whether the individual group members perceive the conflict as good or bad is irrelevant. A group member may perceive an action as dysfunctional because the outcome is personally dissatisfying to him or her. However, for our analysis, it would be functional if it furthers the objectives of the group.

THE CONFLICT PARADOX   If some conflict has been proven to be beneficial to a group's performance, why do most of us continue to look at conflict as undesirable? The answer is that we live in a society that has been built upon the traditional view. Tolerance of conflict is counter to most cultures in developed nations. In North America, the home, school, and church are generally the most influential institutions during the early years when our attitudes are forming. These institutions, for the most part, have historically reinforced anticonflict values and emphasized the importance of getting along with others.

The home has historically reinforced the authority pattern through the parent figure. Parents knew what was right and children complied. Conflict between children or between parents and children has generally been actively discouraged. The traditional school systems in developed countries reflected the structure of the home. Teachers had *the* answers and were not to be challenged. Disagreements at all levels were viewed negatively. Examinations reinforced this view: Students tried to give the answers the teacher expected. The last major influencing institution, the church, also has supported anticonflict values. The religious perspective emphasizes peace, harmony, and tranquility. Church doctrines, for the most part, advocate acceptance rather than argument. This is best exemplified by the teachings of the Roman Catholic Church. According to its beliefs, when the Pope speaks officially (ex cathedra) on religious matters, he is infallible. Such dogma has discouraged questioning the teachings of the Church.

Should we be surprised, then, that the traditional view of conflict continues to receive wide support? Let us now proceed to move beyond definitions and philosophy to describe and analyze the evolutionary process leading to conflict outcomes.

THE CONFLICT PROCESS   The conflict process can be thought of as progressing through four stages: potential opposition, cognition and personalization, behavior, and outcomes. The process is diagrammed in Figure 10-1.

Stage I: Potential Opposition   The first step in the conflict process is the presence of conditions that create opportunities for conflict to arise. They *need not* lead directly to conflict, but one of these conditions is necessary if conflict is to arise. For simplicity's sake, these conditions (which also may be looked at as causes or sources of conflict) have been condensed into three general categories: communication, structure, and personal variables.

Communication.   The communicative source represents those opposing forces that arise from semantic difficulties, misunderstandings, and "noise" in the communication channels. Much of this discussion can be related to our comments on communication and communication networks in Chapter 7.

Figure 10-1
The Conflict Process

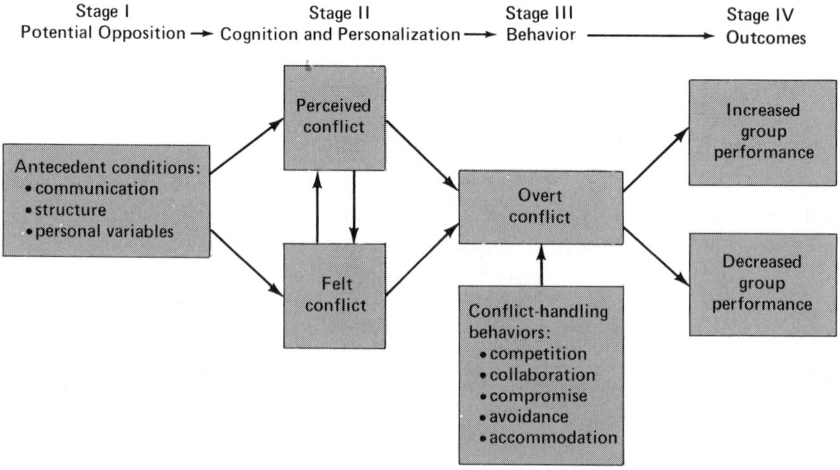

156

One of the major myths that most of us carry around with us is that poor communication is the reason for conflicts. Such a conclusion is not unreasonable, given the amount of time each of us spends communicating. But, of course, poor communication is certainly not the source of *all* conflicts, though there is considerable evidence to suggest that problems in the communication process act to retard collaboration and stimulate misunderstanding.

A review of the research suggests that semantic difficulties, insufficient exchange of information, and noise in the communication channel are all barriers to communication and potential antecedent conditions to conflict. Specifically, evidence demonstrates that semantic difficulties arise as a result of differences in training, selective perception, and inadequate information about others. Research has further demonstrated a surprising finding: The potential for conflict increases when either too little or too much communication takes place. Apparently, an increase in communication is functional up to a point, whereupon it is possible to overcommunicate, resulting in an increase in the potential for conflict. Too much information as well as too little can lay the foundation for conflict. Further, the channel chosen for communicating can have an influence on stimulating opposition. The filtering process that occurs as information is passed between members, and the divergence of communications from formal or previously established channels, offer potential opportunities for conflict to arise.

Structure. The term structure is used, in this context, to include variables such as size; degree of routinization, specialization, and standardization in the tasks assigned to group members; heterogeneity of members; leadership styles; reward systems; and the degree of dependence between groups.

Research indicates that size and specialization act as forces to stimulate conflict. The larger the group and the more specialized its activities, the greater the likelihood of conflict. Tenure and conflict have been found to be inversely related. The potential for conflict tends to be greatest where group members are younger and where turnover is high.

There is some indication that a close style of leadership, that is, tight and continuous observation with restrictive control of the others' behaviors, increases conflict potential, but the evidence is not strong. Too much reliance on participation may also stimulate conflict. Research tends to confirm that participation and conflict are highly correlated, apparently because participation encourages the promotion of differences. Reward systems, too, are found to create conflict when one member's gain is at another's expense. Finally, if a group is dependent on another group (in contrast to the two being mutually independent) or if interdependence allows one group to gain at another's expense, opposing forces are stimulated.

157

Personal Variables. The most important personal factors are individual value systems and individual idiosyncracies and differences.

The evidence indicates that certain personality types—for example, individuals who are highly authoritarian, dogmatic, and who demonstrate low esteem—lead to potential conflict. Most important, and probably the most overlooked variable in the study of social conflict, is the notion of differing value systems. In Chapter 2, we argued that values are the initial foundation upon which individual behavior is built. It seems reasonable that differences in value structure are an important explanation for why conflicts occur. Value differences, for example, are the best explanation of such diverse issues as prejudice, disagreements over one's contribution to the group and the rewards one deserves, or assessments of whether this particular book is any good. The fact that John dislikes blacks and Dana believes John's position indicates his ignorance; that an employee thinks he is worth $30,000 a year but his boss believes him to be worth $24,000; and that Ann thinks this book is interesting to read while Jennifer views it as a "crock of . . . , " are all value judgments. And differences in value systems are important sources for creating the potential for conflict.

Stage II: Cognition and Personalization

If the conditions cited in Stage I generate frustration, then the potential for opposition becomes realized in the second stage. The antecedent conditions can lead to conflict only when one or more of the parties are affected by, and cognizant of, the conflict.

As we noted in our definition of conflict, perception is required. Therefore, one or more of the parties must be aware of the existence of the antecedent conditions. However, because a conflict is perceived does not mean that it is personalized. You may be aware that you and a co-worker are in disagreement. However, it may not make you tense or anxious and it may not influence your affection towards this co-worker. It is at the level where conflict is felt, when individuals become emotionally involved, that parties experience anxiety, tension, frustration, or hostility.

Stage III: Behavior

We are in the third stage of the conflict process when a member engages in action that frustrates the attainment of another's goals or prevents the furthering of the other's interests. This action must be intended; that is, there must be a known effort to frustrate another. At this juncture, the conflict is out in the open.

Overt conflict covers a full range of behaviors, from subtle, indirect, and highly controlled forms of interference to direct, aggressive, violent, and uncontrolled struggle. At the low range, this overt behavior is illustrated by the student who raises his or her hand in class and questions a point the instructor has made. At the high range, strikes, riots, and wars come to mind.

Stage III is also where most conflict-handling behaviors are initiated. Once the conflict is overt, the parties will develop a method for dealing with the conflict. This does not exclude conflict-handling behaviors from being initiated in Stage II, but in most cases, these techniques for reducing the frustration are used not as preventive measures but only when the conflict has become observable. Five conflict handling approaches are typically available to the parties: competition, collaboration, avoidance, accommodation, and compromise.

Figure 10-2 represents one author's effort at identifying the primary conflict-handling orientations. Using two dimensions—*cooperativeness* (the degree to which one party attempts to satisfy the other party's concerns) and *assertiveness* (the degree to which one party attempts to satisfy his or her own concerns)—five conflict-handling orientations are identified: *competition* (assertive and uncooperative), *collaboration* (assertive and cooperative), *avoidance* (unassertive and uncooperative), *accommodation* (unasser-

Figure 10-2
Dimensions of Conflict-Handling Orientations

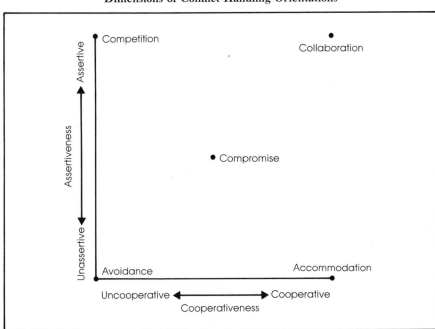

Source: K. Thomas, "Conflict and Conflict Management," in *Handbook of Industrial and Organizational Psychology*, p. 900., ed. M. D. Dunnette. Copyright © 1976 John Wiley & Sons. Reprinted by permission of John Wiley & Sons, Inc.

tive and cooperative), and *compromise* (midway on both assertiveness and cooperativeness dimensions).

Competition. When one party seeks to achieve her goals or further her interests, regardless of the impact on the parties to the conflict, she competes and dominates. These win-lose struggles, in formal groups or in an organization, frequently utilize the formal authority of a mutual superior as the dominant force, and the conflicting parties will each use his or her own power base in order to resolve a victory in his or her favor.

Collaboration. When each of the parties in conflict desires to satisfy fully the concern of all parties, we have cooperation and the search for a mutually beneficial outcome. In collaboration, the behavior of the parties is aimed at solving the problem and at clarifying the differences rather than accommodating various points of view. The participants consider the full range of alternatives; the similarities and differences in viewpoint become more clearly focused; and the causes or differences become outwardly evident. Because the solution sought is advantageous to all parties, collaboration is often thought of as a win-win approach to resolving conflicts. It is, for example, a tool used frequently by marriage counselors. Behavioral scientists, who value openness, trust, and spontaneity in relationships, are also strong advocates of a collaborative approach to resolving conflicts.

Avoidance. A party may recognize that a conflict exists but react by withdrawing, or suppressing the conflict. Indifference or the desire to evade overt demonstration of a disagreement can result in withdrawal: The parties acknowledge physical separation and each stakes out a territory that is distinct from the other's. If withdrawal is not possible or desirous, the parties may suppress, that is, withhold their differences. When group members are required to interact because of the interdependence of their tasks, suppression is a more probable outcome than withdrawal.

Accommodation. When the parties seek to appease their opponents, they may be willing to place their opponents' interests above their own. In order to maintain the relationship, one party is willing to be self-sacrificing. We refer to this behavior as accommodation. When husbands and wives have differences, it is not uncommon for one to accommodate the other by placing a spouse's interest above one's own.

Compromise. When each party to the conflict must give up something, sharing occurs, resulting in a compromised outcome. In compromising, there is no clear winner or loser. Rather, there is a rationing of the object of the conflict or, where the object is not divisible, one rewards the other by yielding something of substitute value. The distinguishing characteristic of compromise, therefore, is the requirement that each party give up something. In negotiations between unions and management, compromise is required in order to reach a settlement and agree upon a labor contract.

Stage IV: Outcomes   The interplay between the overt conflict behavior and conflict-handling behaviors results in consequences. As Figure 10-1 demonstrates, they may be functional in that the conflict has resulted in an improvement in the group's performance. Conversely, group performance may be hindered and the outcome then would be dysfunctional.

Functional Outcomes.   How might conflict increase group performance? It is hard to visualize a situation where open or violent aggression could be functional. But there are a number of instances where it is possible to envision how low or moderate levels of conflict could improve the effectiveness of a group. Because it is often difficult to think of instances where conflict can be constructive, let us consider some examples, and then look at the research evidence.

Conflict is constructive when it improves the quality of decisions, stimulates creativity and innovation, encourages interest and curiosity among group members, provides the medium through which problems can be aired and tensions released, and fosters an environment of self-evaluation and change. The evidence suggests that conflict can improve the quality of decision making by allowing all points, particularly the ones that are unusual or held by a minority, to be weighed in important decisions. Conflict is an antidote for groupthink. It does not allow the group to "rubber stamp" decisions that may be based on weak assumptions, inadequate consideration to relevant alternatives, or other debilities. Conflict challenges the status quo and therefore furthers the creation of new ideas, promotes reassessment of group goals and activities, and increases the probability that the group will respond to change.

Research studies in diverse settings confirm the functionality of conflict. Consider the following findings.

A comparison of six major decisions during the administrations of four different U.S. presidents found that conflict reduced the chance that groupthink would overpower policy decisions. The comparisons demonstrated that conformity among presidential advisers was related to poor decisions, while an atmosphere of constructive conflict and critical thinking surrounded the well-developed decisions.

Not only do better and more innovative decisions result from situations where there is some conflict, there is evidence indicating that conflict can be related positively to productivity. It was demonstrated that, among established groups, performance tended to improve more when there was conflict among members than when there was fairly close agreement. The investigators observed that when groups analyzed decisions that had been made by the individual members of that group, the average improvement among the high-conflict groups was 73 percent greater than that of those groups characterized by low-conflict conditions.[1] Others have found similar results: Groups composed of members with different interests tend to produce higher-quality solutions to a variety of problems than do homogeneous groups.[2]

Conflict has even been shown to be constructive to the operations of labor unions. An examination of local unions found that conflict between members of the local was positively related to the union's power and to member loyalty and participation in union affairs.[3]

The above findings suggest that conflict in the group might be an indication of strength rather than, in the traditional view, of weakness.

Dysfunctional Outcomes. The destructive consequences of conflict upon a group or organization's performance are generally well known. A reasonable summary might state: Uncontrolled opposition breeds discontent, which acts to dissolve common ties, and eventually leads to destruction of the group. And, of course, there is a substantial body of literature to document how the dysfunctional varieties of conflict can reduce group effectiveness. Among the more undesirable consequences are a retarding of communication, reductions in group cohesiveness, and subordination of group goals to the primacy of infighting among members. At the extreme, conflict can bring group functioning to a halt and potentially threaten the group's survival.

This discussion has again returned us to the issue of what is functional and what is dysfunctional. Research on conflict has yet to identify those situations where conflict is more likely to be constructive than destructive. However, the difference between functional and dysfunctional conflict is important enough for us to go beyond the substantive evidence and propose at least two hypotheses. The first is that extreme levels of conflict, exemplified by overt struggle or violence, are rarely, if ever, functional. Functional conflict is probably most often characterized by low to moderate levels of subtle and controlled opposition. Secondly, the type of group activity should be another factor determining functionality. We hypothesize that the more creative or unprogrammed the decision making of the group, the greater the probability that internal conflict is constructive. Groups that

1. J. Hall and M. S. Williams, "A Comparison of Decision-Making Performances in Established and Ad-Hoc Groups," *Journal of Personality and Social Psychology*, February 1966, p. 217.

2. Richard L. Hoffman, "Homogeneity of Member Personality and Its Effect on Group Problem Solving," *Journal of Abnormal and Social Psychology*, January 1959, pp. 27–32; Richard L. Hoffman and Norman R. F. Maier, "Quality and Acceptance of Problem Solutions by Members of Homogeneous and Heterogeneous Groups," *Journal of Abnormal and Social Psychology*, March 1961, pp. 401–07.

3. Arnold Tannenbaum, "Control Structure and Union Functions," *American Journal of Sociology*, May 1956, pp. 127–40.

are required to tackle problems requiring new and novel approaches—for example, in research or advertising—will benefit more from conflict than groups performing highly programmed activities, such as work teams on an automobile assembly line.

IMPLICATIONS FOR MANAGERS

Many people assume that conflict is related to lower group and organizational performance. This chapter has demonstrated that this assumption is frequently fallacious. Conflict can be either constructive or destructive to the functioning of a group or unit. As shown in Figure 10-3, levels of conflict can be either too high or too low.

Figure 10-3
Conflict and Unit Performance

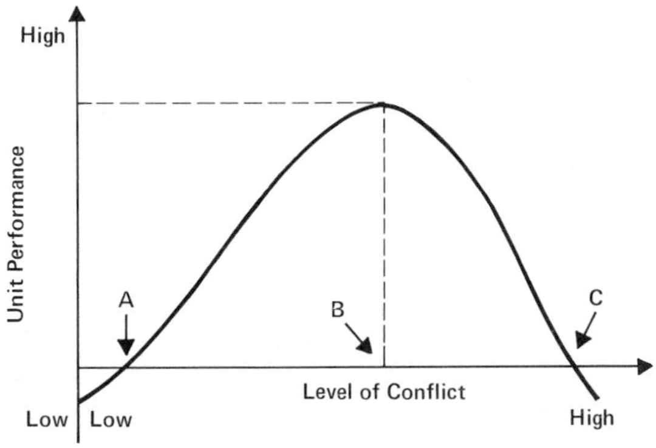

Situation	Level of Conflict	Type of Conflict	Unit's Internal Characteristics	Unit Performance Outcome
A	Low or none	Dysfunctional	Apathetic Stagnant Nonresponsive to change Lack of new ideas	Low
B	Optimal	Functional	Viable Self-critical Innovative	High
C	High	Dysfunctional	Disruptive Chaotic Uncooperative	Low

Table 10-1
When to Use the Five Conflict-Handling Orientations

Conflict-handling Orientation	Appropriate Situations
Competition	1. When quick, decisive action is vital (in emergencies) 2. On important issues where unpopular actions need implementing (in cost cutting, enforcing unpopular rules, discipline) 3. On issues vital to the organization's welfare when you know you're right 4. Against people who take advantage of noncompetitive behavior
Collaboration	1. To find an integrative solution when both sets of concerns are too important to be compromised 2. When your objective is to learn 3. To merge insights from people with different perspectives 4. To gain commitment by incorporating concerns into a consensus 5. To work through feelings that have interfered with a relationship
Avoidance	1. When an issue is trivial, or more important issues are pressing 2. When you perceive no chance of satisfying your concerns 3. When potential disruption outweighs the benefits of resolution 4. To let people cool down and regain perspective 5. When gathering information supersedes immediate decision 6. When others can resolve the conflict more effectively 7. When issues seem tangential or symptomatic of other issues
Accommodation	1. When you find you are wrong and to allow a better position to be heard, to learn, and to show your reasonableness 2. When issues are more important to others than yourself and to satisfy others and maintain cooperation 3. To build social credits for later issues 4. To minimize loss when you are outmatched and losing 5. When harmony and stability are especially important 6. To allow subordinates to develop by learning from mistakes
Compromise	1. When goals are important, but not worth the effort or potential disruption of more assertive modes 2. When opponents with equal power are committed to mutually exclusive goals 3. To achieve temporary settlements to complex issues 4. To arrive at expedient solutions under time pressure 5. As a backup when collaboration or competition is unsuccessful

Source: K. W. Thomas, "Toward Multidimensional Values in Teaching: The Example of Conflict Behaviors," *Academy of Management Review*, July 1977, p. 487. With permission.

Either extreme hinders performance. An optimal level is one in which there is enough conflict to prevent stagnation, stimulate creativity, allow tensions to be released, and initiate the seeds for change, yet not so much as to be disruptive.

What advice can we give to managers faced with excessive conflict and the need to reduce it? Don't assume that there's one conflict-handling approach that will always be best! You should select the resolution technique appropriate for each situation. Table 10-1 offers guidance in making the right selection.

SELECTED REFERENCES

ANDREWS, I. ROBERT, AND DEAN TJOSVOLD, "Conflict Management Under Different Levels of Conflict Intensity," *Journal of Occupational Behaviour,* July 1983, pp. 223–28.

BLAKE, ROBERT R., AND JANE S. MOUTON, *Solving Costly Organizational Conflicts.* San Francisco: Jossey-Bass, 1984.

KING, DONALD, "Three Cheers for Conflict," *Personnel,* January–February 1981, pp. 13–22.

RAHIM, M. AFZALUR, "A Strategy of Managing Conflict in Complex Organizations," *Human Relations,* January 1985, pp. 81–89.

ROBBINS, STEPHEN P., " 'Conflict Management' and 'Conflict Resolution' Are Not Synonymous Terms," *California Management Review,* Winter 1978, pp. 67–75.

STERNBERG, ROBERT J., AND LAWRENCE J. SORIANO, "Styles of Conflict Resolution," *Journal of Personality and Social Psychology,* February 1984, pp. 115–26.

11

FOUNDATIONS OF ORGANIZATIONAL STRUCTURE

<== **IDEAS TO BE FOUND** ==>
IN THIS CHAPTER

- Complexity
- Formalization
- Centralization
- Technology
- Environment
- Power-control
- Mechanistic structures
- Organic structures

Jerry Nichols's job is pretty good. He's got an attractively furnished office on the top floor of a New York skyscraper, a nice view, his own secretary, the prestige that goes with being a securities analyst with a major brokerage firm, and a salary and bonus package that earns him more than $100,000 a year—not bad for a twenty-eight-year-old guy who has been out of school for less than five years.

In contrast to a blue-collar assembly-line worker, Jerry Nichols has a lot of freedom on his job. But in absolute terms, Jerry and the more than 100 million other North Americans who go to work every Monday have a number of restrictions imposed on them by their organizations that limit and regulate their attitudes and behavior. Most employees have a job description that says what they are supposed to do. The organization has rules telling Jerry and the other employees like Jerry what they can and cannot do. There is an authority hierarchy that defines who everyone's boss is and the formal channels through which communications are to pass. These are examples of the structural characteristics that most organizations have. In this chapter, we will demonstrate how an organization's *structure* affects the attitudes and behavior of its members.

WHAT IS STRUCTURE?

An organization's structure is made up of three components. The first has to do with the amount of vertical, horizontal, and spatial differentiation. This is called *complexity*. Next is the degree to which rules and procedures are utilized. This is referred to as *formalization*. The third is *centralization*, which considers where decision-making authority lies. Let's briefly elaborate on each of these components.

Complexity

Complexity can be broken down into three parts. *Horizontal differentiation* considers the degree of horizontal separation between units. *Vertical differentiation* refers to the depth of the organizational hierarchy. *Spatial differentiation* encompasses the degree to which the location of an organization's facilities and personnel are geographically dispersed. The more that an organization is differentiated along these dimensions, the more complex it is.

Horizontal Differentiation. Horizontal differentiation refers to the degree of differentiation between units based on the orientation of members, the nature of the tasks they perform, and their education and training. We can state that the larger the number of different occupations within an organization that require specialized knowledge and skills, the more horizontally complex that organization is. Why? Because diverse orientations make it more difficult for organizational members to communicate and more difficult for management to coordinate their activities. For instance, when organizations create specialized groups or expand departmental designations, they separate groups from each other, making interactions between those groups more complex. If the organization is staffed by people who have similar backgrounds, skills, and training, they are likely to see the world in more similar terms. Conversely, diversity increases the likelihood that they will have different goal emphases, time orientations, and even a different work vocabulary. Job specialization reinforces differences—the chemical engineer's job is clearly different from that of the personnel recruitment interviewer. Their training is different. The language they use on their respective jobs is different. They are typically assigned to different departments, which further reinforces their diverse orientations.

Vertical Differentiation. Vertical differentiation refers to the depth of the structure. Differentiation increases, and so does complexity, as the number of hierarchical levels in the organization increases. The more levels that exist between top management and operatives, the greater the potential for communication distortion, the more difficult it is to coordinate the decisions of managerial personnel, and the more difficult it is for top management to oversee closely the actions of operatives.

Vertical and horizontal differentiation should not be construed as independent of each other. Vertical differentiation may be best understood as a response to an increase in horizontal differentiation. As work is divided into smaller parts, it becomes increasingly necessary to coordinate tasks. Since high horizontal differentiation means members will have diverse training and background, it may be difficult for the individual units to see how their tasks fit into the greater whole. The bricklayers on a large construction site may see themselves as merely laying bricks, not putting up a building. Someone must supervise their tasks to see that they are done according to the architect's plan and consistent with the time schedule. The result is a need for increased coordination which shows itself in the development of vertical differentiation.

Spatial Differentiation. An organization can perform the same activities with the same horizontal and vertical arrangement in multiple locations. Yet, this existence of multiple locations increases complexity. Therefore, the third element in complexity is spatial differentiation, or the degree to which the location of an organization's offices, plants, and personnel are geographically dispersed.

A manufacturing company horizontally differentiates when it separates the marketing function from production. Yet, if essentially identical marketing activities are carried on in six geographically dispersed sales offices—Seattle, Los Angeles, Atlanta, New York, Toronto, and Brussels—while all production is done in a large factory in Cleveland, this organization is more complex than if both the marketing and production activities were performed at the same facility in Cleveland. The spatial concept applies similarly to vertical differentiation. If an organization's senior executives reside in one city, middle managers in a half-dozen cities, and lower-level managers in a hundred different company offices around the world, complexity has increased. Why? Because communication, coordination, and control is easier where spatial differentiation is low.

A final point: Spatial differentiation considers distance as well as numbers. If the state of Delaware had two regional welfare offices located in Dover and Wilmington, these offices would be approximately 45 miles apart. If the state of Alaska had two comparably sized offices in Anchorage and Fairbanks, these offices would be separated by 350 miles. Although the number of offices is the same in both cases, the Delaware welfare organization would be less complex because the distance between the offices is smaller.

Formalization   Formalization refers to the degree to
                                                 which jobs within the organization
are standardized. If a job is highly formalized, then the job incumbent has
a minimum amount of discretion over what is to be done, when it is to be
done, and how he or she should do it. Employees can be expected always
to handle the same input in exactly the same way, resulting in a consistent
and uniform output. There are explicit job descriptions, lots of organizational rules, and clearly defined procedures covering work processes in
organizations where there is high formalization. Where formalization is
low, job behaviors are relatively nonprogrammed and employees have a
great deal of freedom to exercise discretion in their work. Since an individual's discretion on the job is inversely related to the amount of behavior
that is preprogrammed by the organization, the greater the standardization, the less input the employee has into how his or her work is to be
done. Standardization not only eliminates the possibility of employees engaging in alternative behaviors, but even removes the need for employees
to consider alternatives.

The degree of formalization can vary widely between organizations
and within organizations. Certain jobs, for instance, are well known to have
little formalization. College textbook representatives, who call on professors to inform them of new publications, have a great deal of freedom in
their jobs. They have no standard sales pitch, and the extent that rules and
procedures govern their behavior may be little more than the requirement
that they submit a weekly sales report and some suggestions on what pluses
to emphasize for the various new titles. At the other extreme, there are
clerical and editorial positions in the same publishing houses where employees are required to clock in at their work stations by 8:00 A.M. or be
docked a half-hour of pay and, once at that work station, to follow a set of
precise procedures dictated by management.

It is generally true that the narrowest of unskilled jobs—those that
are simplest and most repetitive in nature—are most amenable to high
degrees of formalization. The greater the professionalization of a job, the
less likely it is to be highly formalized. Yet, there are obvious exceptions.
Public accountants and consultants, for instance, typically are required to
keep detailed hour-by-hour records of their activities so their companies
can appropriately bill clients for their services. In general, however, the
relationship holds. The jobs of lawyers, engineers, social workers, librari-
ans, and like professionals tend to rate low on formalization.

Formalization not only differs if the jobs are unskilled or professional,
but also by level in the organization and by functional department. Employees higher in the organization are increasingly involved in activities
that are less repetitive and require more complex solutions. The discretion

that managers have increases as they move up the hierarchy so that formalization is lowest at the highest levels of the organization.

The kind of work that people are engaged in also influences the degree of formalization. Jobs in production are typically more formalized than those in sales or research. Why? Because production tends to be concerned with stable and repetitive activities. Such jobs lend themselves to standardization. In contrast, the sales department must be flexible in order to respond to changing needs of customers, and research must be flexible if it is to be innovative.

Centralization   Centralization is the degree to which decision making is concentrated at a single point in the organization. The concept includes only formal authority—that is, the rights inherent in one's position. Typically, it is said that if top management makes the organization's key decisions with little or no input from lower-level personnel, then the organization is centralized. In contrast, the more that lower-level personnel provide input or are given the discretion to make decisions, the more decentralized the organization. As we shall point out, an organization characterized by centralization is an inherently different structural animal than one where decision making has been pushed down to those managers who are closest to the action.

A small but important point needs to be made before we move on. While they are sometimes confused with one another, the concept of centralization is distinctly different from that of spatial differentiation. Centralization is concerned with the dispersion of authority to make decisions within the organization, not geographic dispersion. While it is generally true that organizations with high spatial differentiation also tend to be decentralized (because it's hard for headquarter's management in New York to oversee and understand the unique problems in its office in Vancouver, for instance), this need not be the case. Information technology can allow top management to stay on top of problems in geographically dispersed locations and make the key decisions that affect personnel in those locations. Conversely, an organization operating entirely in a single building can be decentralized if top management delegates authority to its lower-level managers.

THE DETERMINANTS: WHY DO STRUCTURES DIFFER?   We have identified three components which, when "mixed and matched," create different structural forms. For instance, an organization that is highly complex, formalized, and decentralized certainly has a different structure than an organization of similar size and function that is low in complexity, has few rules and procedures governing personnel, and where decision making is centralized in the top executive suites.

Before we review the various forms that structures can take, we need to understand those forces that influence the form that is chosen. Management is the obvious decision-making body for choosing structure. But there are forces that limit management's choices. In the following pages, we shall present the major forces that researchers have identified as causes or determinants of an organization's structure.

Size　　　　　　A quick glance at the organizations we deal with regularly in our lives would lead most of us to conclude that size has some bearing on an organization's structure. The 325,000 employees of General Electric, for example, do not neatly fit into one building, nor into several departments supervised by a couple of managers. It's pretty hard to envision 325,000 people being organized in any manner other than that which would be labeled as high in complexity. On the other hand, a local appliance repair service that employs half-a-dozen people and generates less than $200,000 a year in revenues is not likely to need decentralized decision making or formalized procedures and regulations.

A little more thought suggests that the same conclusion, that size influences structure, can be arrived at through a more sophisticated reasoning process. As an organization hires more operative employees, it will attempt to take advantage of the economic benefits from specialization. The result will be increased horizontal differentiation. Grouping like functions together will facilitate intragroup efficiencies, but will cause intergroup relations to suffer as each performs its different activities. Management, therefore, will need to increase vertical differentiation to coordinate the horizontally differentiated units. This expansion in size is also likely to result in spatial differentiation. All of this increase in complexity will reduce top management's ability to supervise directly the activities within the organization. The control achieved through direct surveillance, therefore, will be replaced by the implementation of formal rules and regulations. This increase in formalization may also be accompanied by still greater vertical differentiation as management creates new units to coordinate the expanding and diverse activities of organization members. Finally, with top management further removed from the operating level, it becomes difficult for senior executives to make rapid and informative decisions. The solution is to substitute decentralized decision making for centralization. Following this reasoning, we see changes in size leading to major structural changes.

But does it actually happen this way? Does structure change directly as a result of a change in the total number of employees? A review of the evidence indicates that size has a significant influence on all elements of structure.

Size appears to have an impact on complexity at a decreasing rate. That is, increases in an organization's size are accompanied by first rapid and then more gradual increases in differentiation. The biggest effect, however, is on vertical differentiation. As organizations increase their numbers of employees, more levels are added, but at a decreasing rate.

The evidence linking size and formalization is quite strong. There is a logical connection between the two. Management seeks to control the behavior of its employees. This can be achieved by direct surveillance or by the use of formalized regulations. While not perfect substitutes for each other, as one increases, the need for the other should decrease. Because surveillance costs should increase very rapidly as an organization expands in size, it seems reasonable to expect that it would be less expensive for management to substitute formalization for direct surveillance as size increases.

There is also a strong inverse relationship between size and centralization. In small organizations, it's possible for management to exercise control by keeping decisions centralized. As size increases, management is physically unable to maintain control in this manner and, therefore, is forced to decentralize.

Technology

The term *technology* refers to how an organization transfers its inputs to outputs. Every organization has one or more technologies for converting financial, human, and physical resources into products or services. The Ford Motor Company, for instance, makes predominant use of an assembly-line to make its products. On the other hand, colleges may use a number of instruction technologies: the ever-popular formal lecture method, the case analysis method, the experiential exercise method, the programmed learning method, and so forth.

There is no agreement on a universal technology classification. If there is a common denominator among those classifications that attempt to describe the processes or methods that organizations use to transform inputs into outputs it is the *degree of routineness*. By this we mean that technologies tend toward either routine or nonroutine activities. The former are characterized by automated and standardized operations. This describes such diverse processes as mass production assembly lines or repetitive clerical tasks. Nonroutine activities are customized. They include such varied operations as furniture restoring, custom shoemaking, or the design of the "Star Wars" defense system.

Some researchers argue that there is a *technological imperative*, that is, that technology *causes* structure. A more moderate position is that technology *constrains* managers. If managers have a considerable degree of choice over their organization's technology, then there is little basis for the imperative argument. Technology would only control structure to the degree that managers chose a technology that demanded certain structural dimensions. For instance, it has been argued that organizations choose the domain in which they will operate and, hence, the activities that they will engage in. If an organization decides to offer consulting advice tailored to the needs of its clients, it is not likely to use the routine, mass production technology. Similarly, the fact that American Honda Motor Company chose to build a manufacturing facility in Ohio that could produce at least 900 cars a day, each, in turn, retailing in the $9,000-to-$14,000 price range, pretty well eliminated any technology other than one relying heavily on routinized mass production activities. Had American Honda decided to produce only four cars a day at that plant and charge $100,000 or more apiece for each car (as does the production facility at Rolls-Royce), then routine mass production might not be at all appropriate. The point is that choice of domain tends to constrain the organization's technology, but the domain is still chosen. The counterpoint, of course, is that even though domain is chosen, technology is still a major influence on structure. For instance, research laboratories are typically low in formalization, while claims departments in insurance companies are typically high on this structural dimension. A good part of this structural difference can be traced to the fact that research labs use nonroutine technologies and claims department activities are standardized and routine.

What relationships have been found between technology and structure? Although the relationship is not overwhelmingly strong, we do find that routine technology is positively associated with low complexity. The greater the routineness, the fewer the number of occupational groups. Similarly, as the work becomes more sophisticated, customized, and nonroutine, more problems occur that require management's attention. Closer supervision results and, with it, more vertical levels are necessary in the structure. So, nonroutine technology is likely to lead to high complexity.

The technology-formalization relationship is stronger. Studies consistently show routineness to be associated with the presence of rule manuals, job descriptions, and other formalized documentation.

Finally, the technology-centralization relationship is less straightforward. It seems logical that routine technologies would be associated with a centralized structure, whereas nonroutine technologies, which rely more heavily on the knowledge of specialists, would be characterized by delegated decision authority. This position has met with some support. However, a more generalized conclusion is that the technology-centralization relationship is moderated by the degree of formalization. Formal regulations and centralized decision making are both control mechanisms and management can substitute them for each other. Routine technologies should be associated with centralized control if there is a minimum of rules and regulations. However, if formalization is high, routine technology can be accompanied by decentralization. So, we would predict that routine technology would lead to centralization, but only if formalization is low.

Environment An organization's environment represents anything outside the organization itself. The problem of defining an organization's environment, however, is often quite difficult. "Nature has neatly packaged people into skins, animals into hides, and allowed trees to enclose themselves with bark. It is easy to see where the unit is and where the environment is. Not so for social organizations."[1] We'll define the environment as composed of those institutions or forces that affect the performance of the organization, but over which the organization has little control. These typically include suppliers, customers, government regulatory agencies, and the like. But keep in mind that it is not always clear who or what is included in any specific organization's relevant environment.

The environment-structure relationship has received a large amount of attention. The reason for this attention is quite simple: Organizations must adapt to their environments if they are to succeed because organizations are dependent on their environments if they are to survive. They must identify and follow their environments, sense changes in those environments, and make appropriate adjustments as necessary. But changing environments produce uncertainty if management can't predict in what ways their environments are moving. And management doesn't like uncertainty. As a result, management will try to eliminate or at least minimize the impact of environmental uncertainty. Alterations in the organization's structural components represent a major tool that management has for controlling environmental uncertainty. The environmental imperative would propose, therefore, that the degree of environmental uncertainty is *the* determinant of structure. If uncertainty is high, the organization will be designed along flexible lines in order to adapt to rapid changes. If uncertainty is low, management will opt for a structure that will be most efficient and offer the highest degree of managerial control. That would be a structure characterized by high complexity, high formalization, and centralization.

Does the evidence support the above predictions? The answer is "Yes." Environmental uncertainty and organizational complexity are inversely related. This is particularly true for departments within organiza-

---

1. Jeffrey Pfeffer and Gerald R. Salancik, *The External Control of Organizations: A Resource Dependence Perspective* (New York: Harper & Row, 1978), p. 29.

tions. Those departments within the organization that are most dependent on the environment—like marketing or research and development—are typically the lowest in complexity.

Similarly, formalization and environmental uncertainty are inversely related. That is, certain and stable environments lead to high formalization. Why? Because stable environments create a minimal need for rapid response, and economies exist for organizations that standardize their activities.

Centralization is also affected by the environment. If the environment is large and multifaceted, it becomes difficult for management to monitor it. As a result, the structure tends to become decentralized. This explains why the marketing function in organizations is typically decentralized. If a firm has a large number of customers and the needs of these customers are prone to rapid changes, management must be able to respond just as rapidly if it is to keep its customers satisfied. This can best be achieved by pushing key decisions down to the local marketing managers who are closest to the customer. Decentralization allows for more rapid response.

Power-Control

An increasingly popular and insightful approach to the question of what causes structure is to look to a political explanation. Size, technology, and environment, even when combined, can at best explain only 50 to 60 percent of the variability in structure. There is a growing body of evidence that suggests that power and politics can explain why an organization's structure is the way it is better than any of the previous three factors. More specifically, the *power-control* explanation states that an organization's structure is the result of a power struggle by internal constituencies who are seeking to further their own interests. Like all decisions in an organization, the structural decision is not fully rational. Managers do not necessarily choose those alternatives that will maximize the organization's interest. They choose criteria and weight them so that the "best choice" will meet the minimal demands of the organization, and also satisfy or enhance the interests of the decision makers. Size, technology, and environmental uncertainty act as contraints by establishing parameters and defining how much discretion is available. Almost always, within the parameters, there is still a great deal of room for the decision maker to maneuver. The power-control position, therefore, argues that those in power will choose a structure that will maintain or enhance their control. Consistent with this perspective, we should expect structures to change very slowly, if at all. Significant changes would occur only as a result of a political struggle in which new power relations evolve. But this rarely occurs. Transitions in the executive suite are usually peaceful. They are evolutionary rather than revolutionary. However, major shake-ups in top management occasionally do occur. Not surprisingly, they are typically followed by major structural changes.

Predictions based on the power-control viewpoint differ from those based on the three previous approaches in that those approaches were basically contingency models: Structures change to reflect changes in size, technology, or environmental uncertainty. The power-control approach, however, is essentially noncontingent. It assumes little change within the organization's power coalition. Hence, it would propose that structures are relatively stable over time. More importantly, power-control advocates would predict that after taking into consideration size, technology, and environmental factors, those in power would choose a structure that would best serve their personal interests. What type of structure would that be? Obviously one that would be low in complexity, high in formalization, and centralized. These structural dimensions will most likely maximize control in the hands of senior management. A structure with these properties becomes the single "one best way" to organize. Of course, *best* in this context refers to "maintenance of control" rather than enhancement of organizational performance.

MECHANISTIC AND ORGANIC STRUCTURES

Organization structures can be classified as essentially either mechanistic or organic. Mechanistic structures are characterized as being *high* in complexity, formalization, and centralization. In contrast, organic structures are relatively flexible and adaptive; that is, they tend to be *low* in complexity, formalization, and centralization.

The mechanistic-organic dichotomy is a convenient way to classify organizations. Unfortunately, it's an oversimplification. In the real world, there are few pure mechanistic or organic structures. Rather, there are a variety of structural options that tend generally to fall within one or the other classification. Let's look at a few of the more well-known structural designs that represent real-world applications of both categories.

Mechanistic Options

When contingency factors favor a mechanistic design, one of three options is most likely to be considered: the *functional* structure, the *divisional* structure, or the *conglomerate* structure.

The Functional Structure. The functional structure's primary focus is on achieving the efficiencies from division of labor by grouping similar and related occupational specialties together. For example, if a manufacturing firm has vice-presidents for marketing, research and development, finance, production, and human resources, all reporting to a common president, it is employing a functional structure.

The strength of the functional structure lies in the advantages that accrue from specialization. Putting similar specialties together results in

176

economies of scale, minimizes the duplication of personnel and equipment, and allows comfortable and satisfied employees to have the opportunity to talk "the same language" among their peers.

The functional structure's major weakness is that the best interests of the organization are frequently lost in the pursuit of functional goals. Members within individual functions become insulated and have little understanding of what people in other functions are doing. The diversity of interests and perspectives that exist between functions can result in continual conflict as each function tries to assert its importance.

The Divisional Structure. The divisional structure creates self-contained and autonomous units. Each unit or division is headed by a division manager who is responsible for performance and who holds complete strategic and operating decision-making authority. Typically, divisional structures are composed of functional subsets. That is, each divisional unit has its own autonomous functional structure. A central headquarters provides support services to the divisions. This usually includes financial and legal services, but can include any activity in which there are economies to providing centralized operations. Of course, the headquarters also acts as an external overseer to coordinate and control the various divisions. Divisions, therefore, are autonomous within given parameters. Division managers are usually free to direct their divisions any way they see fit, as long as it is within the overall guidelines set down by headquarters.

What primary advantage does the divisional structure offer? It focuses on results. Division managers have full responsibility for a product or service. Its major disadvantage is duplication of activities and resources. Each division, for instance, may have a marketing research department. In the absence of autonomous divisions, all of the organization's marketing research might be centralized and done for a fraction of the cost that divisionalization requires. So the divisional form's duplication of functions increases the organization's costs and reduces efficiency.

The Conglomerate Structure. The conglomerate structure is composed of a diverse set of companies that are completely independent except that they pool their resources. It is like a divisional structure, except that the companies in a conglomerate are even more independent and they have been chosen to provide diversity. For instance, in 1987 Gulf+Western included The Associates (the third largest independent finance company in the U.S.), Simon & Schuster (the publishing company), Paramount Pictures, and Madison Square Garden. Each of Gulf+Western's companies is run by its own chief executive officer. Corporate headquarters provides the financial capital, strategic planning capability, and managerial expertise that might otherwise be unavailable if these companies were independent.

The conglomerate structure can provide financial economies of scale, and can balance risks. Operating companies can be bought and sold independently with little or no effect on the organization's other units. But there is duplication of activities, since there is no sharing of skilled personnel, sophisticated equipment, and facilities across company lines. Perhaps the most important drawback is that the conglomerate's top management cannot be experts in each of the industries their operating companies function in. Top management, therefore, is likely to take a very impersonal approach to its relations with each of its companies' managements. Controls become highly formalized, and operating companies and their employees become abstract statistics on computer reports.

Organic Options   Three examples of organization structures that tend to take organic forms are the *simple* structure, the *matrix* structure, and the *task force*.

The Simple Structure.   An organization that appears to have no structure probably has a simple one. By that we mean that it is low in complexity, has little formalization, and has its authority centralized in a single person. The simple structure is a "flat" organization—typically one with only two or three vertical levels, with a loose body of employees, and with almost everyone reporting to the one individual in whom the decision-making authority is centralized. This structure is most widely practiced in small businesses where the manager and the owner are one and the same.

The strengths of the simple structure are obvious. It's flexible, inexpensive to maintain, and accountability is clear. One of its major weaknesses is that it is really applicable only to small organizations. When confronted with increased size, the simple structure is generally inadequate. Its low formalization and high centralization result in information overload at the top. As size increases, decision making becomes slower and may eventually come to a standstill as the single executive tries to continue making all decisions.

The Matrix Structure.   The functional structure offers the advantages that accrue from specialization. The divisional structure has greatest focus on end results but suffers from duplication of activities and resources. However, if the organization gave each product its own supporting functional structure, then the emphasis on end results would again be great. Each product would have a product manager responsible for everything related to that product. But this, too, would result in redundant positions as each product would require a separate set of functional specialists. The matrix is a structural device for maintaining high accountability while, at the same time, achieving the economies from functional specialization.

A matrix structure is created by superimposing a project or product organization over a functional one. Functional units are used to gain the economies from specialization. But overlaid upon the functional departments are a set of managers who are responsible for specific products, projects, or programs within the organization. The result is that employees have two bosses: their functional department head and the manager overseeing the project, product, or program they are working on.

It's the matrix's ability to be adaptive and flexible that places it in the organic category. It can, for example, permit an aerospace firm to work on dozens of projects, adding new ones and dropping completed ones as needed. The success or failure of any project can be directly linked to its project manager. Meanwhile, specialists are grouped by function, which minimizes the number necessary and allows for specialized resources to be shared and pooled across projects. Of course, these advantages don't come without costs. The matrix is a complex structure that is difficult to coordinate and can be frustrating to employees when their multiple bosses make conflicting demands upon them.

The Task Force Structure. The task force is not an independent structure. It is essentially an organic appendage designed to be used with a mechanistic structure to gain flexibility.

The task force is a temporary structure created to accomplish a specific, well-defined, and complex task involving personnel from various organization subunits. Members serve on the task force until its goal is achieved. They then disband to move on to a new task force, return to their permanent functional department, or leave the organization.

Because the task force is temporary, it can be used to attack problems that cut across functional lines with only minimal disturbance to the organization's mechanistic main frame. It allows the organization the best of organic and mechanistic structures—flexibility and efficiency.

A Buyer's Guide to Structural Options   What conditions make one structural form preferable to another? Table 11-1 summarizes the options we have discussed and notes the conditions that favor each.

Certain structures are designed to work well with specialization and large size. These are mechanistic designs like the functional, divisional, and conglomerate structures.

The simple structure is effective when there are few employees, when the organization is new, and when the environment is simple and dynamic. Small size usually means less repetitive work, so standardization is less attractive. Small size also makes informal communication both convenient and effective. All new organizations tend to adopt the simple struc-

Table 11-1
Structural Options: Strengths and Conditions of Use

Design	Strengths	When to Use
Functional	Economies through specialization	Single-product or service organization
Divisional	High accountability for end results	Large size; multiple-product or multiple-market organization
Conglomerate	Spreads risk through diversification	Large size; operating in highly diverse markets
Simple	Flexible and economical	Small size; formative years of development; a simple and dynamic environment
Matrix	Economies through specialization and accountability for results	Multiple products or programs that rely on functional expertise
Task force	Flexibility	Important tasks that have specific time and performance standards; that are unique and unfamiliar; that require expertise that crosses functional lines.

ture, because management hasn't had the time to elaborate on its structure. Finally, the simple structure works well with a simple and dynamic environment. A simple environment is easily comprehended by a single individual, yet the structure's flexibility allows it to respond rapidly to unpredictable contingencies.

The matrix attempts to gain the advantages of specialization without any disadvantages. When the organization utilizes multiple programs or products and functional departmentalization, it can appoint program or product managers who direct activities across functional lines.

The task force structure is an appendage to a mechanistic structure. It can bring together personnel from across functional lines. It is an ideal vehicle for tackling important tasks that have specific time and performance standards and that are unique and unfamiliar. Once the task is familiar, and if it needs to be repeated, a mechanistic design can be chosen that can handle it in a more standardized and efficient manner.

In Practice   The logic of the contingency approach to organization design suggests that mechanistic structures are well suited to large size, routine technologies, and relatively stable and certain environments. But, in smaller organizations with unique or customized technologies and dynamic and uncertain environments, the mechanistic structure becomes too constraining. Such contingencies dictate the need for an organic structure.

The above assumes management will place organizational performance criteria above the desire to maintain control. But observation indicates that all but the smallest organizations, or those just being formed, are structured along mechanistic lines. The wide popularity of the mechanistic structure is undoubtedly due to a number of factors. First, it works. In spite of the contingencies of size, technology, and environment, mechanistic structures are effective in a wide range of organized activities: manufacturing, service firms, hospitals, schools and colleges, the military, and voluntary associations. Second, large size among organizations prevails. Organizations that succeed and survive tend to grow to large size. Third, the environment may be less dynamic than typically believed. Many changes, for instance, can be forecasted and the outcome therefore much less uncertain. Fourth, the mechanistic structure maintains control. Even given the constraints of a nonroutine technology and an uncertain environment, management can choose to design a structure that will contain the maximum degree of mechanistic qualities. Finally, flexibility can be achieved by using organic appendages like the task force. In this way, the control that mechanistic structures provide doesn't have to be given up.

Our conclusions, therefore, are that (1) management has structural choices; (2) that those choices should be dictated by the organization's size, technology, and environment; (3) but that, in practice, the mechanistic structure is the dominant organizational form.

KEY STRUCTURAL VARIABLES AND THEIR RELEVANCE TO OB

Now we move to the crux of our concern: relating structure to performance and satisfaction. This is no trivial task. The research on the structure-performance relationship, for instance, has been described as "among the most vexing and ambiguous in the field of management and organizational behavior."[2] Seven structural variables have received the

2. Dan R. Dalton, William D. Tudor, Michael J. Spendolini, Gordon J. Fielding, and Lyman W. Porter, "Organization Structure and Performance: A Critical Review," *Academy of Management Review*, January 1980, p. 60.

bulk of the attention. As a result, the following analysis reviews the evidence as it relates only to these variables.[3] This is not a major shortcoming, however, since these seven include the essence of what we have called "organization structure."

Size   If we look at the organization as a whole, there is evidence to suggest that job satisfaction tends to decrease with size. This is intuitively logical, since larger size results in fewer opportunities for individuals to participate in decision making, less proximity and identification with organizational goals, and less clarity between individual effort and an identifiable outcome. Increased size also appears to lead to higher absenteeism, though not necessarily greater turnover. The larger size offers less opportunity for an employee to identify with his or her organization but evidence suggests that larger organizations tend to pay better than smaller ones. The result is that individuals do not leave the larger organization but they do have a propensity to absent themselves more frequently from work. Interestingly, these findings may be moderated by the degree of decentralization. If increased size is accompanied by increased delegation of authority, the negative impact of size tends to be reduced.

The attention paid to the impact of size on performance and attitudes has not been focused solely at the organization level. Concern has also been given to subunit size; that is, the size of intraorganizational work units. Here, there appears to be a definite positive relationship between subunit size and absenteeism and turnover. However, there seems to be no consistent relationship between subunit size and job satisfaction.

Organizational Level   Is satisfaction or performance affected by an employee's position in the vertical hierarchy? For instance, are senior executives more satisfied with their jobs than operatives or low-level supervisors?

In terms of structural variables, the most frequently investigated characteristic has been level in the organizational hierarchy. Although the evidence is far from conclusive, the bulk of the evidence finds that as we go up

---

3. This section has drawn on the findings and insights provided in Lyman W. Porter and Edward E. Lawler III, "Properties of Organization Structure in Relation to Job Attitudes and Job Behavior," *Psychological Bulletin*, July 1965, pp. 23–51; Lawrence R. James and Allan P. Jones, "Organization Structure: A Review of Structural Dimensions and Their Conceptual Relationships with Individual Attitudes and Behavior," *Organizational Behavior and Human Performance*, June 1976, pp. 74–113; Chris J. Berger and Larry L. Cummings, "Organizational Structure, Attitudes, and Behaviors," in *Research in Organizational Behavior*, Vol. 1, ed. Barry M. Staw (Greenwich, Conn.: JAI Press, 1979), pp. 169–208; and Dalton et al., "Organization Structure," pp. 49–64.

the hierarchy, we generally find more satisfied employees. Although one can debate causality, it seems unlikely that satisfied employees are getting more promotions than grumpy employees. It is far more logical to conclude that as one moves up in the organization, pay, formal authority, status, accouterments, and other rewards increase and, with them, job satisfaction.

Line versus Staff The distinction is typically made in organizations between individuals with line authority and those with staff authority. Line personnel possess command authority, while staff personnel support and advise the line. Does this difference affect the attitudes and behavior of those involved?

The early evidence indicated that staff personnel derived less satisfaction from their jobs. This might have been due to the fact that staff jobs were more specialized and offered less opportunity for decision making. More recent studies suggest that there are no consistent, important differences in the satisfaction levels of persons in line and staff positions. It's possible that the traditional distinction between line and staff has in recent years become blurred in many organizations. It is not unusual nowadays for staff personnel to exert tremendous power over line managers as a result of their technical expertise. Therefore, while staff personnel may not enjoy positional authority, their satisfaction is not adversely affected because they have other power sources.

Span of Control The term *span of control* refers to the number of subordinates who report directly to a manager. Does this variable influence employee performance or satisfaction?

A review of the research indicates that it is probably safe to say that there is no evidence to support a relationship between span of control and performance. While it is intuitively attractive to argue that large spans might lead to higher employee performance because these spans provide more distant supervision, more opportunity for personal initiative, and better communication, the research fails to support this notion. At this point it is impossible to state that any particular span of control is best for producing high performance or high satisfaction among subordinates. The most we can say is that there is some, but slight, evidence that a manager's job satisfaction increases as the number of subordinates he or she supervises increases.

Horizontal Differentiation There have not been many studies that have looked at the horizontal differentiation-performance relationship. But among the studies performed, most of the evidence suggests a positive relationship; that is, the greater the special-

183

ization, the higher the performance. But because the measures of performance tend to be questionable, and several studies find no association, the realistic conclusion is that the relationship between horizontal differentiation and performance has not been clearly demonstrated.

Evidence for the impact of horizontal differentiation on satisfaction is only a little more encouraging. Horizontal differentiation has generally been regarded to leading to lower satisfaction in that a large segment of the work force is alienated by having to do narrowly defined and repetitive tasks. However, as we showed in Chapter 4 in our discussion of job design, this conclusion must be moderated by individual differences. Some people prefer structured and narrowly defined work tasks, while others value autonomy and freedom. Again, a clear relationship between horizontal differentiation and satisfaction has not been demonstrated.

Vertical Differentiation

Are there significant differences in employee performance and satisfaction in tall organizations (with many vertical levels) versus flat organizations? There are mixed findings regarding performance. Research reports both positive and negative relationships, making it difficult to generalize. Concerning satisfaction, it appears that vertical differentiation does matter. High-level managers in tall organizations and lower-level managers in flat organizations experience more satisfaction than their opposites.

Centralization

The last independent variable we shall look at is centralization. Although we must qualify our generalizations, there do seem to be some meaningful relationships between centralization and our dependent variables.

The evidence supports the conclusion that centralization is negatively related with performance. Although these studies were conducted with managerial and professional personnel, therefore limiting our ability to generalize to blue-collar and nonprofessional employees, the evidence is nevertheless consistent.

There is limited evidence that, for a large segment of the work force, decentralization generates less job alienation, less dissatisfaction with work, greater satisfaction with supervision, and greater communication frequency among co-workers at the same level in the organization. Yet, even though centralization and satisfaction appear to be inversely related, this conclusion is likely to be moderated by individual differences and the types of tasks that employees perform. For instance, we would predict that this inverse relationship is likely to be stronger among professionals than among blue-collar workers.

IMPLICATIONS FOR MANAGERS

This chapter has demonstrated that, in addition to individual differences and group factors, the structural relationships in which people work have an important bearing on employee attitude and behavior. To the degree that an organization structure reduces ambiguity and clarifies concerns such as "What am I supposed to do?" "How am I supposed to do it?" "Who do I report to?" and "Who do I go to if I have a problem?", it shapes employees' attitudes, and facilitates and motivates them to higher levels of performance. Of course, structure also constrains employees by imposing some limits and controls.

Figure 11-1 represents what we have discussed in this chapter. Size, technology, environment, and power-control determine the type of structure an organization will have. Complexity, formalization, and centralization represent the structural components that can be mixed and matched to form various structural designs. For the most part, structural designs fall into one of two categories: mechanistic or organic. Finally, different structural designs have different effects on employees.

From a managerial perspective, it is important to emphasize that managers have some discretion in the structural decision. Even though the organization's size, technology, and environment constrain structural options, managers still have considerable influence on which structure is implemented. Given this discretion and the fact that structural configurations appear to influence employee performance and satisfaction, managers should consider carefully the behavioral implications when they make structural decisions. Let's now consider some general thoughts.

For a large proportion of the population, high structure—that is, high complexity, high formalization, and centralization—leads to reduced job satisfaction. High vertical differentiation tends to alienate lower-level employees because vertical communication becomes more difficult and one can feel like "low man on the totem pole." On the other hand, upper management undoubtedly finds that the rewards accompanying their positions enhance job satisfaction.

Specialization also tends to be inversely related to satisfaction, espe-

Figure 11-1
Organization Structure Model

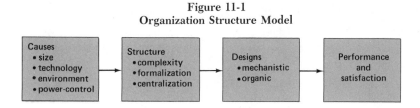

cially where jobs have been divided into minute tasks. This conclusion would have to be moderated to reflect individual differences among employees. While most prefer autonomy, not *all* do.

For individuals who value autonomy and self-actualization, large size, when accompanied by high centralization, results in lower satisfaction. As we have noted, there are fewer opportunities to participate in decision making, less proximity and identification with organizational goals, and less feeling that individual effort is linked to an identifiable outcome. In other words, the larger the organization, the more difficult it is for the individual to see the impact of his or her contribution to the final goods or service produced.

For certain types of activities, the organic structure will result in more effective performance. For instance, if tasks are nonroutine and there exists a great deal of environmental uncertainty, the organization can be more responsive when structured along organic rather than mechanistic lines. But this more responsive structure provides both advantages and disadvantages to employees. There are rarely restrictive job descriptions or excessive rules and regulations; and the structure does not require workers to obey commands that are issued by distant executives. But there are usually overlapping layers of responsibility and this wrecks havoc with individuals who need the security of standardized tasks. To maximize employee performance and satisfaction, individual differences should be taken into account. Individuals with a high degree of bureaucratic orientation tend to place a heavy reliance on higher authority, prefer formalized and specific rules, and prefer formal relationships with others on the job. These people are better suited to mechanistic structures. Individuals with a low degree of bureaucratic orientation are better suited to organic structures.

SELECTED REFERENCES

DAFT, RICHARD L., *Organization Theory and Design* (2nd ed.). St. Paul, Minn.: West Publishing, 1986.

HALL, RICHARD H., *Organizations: Structure and Process* (4th ed.). Englewood Cliffs, N.J.: Prentice-Hall, 1987.

MEDCOF, JOHN W., "The Power Motive and Organizational Structure: A Micro-Macro Connection," *Canadian Journal of Administrative Science,* June 1985, pp. 95–113.

MINTZBERG, HENRY, *Structure in Fives*. Englewood Cliffs, N.J.: Prentice-Hall, 1983.

PFEFFER, JEFFREY, *Organizational Design*. Arlington Heights, Ill.: AHM Publishing, 1978.

ROBBINS, STEPHEN P. *Organization Theory: Structure, Design, and Applications* (2nd ed.). Englewood Cliffs, N.J.: Prentice-Hall, 1987.

PERFORMANCE APPRAISAL AND REWARD SYSTEMS

Would you study differently for a course if your goal was *to learn as much as you could about the subject* rather than *to make a high grade on the tests in the course?* When I ask that question of students, I frequently get an affirmative answer. When I inquire further, I am typically told that making a high grade is only partially determined by knowledge of the material. You also need to know what the instructor thinks is important. I have been told by many a student that, "If you want to do well in a course, you do best to study what the instructor tests for." In some cases, that approach will also result in learning as much as you can about the subject. But in many courses, studying to make a high grade means studying much differently than if you were studying for general knowledge.

Let me propose another question. Assume you are taking two similar classes, both with enrollments of about twenty. In one class, the grade is determined totally by your scores on the midterm and final. In the other class, the midterm and final each count only 25 percent, with the remaining 50 percent being allocated for class participation. Would your in-class behavior be different in the two classes? I would predict that most students would talk more—ask questions, answer questions, offer examples, elaborate on points made by the instructor—in the class where participation was so highly weighted.

The previous paragraphs are meant to illustrate how the system's appraisal and reward practices influence behavior. Studying and in-class behavior are modified to take into consideration the criteria that the instructor appraises and the linking of those appraisals to desirable rewards (high grades). It's not unusual, in fact, for the more experienced student to behave five different ways in five different classes in order to obtain five high grades. The reason studying and in-class behaviors vary is certainly in large measure directly attributable to the different performance appraisal and reward systems that instructors use.

What applies in the school context also applies to employees at work. In this chapter, we shall show how performance appraisal and reward systems influence the attitudes and behaviors of people in organizations.

PERFORMANCE APPRAISAL

Why do organizations appraise the performance of their employees? *How* do they appraise? *What* potential problems can arise to subvert the intentions of objective appraisals? *How* can managers overcome these problems? These are the key questions addressed in this section.

Purposes of Performance Appraisal

Performance appraisal serves a number of purposes in organizations. Management uses appraisals for general personnel decisions. Appraisals provide information for such important decisions as promotions, transfers, and terminations. Appraisals identify training and development needs. They pinpoint employee skills and competencies that are currently inadequate, but for which programs can be developed to remedy. Performance appraisals can be used as a criterion against which selection and development programs are validated. Newly hired employees who perform poorly can be identified through performance appraisal. Similarly, the effectiveness of training and development programs can be determined by assessing how well those employees who have participated do on their performance appraisals. Appraisals also fulfill the purpose of providing feedback to employees on how the organization views their performance. Finally, performance appraisals are used as the basis for reward allocations. Decisions about who gets merit pay increases and other rewards are determined by performance appraisals.

Each of these functions of performance appraisal is important. Yet their importance to us depends on the perspective we're taking. Several are clearly most relevant to personnel management decisions. But our interest is in organizational behavior. As a result, we shall be emphasizing performance appraisal in its role as a determinant of reward allocations.

Performance Appraisal and Motivation

In Chapter 3, considerable attention was given to the expectancy model of motivation. We argued that this model currently offers the best explanation of what conditions the amount of effort an individual will exert on his or her job. A vital component of this model is performance, specifically the effort-performance and performance-reward linkages. Do people see effort leading to performance, and performance to the rewards that they value? Clearly, they have to know what is expected of them. They need to know how their performance will be measured. Further, they must feel confident that if they if they exert an effort within their capabilities that it will result in a satisfactory performance as defined by the criteria by which they are being measured. Finally, they must feel confident that if they perform as they are being asked, they will achieve the rewards they value.

In brief, if the objectives that employees are seeking are unclear, if the criteria for measuring those objectives are vague, and if the employees lack confidence that their efforts will lead to a satisfactory appraisal of their performance, or believe that there will be an unsatisfactory payoff by the organization when their performance objectives are achieved, we can expect individuals to work considerably below their potential.

Performance Appraisal Methods

Obviously, performance appraisals are important. But how do you evaluate an employee's performance? That is, what are the specific techniques for appraisal? The following reviews the major performance appraisal methods.

Written Essays.

Probably the simplest method of appraisal is to write a narrative describing an employee's strengths, weaknesses, past performance, potential, and suggestions for improvement. The written essay requires no complex forms or extensive training to complete. But the results often reflect the ability of the writer. A good or bad appraisal may be determined as much by the evaluator's writing skill as by the employee's actual level of performance.

Critical Incidents.

Critical incidents focus the evaluator's attention on those behaviors that are key in making the difference between executing a job effectively or ineffectively. That is, the appraiser writes down anecdotes that describe what the employee did that was especially effective or ineffective. The key here is that only specific behaviors, and not vaguely defined personality traits, are cited. A list of critical incidents provides a rich set of examples from which the employee can be shown those behaviors that are desirable and those that call for improvement.

Graphic Rating Scales. One of the oldest and most popular methods of appraisal is the use of graphic rating scales. In this method, a set of performance factors, such as quantity and quality of work, depth of knowledge, cooperation, loyalty, attendance, honesty, and initiative, are listed. The evaluator then goes down the list and rates each on incremental scales. The scales typically specify five points, so a factor like *job knowledge* might be rated 1 ("poorly informed about work duties") to 5 ("has complete mastery of all phases of the job").

Why are graphic rating scales so popular? Though they don't provide the depth of information that essays or critical incidents do, they are less time-consuming to develop and administer. They also allow for quantitative analysis and comparison.

Behaviorally Anchored Rating Scales. Behaviorally anchored rating scales have received a great deal of attention in recent years. These scales combine major elements from the critical incident and graphic rating scale approaches: The appraiser rates the employees based on items along a continuum, but the points are examples of actual behavior on the given job rather than general descriptions or traits.

Behaviorally anchored rating scales specify definite, observable, and measurable job behavior. Examples of job-related behavior and performance dimensions are found by asking participants to give specific illustrations of effective and ineffective behavior regarding each performance dimension. These behavioral examples are then translated into a set of performance dimensions, each dimension having varying levels of performance. The results of this process are behavioral descriptions, such as anticipates, plans, executes, solves immediate problems, carries out orders, and handles emergency situations.

Multi-Person Comparisons. Multi-person comparisons evaluate one individual's performance against one or more others. It is a relative rather than an absolute measuring device. The three most popular comparisons are group order ranking, individual ranking, and paired comparisons.

The group order ranking requires the evaluator to place employees into a particular classification, such as top one-fifth or second one-fifth. This method is often used in recommending students to graduate schools. Evaluators are asked to rank the student in the top 5 percent, the next 5 percent, the next 15 percent, and so forth. But when used by managers to appraise employees, managers deal with all their subordinates. Therefore, if a rater has twenty subordinates, only four can be in the top fifth and, of course, four must also be relegated to the bottom fifth.

The individual ranking approach rank orders employees from best to worst. If the manager is required to appraise thirty subordinates, this approach assumes that the difference between the first and second employee is the same as that between the twenty-first and twenty-second. Even though some of the employees may be closely grouped, this approach allows for no ties. The result is a clear ordering of employees, from the highest performer down to the lowest.

The paired comparison approach compares each employee with every other employee and rates each as either the superior or the weaker member of the pair. After all paired comparisons are made, each employee is assigned a summary ranking based on the number of superior scores he or she achieved. This approach ensures that each employee is compared against every other, but it can obviously become unwieldy when many employees are being compared.

Multi-person comparisons can be combined with one of the other methods to blend the best from both absolute and relative standards. For example, a college might use the graphic rating scale and the individual ranking method to provide more accurate information about its students' performance. The student's relative rank in the class could be noted next to an absolute grade of A,B,C,D, or F. A prospective employer or graduate school could then look at two students who each got a "B" in their different financial accounting courses and draw considerably different conclusions about each where next to one grade it says "ranked 4th out of 26," while the other says "ranked 17th out of 30." Obviously, the latter instructor gives out a lot more high grades!

Potential Problems   While organizations may seek to make the performance appraisal process free from personal biases, prejudices, or idiosyncracies, a number of potential problems can creep into the process. To the degree that the following factors are prevalent, an employee's evaluation is likely to be distorted.

Single Criterion.   The typical employee's job is made up of a number of tasks. An airline flight attendant's job, for example, includes welcoming passengers, seeing to their comfort, serving meals, and offering safety advice. If performance on this job were assessed by a single criterion measure—for example, the time it took to provide food and beverages to a hundred passengers—the result would be a limited evaluation of that job. More important, flight attendants whose performance appraisal included assessment on only this single criterion would be motivated to ignore those other tasks composing the job. Similarly, if a football quarterback were appraised only on his percentage of completed passes, he would be likely to throw short passes and only in situations where he felt assured that they would be caught. Our point is that when employees are appraised on a single job criterion, even though successful performance on that job requires good performance on a number of criteria, employees will emphasize the single criterion to the exclusion of other relevant factors.

Leniency Error. Every appraiser has his or her own value system that acts as a standard against which appraisals are made. Relative to the true or actual performance of an individual, some evaluators mark high and others low. The former is referred to as positive leniency error, and the latter as negative leniency error. When evaluators are positively lenient in their appraisal, an individual's performance becomes overstated; that is, rated higher than it actually should. Similarly, a negative leniency error understates performance, giving the individual a lower appraisal.

If all individuals in an organization were appraised by the same person, there would be no problem. Although there would be an error factor, it would be applied equally to everyone. The difficulty arises when we have different raters with different leniency errors making judgments. For example, Jones and Smith are performing the same job for different supervisors, but they have absolutely identical job performance. If Jones' supervisor tends to err toward positive leniency, while Smith's supervisor errs toward negative leniency, we might be confronted with two dramatically different evaluations.

Halo Error. The halo error is the tendency for an evaluator to let the assessment of an individual on one trait influence his or her appraisal of that person on other traits. For example, if an employee tends to be trustworthy and dependable, we might become biased toward that individual and rate him or her high on many other desirable attributes.

People who design teaching appraisal forms for college students to fill out in evaluating the effectiveness of their instructors each semester must confront the halo effect. Students tend to rate a faculty member as outstanding on all criteria when they are particularly appreciative of a few things he or she does in the classroom. Similarly, a few bad habits like showing up late for lectures or being slow in returning papers, might result in students' appraising the instructor as lousy across the board.

Similarity Error. When the evaluator rates other people by giving special consideration to those qualities that he perceives in himself, he is making a similarity error. For example, the evaluator who perceives himself as aggressive may appraise others by looking for aggressiveness. Those who demonstrate this characteristic tend to benefit, while other are penalized.

Again, this error would tend to be cancelled out if the same evaluator appraised all the people in the organization. However, interrater reliability obviously suffers when various evaluators are utilizing their own similarity criteria.

Low Differentiation. It is possible that, regardless of whom the appraiser evaluates and what traits are used, the pattern of evaluation remains the same. It is possible that the evaluator's ability to appraise objectively and accurately has been impeded by social differentiation; that is, by the evaluator's style of rating behavior.

It has been suggested that evaluators may be classified as either high differentiators, who use all or most of the scale, or low differentiators, who use a limited range of the scale.

Low differentiators tend to ignore or suppress differences, perceiving the universe as more uniform than it really is. High differentiators, on the other hand, tend to utilize all available information to the utmost extent and thus are better able to perceive anomalies and contradictions.

This finding tells us that evaluations made by low differentiators need to be carefully inspected and that the people working for a low differentiator have a high probability of being appraised as significantly more homogeneous than they really are.

Forcing Information to Match Nonperformance Criteria. While rarely advocated, it is not an infrequent practice to find the formal appraisal taking place *following* the decision about the individual's performance! This may sound illogical, but it shows that subjective, yet formal, decisions are often arrived at prior to the gathering of objective information to support that decision. For example, if the evaluator believes that the appraisal should not be based on performance, but rather seniority, he may be unknowingly adjusting each performance appraisal to bring it into line with the employee's seniority rank. In this and other cases, the evaluator is increasing or decreasing performance appraisals to align with the nonperformance criteria actually being utilized.

Overcoming the Problems

The fact that organizations can encounter problems with performance appraisals should not lead managers to give up on the process. Some things can be done to overcome most of the problems we have identified.

Use Multiple Criteria. Since successful performance on most jobs requires doing a number of things well, all those things should be identified and evaluated. The more complex the job, the more criteria that will need to be identified and evaluated. But everything need not be assessed. The critical activities that lead to effective or ineffective performance are the ones that need to be appraised.

De-emphasize Traits. Many traits often considered to be related to good performance may, in fact, have little or no performance relationship. Traits like loyalty, initiative, courage, reliability, and self-expression are intuitively appealing characteristics in employees. But the relevant question is: Are individuals who are appraised as high on those traits better performers than those who rate low? We can't answer this question. We know that there are employees who rate high on these characteristics and are poor performers. We can find others who are excellent performers but do not score well on traits like these. Our conclusion is that traits like loyalty and initiative may be prized by managers, but there is no evidence to support that certain traits will be adequate synonyms for performance in a large cross section of jobs.

Another weakness in traits is the judgment itself. What is "loyalty"? When is an employee "reliable"? What one considers "loyalty," another may not. So traits suffer from weak agreement among evaluators.

Emphasize Behavior. Whenever possible, it is better to use measures based on behavior rather than traits for appraisals. Why? They can deal with the two major objections to traits. First, because measures based on behavior focus on specific examples—both good and bad—of performance we avoid the problem of using inappropriate substitutes for active performance. Second, because we are appraising specific examples of behavior, we increase the likelihood that two or more evaluators will see the same thing. You might consider a given employee as friendly, while I rate her standoffish. But when asked to rate her in terms of specific behaviors, we might both agree that she "frequently says 'Good morning' to customers," "rarely gives advice or assistance to co-workers," and "almost always avoids idle chatter with co-workers."

Use Multiple Evaluators. As the number of evaluators increases, the probability of attaining more accurate information increases. If rater error tends to follow a normal curve, an increase in the number of appraisers will tend to show the majority congregating about the middle. You see this approach being used in athletic competitions in such sports as diving and gymnastics. A multiple set of evaluators judge a performance, the highest and lowest scores are dropped, and the final performance appraisal is derived from the cumulative scores of those remaining. The logic of multiple evaluators applies to organizations as well.

If an employee has had ten supervisors, nine having rated her excellent and one poor, we can discount the value of the one poor appraisal. Therefore, by moving employees about within the organization to gain a number of evaluations, we increase the probability of achiving more valid and reliable appraisals.

Appraise Selectively. Appraisers should evaluate in only those areas in which they have some expertise. If raters make appraisals on *only* those dimensions on which they are in a good position to rate, we increase interrater agreement and make the evaluation a more valid process. This approach also recognizes that different organizational levels often have different orientations toward ratees and observe them in different settings. In general, therfore, we would recommend that appraisers should be as close as possible, in terms of organizational level, to the individual being evaluated. Conversely, the more levels that separate the evaluator and evaluatee, the less opportunity the evaluator has to observe the individual's behavior and, not surprisingly, the greater the possibility for inaccuracies.

The specific application of these concepts would result in having immediate supervisors or co-workers as the major contributors to the appraisal and having them evaluate those factors that they are best qualified to judge. For example, when professors are evaluating secretaries within a university, they could use criteria like judgment, technical competence, and conscientiousness, whereas peers (other secretaries) could use criteria like job knowledge, organization, cooperation with co-workers, and responsibility. Such an approach is both logical and more reliable, since people are appraising only those dimensions about which they are in a good position to make judgments.

Train Appraisers. If you can't *find* good appraisers, the alternative is to *make* good appraisers. By training appraisers, we can make them more accurate raters.

Common errors such as halo and leniency have been minimized or eliminated in workshops where managers can practice observing and rating behaviors. These workshops would typically run from one to three days, but allocating many hours to training may not always be necessary. One case has been cited where both halo and leniency errors were decreased immediately after exposing evaluators to explanatory training sessions lasting only five minutes.[1] But the effects of training do appear to diminish over time. This suggests the need for regular training refresher sessions.

Don't Forget Performance Feedback! A few years back, a nationwide motel chain advertised that when it came to motel rooms, "the best surprise is no surprise." This logic also holds for performance appraisals. Employees like

---

1. H. John Bernardin, "The Effects of Rater Training on Leniency and Halo Errors in Student Rating of Instructors," *Journal of Applied Psychology,* June 1978, pp. 301–08.

to know how they are doing. They expect feedback. This is typically done in the annual review. But this review frequently creates problems. In some cases, it's a problem merely because managers put off such reviews. This is particularly likely if the appraisal is negative. But the annual review is additionally troublesome if the manager saves up information related to performance and unloads it during the appraisal review. In such instances, it is not surprising that the manager may try to avoid addressing stressful issues that, even if confronted, may only be denied or rationalized by the employee. Much of this problem can be avoided by giving feedback to employees on an ongoing basis; for example, providing daily output reports with comparative data on actual units produced and the goal for the day, or bringing up problems as they occur rather than allowing them to accumulate for the annual review.

Regardless of whether feedback is provided annually or on an ongoing basis, management needs to offer performance feedback to employees. Yet, appraising another person's performance is one of the most emotionally charged of all management activities. The impression the subordinate receives about his assessment has a strong impact on his self-esteem and, importantly, on his subsequent performance. Of course, conveying good news is considerably less difficult for both the manager and the subordinate than revealing that performance has been below expectations. In this context, the discussion of the evaluation can have negative as well as positive motivational consequences. Statistically speaking, half of all employees are below the median, yet evidence tells us that the average employee's estimate of her own performance level generally falls around the seventy-fifth percentile.[2] A survey of over 800,000 high school seniors also found that people seem to see themselves as better than average. Seventy percent rated themselves above average on leadership, and when asked to rate themselves on "ability to get along with others," none rated himself or herself below average. Sixty percent rated themselves in the top 10 percent, and 25 percent saw themselves among the top 1 percent! Similarly, a survey of 500 clerical and technical employees found that 58 percent rated their own performance as falling in the top 10 percent of their peers doing comparable jobs and a total of 81 percent placed themselves in the top 20 percent.[3]

The inevitable conclusion is that employees tend to be unrealistic and inflate the assessment of their own performance. This puts the manager in the uncomfortable position of recognizing that even good news may not be good enough! Some suggestions for making the best of a tough situation are listed in Table 12-1.

2. Ronald J. Burke, "Why Performance Appraisal Systems Fail," *Personnel Administration*, June 1972, pp. 32–40.
3. "How Do I Love Me? Let Me Count the Ways," *Psychology Today*, May 1980, p. 16.

Table 12-1
A Manager's Guide Toward More Effective Performance
Appraisal Reviews

1. Don't let problems fester until the annual review. Give daily or weekly feedback. The annual review is *not* the place to spring surprises.
2. Separate performance feedback reviews from pay reviews. In their eagerness to find out how much of a pay increase they are to receive, employees tend to tune out appraisals of their performance when combined.
3. Allow employees to engage in self-evaluation. Ask them how they are doing, how you and the organization can help them perform better, and how much cooperation they get from their peers.
4. When you have to be critical, focus the criticism on specific examples of behavior rather than on the individual personally.
5. Treat the review as only a point in an on-going process. Use it to achieve agreement about what constitutes satisfactory performance in the future.

Source: Based on Beth Brophy, "The Rite of Annual Reviews," *U.S. News & World Report*, February 2, 1986, p. 59.

REWARD SYSTEMS   Our knowledge of motivation tells us that people do what they do to satisfy needs. Before they do anything, they look for the payoff or reward. Because many of these rewards—salary increases, promotions, and preferred job assignments, to name a few—are organizationally controlled, we should consider rewards as an important force influencing the behavior of employees.

Determinants of Rewards   Most organizations believe that their reward systems are designed to reward merit. The problem is that we find differing definitions of merit. Some define merit as being "deserving," while to others merit is being "excellent." One person's merit is another person's favoritism. A consideration of "deserving" may take into account such factors as intelligence, effort, or seniority. The problem is that what is deserving may differ from what is excellent—a problem that is exacerbated by the difficulty of defining excellence. If excellence refers to performance, we concede how unsatisfactory our efforts have been to measure performance. Creation of quantifiable and meaningful performance measures of almost all white-collar and service jobs, and many blue-collar jobs, have eluded us. Thus, while few will disagree with the viewpoint that rewards should be based on merit, what constitutes merit is highly debatable.

In the next several pages we shall briefly assess the role of performance as a prerequisite for rewards and then discuss other popular criteria by which rewards are distributed. In Chapter 3, we argued that motivation will be highest when performance and rewards are closely linked. But, in reality, performance is only *one* of many criteria upon which organizational rewards are based.

Performance. Performance is the measurement of results. It asks the simple question: Did you get the job done? To reward people in the organization, therefore, requires some agreed-upon criterion for defining their performance. Whether this criterion is valid or not in representing performance is not relevant to our definition; as long as rewards are allocated based on factors that are directly linked to doing the job successfully, we are using performance as the determinant. For many jobs, productivity is used as a single criterion. But as jobs become less standardized and routine, productivity becomes more difficult to measure, and hence, defining performance becomes increasingly complex.

Yet, for senior managers in corporations or those who oversee distinct business units, there is increased attention being paid to linking rewards (particularly pay) to performance.[4] Companies as diverse as American Broadcasting, Security Pacific National Bank, Sears, Roebuck, and Dow Chemical are measuring the economic performance of their business units, comparing the results against the competition, and awarding rewards accordingly.

Effort. It is not uncommon for a report card in grammar school to include effort as one of the categories used in grading students. Organizations rarely make their rewarding of effort that explicit, yet it is certainly a major determinant in the reward distribution.

The rewarding of effort represents the classical example of rewarding means rather than ends. In organizations where performance is generally of low caliber, rewarding effort may be the only criterion by which to differentiate rewards. For example, a major eastern university was attempting to increase its research efforts and had designated obtaining funded research grants as a critical benchmark toward this end. Upon selection of this objective, all faculty members were informed that rewards for the coming year were going to be based on performance in obtaining grants. Unfortunately, after the first year of the program, even though approximately 20 percent of the faculty had made grant applications, none were approved. When the time came for performance evaluation and the distribution of rewards, the dean chose to give the majority of the funds available for pay raises to those faculty members who had applied for grants. Here is a case where performance, defined in terms of obtaining funded research grants, was zero, so the dean chose to allocate rewards based on effort.

This practice is more common than you might think. Effort can count

---

4. "Executive Compensation: Looking to the Long Term Again," *Business Week*, May 9, 1983, pp. 80–83.

more than actual performance when it is believed that those who try should be encouraged. The employee who is clearly perceived by her superiors to be working less than her optimum can often expect to be rewarded less than some other employee who, while producing less, is giving out a greater effort. Even where it is clearly stated that performance is what will be rewarded, people who make evaluations and distribute rewards are only human. Therefore, they are not immune to sympathizing with those who try hard, but with minimal success, and allowing this to influence their evaluation and reward decisions.

Seniority. Seniority, job rights, and tenure dominate most civil service systems in the United States, and while they do not play as important a role in business corporations, the length of time on the job is still a major factor in determining the allocation of rewards. Seniority's greatest virtue is that, relative to other criteria, it is easy to determine. We may disagree whether the quality of Smith's work is higher or lower than that of Jones, but we would probably not have much debate over who has been with the organization longer. So seniority represents an easily quantifiable criterion that can be substituted for performance.

Skills Held. Another practice not uncommon in organizations is to allocate rewards based on the skills of the employee. Regardless of whether the skills are used, those individuals who possess the highest levels of skill or talent will be rewarded commensurately. Where such practices are used, it is not unusual to see individuals become "credential crazy." The requirement that an individual needs a college degree in order to attain a certain level within the organization is utilizing skills as a determinant of rewards. Similarly, the requirement that an individual has to pass certain skill tasks by demonstrating an acceptable score in order to maintain a particular position in the organization is again using skills as a reward criterion. If it is necessary for a secretary to demonstrate that he or she can take shorthand at 120 words per minute to be eligible for consideration as secretary to a department head, and if department heads do all their dictation into a dictating machine rather than giving it directly to the secretary, we see an example of a skill being utilized as a reward criterion when, in effect, it is irrelevant.

When individuals enter an organization, their skill level is usually a major determinant of the compensation they will receive. In such cases, the marketplace or competition has acted to make skills a major element in the reward package. These externally imposed standards can evolve from the community or from occupational categories themselves. In other words, the relationship of demand and supply for particular skills in the community can significantly influence the rewards the organization must expend to acquire those skills. Also, the demand-supply relationship for an entire occupational category throughout the country can affect rewards.

Job Difficulty. The complexity of the job can be a criterion by which rewards are distributed. For example, those jobs that are highly repetitive and quickly learned may be viewed as less deserving of rewards than those that are more complex and sophisticated. Jobs that are difficult to perform or are undesirable due to stress or unpleasant working conditions may have to carry with them higher rewards in order to attract workers to them.

Discretionary Time. The greater the discretion called for on a job, the greater the impact of mistakes and the greater the need for good judgment. In a job that has been completely programmed—that is, where each step has been accorded a procedure and there is no room for decision making by the incumbent—there is little discretionary time. Such jobs require less judgment, and lower rewards can be offered to attract people to take these positions. As discretionary time increases, greater judgmental abilities are needed, and rewards must commensurately be expanded.

Types of Rewards The types of rewards that an organization can allocate are more complex than is generally thought. Obviously, there is direct compensation. But there are also indirect compensation and nonfinancial rewards. Each of these types of rewards can be distributed on an individual, group, or organization-wide basis. Figure 12-1 presents a structure for looking at rewards.

Intrinsic rewards are those that individuals receive for themselves. They are largely a result of the worker's satisfaction with his or her job. As noted in Chapter 4, techniques like job enrichment or any efforts to redesign or restructure work to increase its personal worth to the employee may make his or her job more intrinsically rewarding.

As previously noted, extrinsic rewards include direct compensation, indirect compensation, and nonfinancial rewards. Of course, an employee expects some form of direct compensation: a basic wage or salary, overtime and holiday premium pay, bonuses based on performance, profit sharing, and/or possibly opportunities to receive stock options. Employees will expect their direct compensation generally to align with their assessment of their contribution to the organization and, additionally, will expect it to be relatively comparable with the direct compensation given to other employees with similar abilities and performance.

The organization will provide employees with indirect compensation: insurance, paid holidays and vacations, services, and perquisites. Inasmuch as these are generally made uniformly available to all employees at a given

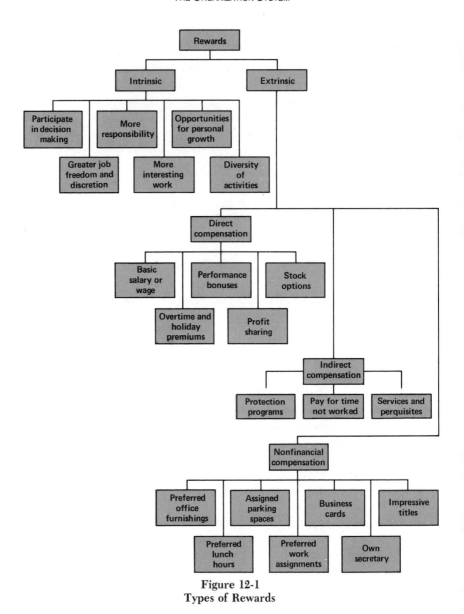

Figure 12-1
Types of Rewards

job level, regardless of performance, they are really not motivating rewards. However, where indirect compensation is controllable by management and is used to reward performance, then it clearly needs to be considered as a motivating reward. To illustrate, if a company-paid membership in a country club is not available to all middle- and upper-level executives, but only to those who have shown particular performance ratings, then it is a motivating reward. Similarly, if company-owned automobiles and aircraft are made available to certain employees based on their performance rather than their "entitlement," we should view these indirect compensations as motivating rewards for those who might deem these forms of compensation as attractive.

As with direct compensation, indirect compensation may be viewed in an individual, group, or organizational context. However, if rewards are to be linked closely with performance, we should expect individual rewards to be emphasized. On the other hand, if a certain group of managers within the organization has made a significant contribution to the effective performance of the organization, a blanket reward like a membership in a social club might be appropriate. Again, it is important to note that since rewards achieve the greatest return when they are specifically designed to meet the needs of each individual, and since group and organizational rewards tend toward homogeneity (they tend to treat all people alike), these types of rewards must, by definition, be somewhat less effective than individual rewards. The only exceptions to that statement are those instances where there is a great need for cohesiveness and group congeniality. In such instances, individuals may find group rewards more personally satisfying than individual rewards.

The classification of nonfinancial rewards tends to be a smorgasbord of desirable "things" that are potentially at the disposal of the organization. The creation of nonfinancial rewards is limited only by managers' ingenuity and ability to assess "payoffs" that individuals in the organization find desirable and that are within the managers' discretion.

The old saying "One man's food is another man's poison" certainly applies to rewards. What one employee views as highly desirable, another finds superfluous. Therefore *any* reward may not get the desired result; however, where selection has been done assiduously, the benefits to the organization by way of higher worker performance should be impressive.

Some workers are very status conscious. A paneled office, a carpeted floor, a large walnut desk, or a private bathroom may be just the office furnishings that stimulate an employee toward top performance. Status-oriented employees may also value an impressive job title, their own business cards, their own secretary, or a well-located parking space with their name clearly painted underneath the "Reserved" sign.

Some employees value having their lunch at, say, 1 P.M. to 2 P.M. If lunch is normally from 11 A.M. to 12 noon, the benefit of being able to take their lunch at another, more desirable time can be viewed as a reward. Having a chance to work with congenial colleagues or getting a desired work assignment are rewards that are within the discretion of management and, when carefully aligned to individual needs, can provide stimulus for improved performance.

IMPLICATIONS FOR MANAGERS   Managers should consider the effect of an organization's employee appraisal methods and how rewards are distributed when these systems are designed.

People do not work gratis. They expect payoffs: salary, fringe benefits, promotion opportunities, recognition, social contact, and so forth. If employees perceive that their efforts are accurately appraised, and if they further perceive that the rewards they value are closely linked to their appraisals, management will have optimized the motivational properties from the organization's appraisal and reward procedures and policies. More specifically, based on the contents of this chapter and our discussion of motivation in Chapter 3, we can conclude that rewards are likely to lead to effective performance and satisfaction when they are (1) perceived as equitable by the employee, (2) tied to performance, and (3) tailored to the needs of the individual. These conditions should foster a minimum of dissatisfaction among employees, reduced withdrawal patterns, and increased organizational commitment. If these conditions don't exist, the probability of withdrawal behavior increases, and the prevalence of marginal or barely adequate performance increases. If workers perceive that their efforts are not recognized or rewarded, and if they view their alternatives as limited, they may continue working but perform at a level considerably below their capabilities.

SELECTED REFERENCES

BELCHER, DAVID W., AND THOMAS ATCHISON, *Compensation Administration* (4th ed.). Englewood Cliffs, N.J.: Prentice-Hall, 1987.

CARROLL, STEPHEN J., AND CRAIG E. SCHNEIER, *Performance Appraisal and Review Systems*. Glenview, Ill.: Scott, Foresman, 1982.

CASCIO, WAYNE F., *Applied Psychology in Personnel Management* (3rd ed.). Englewood Cliffs, N.J.: Prentice-Hall, 1987.

DECENZO, DAVID, AND STEPHEN P. ROBBINS, *Personnel/Human Resource Management* (3rd ed.). Englewood Cliffs, N.J.: Prentice-Hall, 1988.

PEARCE, JONE L., AND LYMAN W. PORTER, "Employee Response to Formal Performance Appraisal Feedback," *Journal of Applied Psychology*, May 1986, pp. 211–18.

SCHNEIER, CRAIG E., RICHARD W. BEATTY, AND LLOYD S. BAIRD, "How to Construct a Successful Performance Appraisal System," *Training and Development Journal*, April 1986, pp. 38–42.

13

ORGANIZATIONAL CULTURE

Just as individuals have personalities, so too do organizations. In Chapter 2, we found that individuals had relatively enduring and stable traits that helped us to predict their attitudes and behaviors. In this chapter, we propose that organizations, like people, can be characterized in terms like rigid, friendly, warm, innovative, or conservative. These traits, in turn, can then be used to predict attitudes and behaviors of the people within these organizations.

The theme of this chapter is that there is a systems variable in organizations that, while hard to define or describe precisely, nevertheless exists and which employees generally describe in common terms. We call this variable *organizational culture*. Just as tribal cultures have totems and taboos that dictate how each member will act toward fellow members and outsiders, organizations have cultures that govern how members behave. Just what organizational culture is, how it has an impact on employee attitudes and behavior, where it comes from, and whether or not it can be managed will be discussed in the following pages.

DEFINING ORGANIZATIONAL CULTURE There seems to be wide agreement that organizational culture refers to a system of shared meaning held by members that distinguishes the organization from other organizations. This system of shared meaning is, on closer analysis, a set of key characteristics that the organization values. There appear to be seven characteristics that, when mixed and matched, expose the essence of an organization's culture:

1. **Individual autonomy**—the degree of responsibility, independence, and opportunities for exercising initiative that individuals in the organization have

2. **Structure**—the degree of rules and regulations, and the amount of direct supervision, that is used to oversee and control employee behavior

3. **Support**—the degree of assistance and warmth managers provide for their subordinates

4. **Identity**—the degree to which members identify with the organization as a whole rather than with their particular work group or field of professional expertise

5. **Performance-reward**—the degree to which reward allocations in the organization (salary increases, promotions) are based on employee performance criteria

6. **Conflict tolerance**—the degree of conflict present in relationships between peers and work groups as well as the willingness to be honest and open about differences

7. **Risk-tolerance**—the degree to which employees are encouraged to be aggressive, innovative, and risk-seeking

Each of these characteristics exists on a continuum from low to high. By appraising the organization on these seven characteristics, then, a composite picture of the organization's culture is formed. This picture becomes the basis for feelings of shared understanding that members have about the organization, how things are done in it, and the way members are supposed to behave. Table 13-1 demonstrates how these characteristics can be mixed to create highly diverse organizations.

Culture is a Descriptive Term Organizational culture is a descriptive term. It is concerned with how employees perceive the seven characteristics, not whether they like them or not. This is important because it differentiates culture from job satisfaction. Research on organizational culture has sought to measure how employees see their organization: Is it highly structured? Does it reward innovation? Does it stifle conflicts? Job satisfaction, on the other hand, seeks to mea-

Table 13–1
Descriptions of Two Highly Diverse Organizational Cultures

Organization A	Organization B
This organization is a manufacturing firm. There are extensive rules and regulations that employees are required to follow. Managers supervise employees closely to ensure there are no deviations. People are allowed little discretion on their jobs. Employees are instructed to bring any unusual problem to their supervisor, who will then determine the solution. Management has no confidence in the honesty or integrity of its employees, so controls are tight. Managers and employees alike tend to be hired by the organization early in their careers, rotated into and out of various departments on a regular basis, and are generalists rather than specialists. Effort, loyalty, cooperation, and avoidance of errors are highly valued and rewarded.	This organization is also a manufacturing firm. Here, however, there are few rules and regulations. Employees are seen as hardworking and trustworthy, thus supervision is loose. Employees are encouraged to solve problems themselves, but to feel free to consult with their supervisors when assistance is needed. Employees are also encouraged to develop their unique specialized skills. Interpersonal and interdepartmental differences are seen as natural occurrences. Promotions and other valuable rewards go to those employees who make the largest contributions to the organization, even when these employees are generally acknowledged to have strange ideas, unusual personal mannerisms, or unconventional work habits.

sure affective responses to the work environment. That is, the former describes, while the latter evaluates.

Do Organizations Have Uniform Cultures?

Organizational culture represents a common perception held by the organization's members. This was made explicit when we defined culture as a system of *shared* meaning. We should expect, therefore, that individuals with different backgrounds or at different levels in the organization will tend to describe the organization's culture in similar terms.

Acknowledgment that organizational culture has common properties does not mean, however, that there cannot be subcultures within any given culture. Most large organizations have a dominant culture and numerous sets of subcultures.

A *dominant culture* expresses the core values that are shared by a majority of the organization's members. When we talk about an *organization's* culture, we are referring to its dominant culture. It is this macro view of culture that gives an organization its distinct personality. *Subcultures* tend to develop in large organizations to reflect common problems, situations, or experiences that members face. These subcultures are likely to be defined by department designations and geographical separation. The purchasing department, for example, can have a subculture that is uniquely shared by members of that department. It will include the core values of the dominant culture plus additional values unique to members of the purchasing department. Similarly, an office or unit of the organization that is physically separated from the organization's main operations may take on a different personality. Again, the core values are essentially retained but modified to reflect the separated unit's distinct situation.

If organizations had no dominant culture and were composed only of numerous subcultures, the value of organizational culture as an independent variable would be significantly lessened. Why? Because there would be no uniform interpretation of what represented appropriate or inappropriate behavior. It is the shared meaning aspect of culture that makes it such a potent device for guiding and shaping behavior. But we cannot ignore the reality that many organizations also have subcultures that can influence the behavior of members.

Strong vs. Weak Cultures   It has become increasingly popular to differentiate between strong and weak cultures. The argument here is that strong cultures have a greater impact on employee behavior and are more directly related to reduced turnover.

A *strong culture* is characterized by the organization's core values being both intensely held and widely shared. The more members that accept the core values and the greater their commitment to those values, the stronger the culture is. Consistent with this definition, a strong culture will obviously have a greater influence on the behavior of its members. Religious organizations, cults, and Japanese companies are examples of organizations that have very strong cultures. When a James Jones can entice nine hundred members of his Guyana cult to commit mass suicide, we see a behavioral influence considerably greater than that typically attributed to leadership. The culture of Jonestown had a degree of sharedness and intensity that allowed for extremely high behavioral control. Of course, the same strong cultural influence that can lead to the tragedy of a Jonestown can be directed positively to create immensely successful organizations like IBM, Mary Kay Cosmetics, and Sony.

A specific result of a strong culture should be lower employee turnover. A strong culture demonstrates high agreement among members about what the organization stands for. Such unanimity of purpose builds cohesiveness, loyalty, and organizational commitment. These, in turn, lessen the propensity for employees to leave the organization.

Culture vs. Formalization   A strong organizational culture increases behavioral consistency. In this sense, we should recognize that a strong culture can act as a substitute for formalization.

In Chapter 11, we discussed how formalization's rules and regulations act to regulate employee behavior. High formalization in an organization creates predictability, orderliness, and consistency. Our point is that a strong culture achieves the same end without the need for written documentation. Therefore, we should view formalization and culture as two different roads to a common destination. The stronger an organization's culture, the less management need be concerned with developing formal rules and regulations to guide employee behavior. Those guides will have been internalized in employees when they accept the organization's culture.

WHAT DOES CULTURE DO? We've alluded to organizational culture's impact on behavior. We've also explicitly argued that a strong culture should be associated with reduced turnover. In this section, we will more carefully review the functions that culture performs and assess whether culture can be a liability for an organization.

Culture's Functions Culture performs a number of functions within an organization. First, it has a boundary defining role; that is, it creates distinctions between one organization and others. Second, it conveys a sense of identity for organization members. Third, culture facilitates the generation of commitment to something larger than one's individual self-interest. Fourth, it enhances social system stability. Culture is the social glue that helps hold the organization together by providing appropriate standards for what employees should say and do. Finally, culture serves as a sense-making and control mechanism that guides and shapes the attitudes and behavior of employees. It is this last function that is of particular interest to us. As the following quote makes clear, culture defines the rules of the game:

> Culture by definition is elusive, intangible, implicit, and taken for granted. But every organization develops a core set of assumptions, understandings, and implicit rules that govern day-to-day behavior in the workplace. . . . Until newcomers learn the rules, they are not accepted as full-fledged members of the organization. Transgressions of the rules on the part of high-level executives or front-line employees result in universal disapproval and powerful penalties. Conformity to the rules becomes the primary basis for reward and upward mobility.[1]

1. Terrence E. Deal and Allan A. Kennedy, "Culture: A New Look Through Old Lenses," *Journal of Applied Behavioral Science,* November 1983, p. 501.

As we'll show later in this chapter, who is made job offers to join the organization, who is appraised as a high performer, and who gets the promotions are strongly influenced by the individual-organization "fit"; that is, whether the applicant or employee's attitudes and behavior are compatible with the culture. It is not a coincidence that employees at Disneyland and Disney World appear to be almost universally attractive, clean, wholesome, with bright smiles. That's the image Disney seeks. The company selects employees who will maintain that image. And once on the job, both the informal norms and formal rules and regulations ensure that Disney employees will act in a relatively uniform and predictable way.

Culture as a Liability

We are treating culture in a nonjudgmental manner. We haven't said that it's good or bad, only that it exists. Many of its functions, as outlined, are valuable for both the organization and the employee. Culture enhances organizational commitment and increases the consistency of employee behavior. These are clearly benefits to an organization. From an employee's standpoint, culture is valuable because it reduces ambiguity. It tells employees how things are done and what's important. But we shouldn't ignore the potentially dysfunctional aspects of culture, especially a strong one, on an organization's effectiveness.

Culture is a liability where the shared values are not in agreement with those that will further the organization's effectiveness. This is most likely to occur when the organization's environment is dynamic. When the environment is undergoing rapid change, the organization's entrenched culture may no longer be appropriate. So consistency of behavior is an asset to an organization when it faces a stable environment. It may, however, burden the organization and make it difficult to respond to changes in the environment.

CREATING AND SUSTAINING CULTURE

An organization's culture doesn't pop out of thin air. Once established, it rarely fades away. What forces influence the creation of a culture? What reinforces and sustains these forces once they are in place? We'll answer both of these questions in this section.

How a Culture Begins

An organization's current customs, traditions, and general way of doing things are largely due to what it has done before and the degree of success it had with those endeavors. This leads us to the ultimate source of an organization's culture: its founders!

The founders of an organization traditionally have a major impact in establishing the early culture. They have a vision or mission of what the organization should be. They are unconstrained by previous customs of doing things or ideologies. The small size that typically characterizes any new organization further facilitates the founders' imposing their vision on all organizational members. Because the founders have the original idea, they also typically have biases on how to get the idea fulfilled. The organization's culture results from the interaction between the founders' biases and assumptions and what the original members learn subsequently from their own experiences.

Henry Ford at the Ford Motor Company, Thomas Watson at IBM, J. Edgar Hoover at the FBI, Thomas Jefferson at the University of Virginia, Edwin Land at Polaroid, Ray Kroc at McDonald's, David Packard at Hewlett-Packard, and Steven Jobs at Apple Computer are just a few obvious examples of individuals who have had immeasurable impact in shaping their organization's culture. For instance, Watson's views on research and development, product innovation, employee attire, and compensation policies are still evident at IBM, though he died in 1956. Polaroid's innovative and risk-assuming culture is a direct reflection of Edwin Land's personal beliefs. McDonald's commitment to the values of quality, service, and cleanliness were originally proposed by Ray Kroc. The formality found today at the University of Virginia is due, in large part, to the original culture created by its founder, Thomas Jefferson. Apple's informal and creative culture was established by Steve Jobs.

Keeping a Culture Alive   Once a culture is in place, there are practices within the organization that act to maintain it by giving employees a set of similar experiences. For example, many of an organization's human resource practices reinforce its culture. The selection process, performance evaluation criteria, reward practices, training and career development activities, and promotion procedures ensure that those hired fit in with the culture, reward those who support it, and penalize (and even expel) those who challenge it. Three forces play a particularly important part in sustaining a culture—selection practices, the actions of top management, and socialization methods. Let's take a closer look at each.

Selection.   The explicit goal of the selection process is to identify and hire individuals who have the knowledge, skills, and abilities to perform the jobs within the organization successfully. But, typically, more than one candidate will be found who meets any given job's requirements. When that point is reached, it would be naive to ignore that the final decision about who is hired will be significantly influenced by the decision maker's judgment of how well the candidates will fit into the organization. This attempt to ensure a proper match, whether purposely or inadvertently, results in the hiring of people who have common values (ones essentially consistent with those of the organization) or accept at least a good portion of those values. In addition, the selection process provides information to applicants about the organization. Candidates learn about the organization, and, if they perceive a conflict between their values and those of the organization, they can choose to remove themselves from the applicant pool. Selection, therefore, becomes a two-way street, allowing either employer or applicant to abrogate a marriage if there appears to be a mismatch. In this way, the selection process sustains an organization's culture by selecting out those individuals who might attack or undermine its core values.

Bain & Co., a large Boston management consulting firm, originally hired only new graduates from Harvard Business School. This practice not only provided bright and talented people, it also reinforced Bain's culture. Many of the values instilled at Harvard—competition, verbal dexterity, hard work, ambition—were also core values at Bain. The selection of recent Harvard graduates increased the likelihood of Bain's having people who would fit in with Bain's culture and contribute to maintaining it. Other examples of the role that selection plays in sustaining culture are widely evident. Corporations tend to recruit and select management personnel from within their own industry, thus enhancing common perceptions. The top Wall Street law firms still hire graduates predominantly from the prestigious eastern law schools, ensuring homogeneity of both partners and associates. College fraternities and sororities assess potential members' socio-economic status, personality, and physical appearance to find those compatible with the organization's image of itself. Personal contacts or "friends of friends" are a major source of job information for white-collar workers, which increases the likelihood that the organization will hire like-minded individuals. It should not be surprising to learn that a study of the U.S. Federal Trade Commission found that the FTC attached more significance to regional background, old school ties, and political endorsements when recruiting attorneys than to their ability as reflected in grades or in the quality of law schools they attended.[2] These examples all confirm our contention that organizations use their personnel selection process to hire those who will fit in and accept the organization's values, norms, and customs, while at the same time screening out those who might challenge the system.

2. Cited in William Evan, *Organization Theory* (New York: John Wiley, 1976), p. 162.

Top Management. The actions of top management also have a major impact on the organization's culture. Through what they say and how they behave, senior executives establish norms that filter down through the organization about whether risk taking is desirable; how much freedom managers should give their subordinates; what is appropriate dress; what actions will pay off in terms of pay raises, promotions, and other rewards; and the like.

Socialization. No matter how good a job the organization does in recruiting and selection, new employees are not fully indoctrinated in the organization's culture. Maybe most important, because they are least familiar with the organization's culture, new employees are potentially most likely to disturb the beliefs and customs that are in place. The organization will, therefore, want to help new employees adapt to its culture. This adaptation process is called *socialization.*

All Marines must go through boot camp, where they prove their commitment. Of course, at the same time, the Marine trainers are indoctrinating new recruits in the "Marine way." The success of any cult depends on effective socialization. New Moonies undergo a "brainwashing" ritual that substitutes group loyalty and commitment in place of family. New Disneyland employees spend their first two full days of work watching films and listening to lectures on how Disney employees are expected to look and act.

As we discuss socialization, keep in mind that the most critical socialization stage is at the time of entry into the organization. This is when the organization seeks to mold the outsider into an employee in "good standing." Those employees who fail to learn the essential or pivotal role behaviors risk being labled nonconformists or rebels, which often leads to expulsion. But the organization will be socializing every employee, though maybe not as explicitly, throughout his or her entire career in the organization. This further contributes to sustaining the culture.

Socialization can be conceptualized as a process made up of three stages: prearrival, encounter, and metamorphosis. The first stage encompasses all the learning that occurs before a new member joins the organization. In the second stage, the new employee sees what the organization is really like and confronts the likelihood that expectations and reality may diverge. In the third stage, the relatively long-lasting changes take place. The new employee masters the skills required for his or her job, successfully performs his or her new roles, and makes the adjustments to his or her work group's values and norms. This three-stage process has an impact on the new employee's work productivity, commitment to the organization's objectives, and his or her decision to stay with the organization. Figure 13-1 depicts this process.

Socialization Process   Outcomes

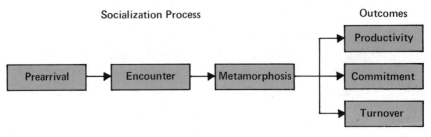

Figure 13-1
A Socialization Model

The *prearrival stage* occurs before the employee joins the organization, so that he or she arrives with an established set of values, attitudes, and expectations. These cover both the work to be done and the organization. For instance, in many jobs, particularly professional work, new members will have undergone a considerable degree of prior socialization in training and in school. One major purpose of a business school, for example, is to socialize business students into the attitudes and behaviors that business firms want. If business executives believe that successful employees value the profit ethic, are loyal, will work hard, desire to achieve, and willingly accept directions from their superiors, they can hire individuals out of business schools who have been premolded in this pattern. But prearrival socialization goes beyond the specific job. The selection process is used in most organizations to inform prospective employees about the organization as a whole. In addition, as noted previously, the selection process also acts to ensure the inclusion of the right type—those who will fit in. "Indeed, the ability of the individual to present the appropriate face during the selection process determines his ability to move into the organization in the first place. Thus, success depends on the degree to which the aspiring member has correctly anticipated the expectations and desires of those in the organization in charge of selection."[3]

Upon entry into the organization, the new member enters the *encounter stage*. Here the individual confronts the possible dichotomy between her expectations about her job, her co-workers, her boss, and the organization in general, and reality. If expectations prove to have been more or less accurate, the encounter stage merely provides a reaffirmation of the perceptions gained earlier. However, this is often not the case. Where expectations and reality differ, the new employee must undergo

3. John Van Maanen and Edgar H. Schein, "Career Development," in *Improving Life at Work*, ed. J. Richard Hackman and J.L. Suttle (Santa Monica, Calif.: Goodyear, 1977), p. 59.

socialization that will detach her from her previous assumptions and replace these with another set that the organization deems desirable. At the extreme, a new member may become totally disillusioned with the actualities of her job and resign. Proper selection should significantly reduce the probability of the latter occurrence.

Finally, the new member must work out any problems discovered during the encounter stage. This may mean going through changes; hence, we call this the *metamorphosis stage*. The choices presented in Table 13-2 are alternatives designed to bring about the desired metamorphosis. But what is a desirable metamorphosis? We can say that metamorphosis, and the entry socialization process, are complete when the new member has become comfortable with the organization and her job. She has internalized the norms of the organization and her work group, and she understands and accepts these norms. The new member feels accepted by her peers as a trusted and valued individual. She is self-confident that she has the competence to complete her job successfully. She understands the system—not only her own tasks, but the rules, procedures, and informally accepted practices as well. Finally, she knows how she will be evaluated; that is, what criteria will be used to measure and appraise her work. She knows what is expected of her and what constitutes a job well done. As Figure 13-1 shows, successful metamorphosis should have a positive impact on the new employee's productivity and her commitment to the organization and reduce her propensity to leave the organization.

Summary: How Cultures Form   Figure 13-2 summarizes how an organization's culture is established and sustained. The original culture is derived from the founder's philosophy. This, in turn, strongly influences the criteria used in hiring. The actions of the current top management set the general climate of what is acceptable behavior and what is not. How employees are to be socialized will depend on the degree of success achieved in matching new employees' values to

Figure 13-2
How Organization Cultures Form

Table 13-2
Entry Socialization Options

Formal or Informal? New employees may be put directly into their jobs, with no effort made to differentiate them from those who have been doing the job for a considerable length of time. Such cases represent examples of informal socialization—it takes place on the job and the new member gets little or no special attention. In contrast, socialization can be formal. The more formal the program, the more the new employee is segregated from the ongoing work setting and differentiated in some way to make explicit her newcomer's role. The more formal a socialization program, the more likely it is that management has participated in its design and execution and, hence, the more likely that the recruit will experience the learning that management desires. In contrast, the more informal the program, the more success will depend on the new employee selecting the correct socialization agents.

Individual or Collective? Another choice to be made by management is whether to socialize new members individually or to group them together and process them through an identical set of experiences. The individual approach is likely to develop far less homogeneous views than collective socialization. As with the informal structure, individual socializing is more likely to preserve individual differences and perspectives.

Fixed or Variable Time Period? A third major consideration for management is whether the transition from outsider to insider should be done on a fixed or variable time period. A fixed schedule reduces uncertainty for the new member since transition is standardized. Successful completion of certain standardized steps means that she will be accepted to full-fledged membership. Variable schedules, in contrast, give no advanced notice of their transition timetable. Variability characterizes the socialization for most professionals and managerial personnel.

Serial or Disjunctive? When an experienced organizational member, familiar with the new member's job, guides or directs a new recruit, we call this serial socialization. In this process, the experienced member acts as a tutor and model for the new employee. When the recruit does not have predecessors available to guide her or to model her behavior upon, we have disjunctive socialization. Serial socialization maintains traditions and customs. It is preferred by organizations that seek to minimize the possibility of change over time. On the other hand, disjunctive socialization is likely to produce more inventive and creative employees because recruits are not burdened by traditions.

Investiture or Divestiture? Does management seek to confirm or dismantle the incoming identity of the new member? Investiture rites ratify the usefulness of the characteristics that the person brings to the new job. These individuals have been selected on the basis of what they can bring to the job. The organization does not want to change these recruits, so entry is made as smooth and trouble free as possible. If this is the goal, socialization efforts concentrate on reinforcing that "we like you just the way you are." Far more often there is a desire to strip away certain entering characteristics of a recruit. The selection process identified the candidate as a potential high performer; now it is necessary to make those minor modifications to improve the fit between the candidate and the organization. This fine-tuning may take the shape of requiring the recruit to sever old friendships; accepting a different way of looking at her job, peers, or the organization's purpose; doing a number of demeaning jobs to prove her commitment; or even undergoing harassment and hazing by more experienced personnel to verify that she fully accepts her role in the organization.

Source: Adapted from John Van Maanen, "People Processing: Strategies of Organizational Socialization," *Organizational Dynamics,* Summer 1978 (New York: AMACOM, a division of American Management Associations), pp. 19–36.

those of the organization in the selection process and top management's preference for socialization methods.

HOW EMPLOYEES LEARN CULTURE

Culture is transmitted to employees in a number of forms, the most potent being stories, rituals, material symbols, and language.

Stories

If you worked at the Ford Motor Co. during the 1970s, you would have undoubtedly heard the story about Henry Ford II reminding his executives, when they got too arrogant, that "it's *my* name that's on the building." The message was clear: Henry Ford II ran the company!

IBM employees tell the story of a plant security supervisor who challenged Thomas Watson, Jr., the all-powerful chairman of IBM's board. The supervisor, a twenty-two-year-old woman, was required to make certain that people entering security areas wore the correct clearance identification. One day, surrounded by his usual entourage, Watson approached the doorway to an area where the supervisor was on guard. He wore an orange badge acceptable elsewhere in the plant, but not a green badge, which alone permitted entrance at her door. Although she knew who Watson was, she told him what she had been instructed to say to anyone without proper clearance: "You cannot enter. Your admittance is not recognized." The men accompanying Watson were taken back. Would this young security guard be fired on the spot? "Don't you know who he is?" someone asked. Watson raised his hand for silence while one of the party strode off and returned with the appropriate badge. The message to IBM employees: No matter who you are, you obey the rules.

Stories like these circulate through many organizations. They contain a narrative of events about the organization's founders, the present top management, and key decisions that affect the organization's future course. They anchor the present in the past and provide explanations and legitimacy for current practices.

Rituals

Rituals are repetitive sequences of activities that express and reinforce the key values of the organization, what goals are most important, which people are important and which are expendable.

College faculty members undergo a lengthy ritual in their quest for permanent employment or tenure. Typically, the faculty member is on probation for six years. At the end of that period, the member's colleagues must make one of two choices: extend a tenured appointment or issue a

217

one-year terminal contract. What does it take to obtain tenure? It usually requires satisfactory teaching performance, service to the department and university, and scholarly activity. But, of course, what satisfies the requirements for tenure in one department at one university may be appraised as inadequate in another. The key is that the tenure decision, in essence, asks those who are tenured to assess whether the candidate has demonstrated, based on six years of performance, whether he or she fits in. Colleagues who have been socialized properly will have proved themselves worthy of being granted tenure. Every year, hundreds of faculty members at colleges and universities are denied tenure. In some cases, this action is a result of poor performance across the board. More often, however, the decision can be traced to the faculty member not doing well in those areas that the tenured faculty believe are important. The instructor who spends dozens of hours each week preparing for class, achieves outstanding evaluations by students, but neglects his or her research and publication activities, may be passed over for tenure. What has happened, simply, is that the instructor has failed to adapt to the norms set by the department. The astute faculty member will assess early in the probationary period what attitudes and behaviors his or her colleagues want and will then proceed to give it to them. And, or course, by doing so the tenured faculty have made significant strides toward standardizing tenure candidates.

Material Symbols   Bank of America is a conservative firm. Aggressive risk taking is not central to its culture. Its executives drive four-door, American-made sedans. In 1983, Bank of America purchased the discount brokerage firm of Charles Schwab & Co. In contrast to B of A, Schwab built its reputation on aggressiveness. It sought out and hired only outgoing and what some might call "flashy" brokers. Top executives at Schwab, like those at Bank of America, drove company cars. Only theirs were Ferraris, Porsches, and BMWs. The cars' images fit both the people who drove them and the cultural values Schwab sought to maintain.

Tandem Computers' headquarters in Cupertino, California, doesn't look like your typical head office operation. It has jogging trails, a basketball court, space for dance and yoga classes, and a large swimming pool—all for its employees' enjoyment. Every Friday afternoon at 4:30, employees partake in the weekly beer bust, courtesy of the company.

Four-door sedans, Ferraris, and a swimming pool at the office are material symbols that help to reinforce these organizations' cultures. The design and physical layout of spaces and buildings, furniture, executive perks, and attire are material symbols that convey to employees who is important, the degree of egalitarianism desired by top management, and the kinds of behaviors (risk taking, conservative, authoritarian, participative, individualistic, social) that are appropriate.

Language   Many organizations and units within organizations use language as a way to identify members of a culture or subculture. By learning this language, members attest to their acceptance of the culture and, in so doing, help to preserve it.

The kitchen personnel in a large hotel use terminology foreign to hotel people outside this area. Members of the U.S. Army sprinkle their language liberally with jargon that readily identifies its members. Many organizations, over time, develop unique terms to describe equipment, offices, key personnel, suppliers, customers, or products that relate to its business. New employees are frequently overwhelmed with acronyms and jargon that, after six months on the job, have become fully part of their language. But once assimilated, this terminology acts as a common denominator that unites members of a given culture or subculture.

IMPLICATIONS FOR MANAGERS   There seems to be little doubt that culture has a strong influence on employee behavior. But what can management do to design a culture that molds employees in the way that management wants?

When an organization is just being established, management has a great deal of influence. There are no established traditions. The organization is small. There are few, if any, subcultures. Everyone knows the founder and is directly touched by his or her vision of what the organization is. Not surprisingly, under these conditions management has the opportunity to create a culture that will best facilitate the achievement of the organization's goals.

However, when the organization is well established, so too is its dominant culture. Given that this culture is made up of relatively stable and permanent characteristics, it becomes very resistant to change. It took time to form; and once established, it tends to become entrenched. Strong cultures are particularly resistant to change because employees become so committed to them. So, if a given culture, over time, becomes inappropriate to an organization and a handicap to management, there may be little management can do to change it. This is especially true in the short run. Under the most favorable conditions, cultural changes have to be measured in years, not weeks or months.

What would those "favorable conditions" be that *might* facilitate changing a culture? The evidence suggests that cultural change is most likely to take place when most or all of the following conditions exist:

A dramatic crisis This can be the shock that undermines the status quo and calls into question the relevance of the current culture. Examples of these crises might be a surprising financial setback, the loss of a major customer, or a dramatic technological breakthrough by a competitor.

Turnover in leadership New top leadership, who can provide an alternative set of key values, may be perceived as more capable of responding to the crisis. This would definitely encompass the organization's chief executive but also might need to include all senior management positions.

Young and small organization The younger the organization is, the less entrenched will be its culture. Similarly, it's easier for management to communicate its new values when the organization is small.

Weak culture The more widely held a culture is and the higher the agreement among members on its values, the more difficult it will be to change. Conversely, weak cultures are more amenable to change than strong ones.

Keep in mind that even if these conditions exist, there is no assurance that the culture will change. Moreover, any significant change will take a long time. So, especially in the short and intermediate term, an organization's culture should be treated as an important influence on employee behavior and something that management has little influence over.

SELECTED REFERENCES

DEAL, TERRENCE E., AND ALLAN A. KENNEDY, *Corporate Cultures: The Rites and Rituals of Corporate Life*. Reading, Mass.: Addison-Wesley, 1982.

FELDMAN, STEVEN P., "Culture and Conformity: An Essay on Individual Adaptation in Centralized Bureaucracy," *Human Relations*, April 1985, pp. 341–56.

FROST, PETER J., LARRY F. MOORE, MERYL REIS LOUIS, CRAIG C. LUNDBERG, AND JOANNE MARTIN, eds., *Organizational Culture*. Beverly Hills, Calif.: Sage Publications, 1985.

KILMANN, RALPH H., MARY J. SAXTON, ROY SERPA AND ASSOCIATES, eds., *Gaining Control of the Corporate Culture*. San Francisco: Jossey-Bass, 1985.

PASCALE, RICHARD, "The Paradox of 'Corporate Culture': Reconciling Ourselves to Socialization," *California Management Review*, Winter 1985, pp. 26–41.

SCHEIN, EDGAR H., *Organizational Culture and Leadership*. San Francisco: Jossey-Bass, 1985.

14

ORGANIZATIONAL CHANGE AND DEVELOPMENT

In the 1960s, the term "organizational development" (OD) became an increasingly popular term to describe the facilitating of system-wide change in an organization. Today, the term is used for a variety of change activities. To some, it is merely a catchy name given to the sensitivity training or small group discussion methods that gained popularity in the late 1950s. At the other extreme, it has been defined in such a general way that it encompasses almost the entire management process. For example, OD has been described as "a complex network of events that enhances the ability of organizational members to manage the culture of their organization, to be creative in solving problems, and to assist their organization in adapting to the external environment."[1] A closer look finds that OD is a systems-oriented approach to change, with heavy emphasis on humanistic-democratic values, and the belief that facilitating the integration of individual and organizational objectives will increase the organization's effectiveness.

1. Wendell French, *The Personnel Management Process*, 3rd ed. (Boston: Houghton Mifflin, 1974), p. 56.

In this chapter we shall review the importance of change to an organization, consider the key objectives of OD, and then proceed to describe the smorgasbord of techniques that have been proposed for bringing about change.

CHANGE AND OD We know that organizations exist in an environment of change. Technology, government regulation, competition, consumer tastes, and spending patterns are some of the more obvious factors that change over time and that organizations must adapt to if they are to survive. The issue is not whether organizations face change—they do! The issue is only one of degree. Those organizations that operate in relatively certain environments need to be less concerned than those that operate in turbulent and dynamic environments. But how is organization-wide change brought about? Organizational development represents a process of preparing for and managing change. It acknowledges that change cannot take place in a vacuum; that is, changes in structure, technology, and people interact. If OD is successful, the attitudes and values of individuals, as well as the structure of the organization, will be more adaptive. When we review the popular OD techniques, we find that they draw heavily upon topics touched on previously in our discussion of learning, motivation, job design, group dynamics, conflict, and organization structure.

In very general terms, planned change can be described as consisting of three stages: unfreezing, changing, and refreezing.

1. **Unfreezing** creates the awareness of the need to change. The status quo is disturbed by reducing the strength of current values, attitudes, or behaviors.
2. **Changing** is the action-oriented stage. Specific changes are brought about through the development of new values, attitudes, or behaviors.
3. **Refreezing** stabilizes the change that has been brought about. The new state becomes the status quo and must be sustained.

Efforts to bring about change will frequently meet with resistance. We have noted in previous chapters that people dislike uncertainty, yet change increases uncertainty. Individuals are required to trade the known for the unknown. Employees want to know how a different work assignment, a transfer, or new co-workers will affect them. Individuals and groups fear that a change may adversely affect their self-interest. As a result, employees will frequently create significant barriers to block change, even if this change may later prove to be beneficial to them.

Several classic studies have offered insight into how this resistance to change may be managed. A study designed to change food-buying habits among housewives found that 32 percent of housewives exposed to a group-decision method changed to a new variety of meats, in contrast to only 3 percent of the women who received information through the lecture method.[2] The researcher concluded that involvement and group pressure reduced the housewives' resistance to change. Similarly, an experiment in a textile factory established three approaches for bringing about change in work methods.[3] In the first group, the change was made autocratically by management and announced to the employees. The second involved employee participation through elected representatives. These representatives, with management, worked out the details of the change; then tried the new methods and trained others in the new procedures. In the third approach, there was full participation. All employees shared in the designing of new methods with management. The results of this experiment strongly favored the value of participation. In the first group, output actually dropped from the previous 60 units per hour to 48 units. However, the participation-by-representation group generated 68 units per hour and the total-participation group averaged 73 units per hour. Interestingly, when the members of autocratic and representative groups were later allowed total participation, their productivity increased to the level of the total-participation group. As with the study to change food habits, this factory experiment attests to the value of participation in reducing resistance to change.

Though both of the above studies are more than thirty years old, their findings have not been overlooked by students of OD. As we shall see, OD techniques have a generous bias toward participatory methods. There is a strong belief held by those people actively engaged in OD that changes are more likely to be accepted by individuals who have been given a voice in determining the content and process of the change.

THE MANAGER AS CHANGE AGENT

Changes within an organization need a catalyst. We call the person or persons who act as catalysts and assume the responsibility for managing the change process the *change agent*.

Any manager can be a change agent. As we review the topic of change, we will assume that it is initiated and carried out by a manager

2. Kurt Lewin, "Group Decision and Social Change," in *Readings in Social Psychology*, 2nd ed., eds. G. E. Swanson, T. M. Newcome, and E. L. Hartley, (New York: Holt, 1952), pp. 459–73.

3. Lester Coch and John R. P. French, Jr., "Overcoming Resistance to Change," *Human Relations*, November 1948, pp. 512–32.

within the organization. However, keep in mind that the change agent can be a nonmanager—an internal staff specialist whose expertise is in change implementation—or an outside consultant. For major, system-wide change efforts, internal management often will hire the services of outside consultants to provide advice and assistance. Because they are from the outside, these individuals can offer an objective perspective usually missing from insiders. However, outside consultants are disadvantaged because they usually have an inadequate understanding of the organization's history, culture, operating procedures, and personnel. Outside consultants also may be prone to initiate more drastic changes—which can be a benefit or disadvantage—because they do not have to live with the repercussions after the change is implemented. In contrast, internal managers, when acting as the change agent, may be more thoughtful (and possibly cautious), because they must live with the consequences of their actions.

OD OBJECTIVES Organizational development efforts are generally directed toward two ends: (1) improvement in an organization's effectiveness and, (2) improvement in the satisfaction of its members. A major value issue underlying these objectives is that they can best be attained by humanizing organizations and encouraging personal growth. When this is translated into operational language, we find the OD literature laden with terms like collaboration, confrontation, authenticity, trust, support, and openness. For example, one author has defined the objectives of a typical OD program as follows:

1. To increase the level of trust and support among organizational members
2. To increase the incidence of confrontation of organizational problems, both within groups and among groups, in contrast to "sweeping problems under the rug"
3. To create an environment in which authority of assigned role is augmented by authority based on knowledge and skill
4. To increase the openness of communications laterally, vertically, and diagonally
5. To increase the level of personal enthusiasm and satisfaction in the organization
6. To find synergistic solutions to problems
7. To increase the level of self- and group responsibility in planning and implementation.[4]

4. Wendell French, "Organization Development: Objectives, Assumptions and Strategies," *California Management Review*, Winter 1969, p. 24.

The previous description of OD objectives is heavily biased toward humanistic-democratic values. The change agent may be directive in OD; however, the literature emphasizes collaboration. Concepts like power, authority, control, conflict, and coercion are held in relatively low esteem among OD supporters. As a result, the OD techniques we shall review tend to emphasize power equalization (reducing hierarchical authority and control), the work group (rather than the individual), and the collaborative process.

But, of course, OD also is concerned with improving organizational performance. If it is true that the major hurdles to high organizational performance are dysfunctional conflicts, poor communication, structural rigidity, failure of members to know themselves and how they have an impact on others, and inadequate understanding of the attitudes and values of others, then OD should offer techniques for improving an organization's effectiveness. The OD techniques that we shall discuss are purported to increase member satisfaction and the meaningfulness of work. We shall review the evidence pertaining to these techniques and consider their ability to bring about change.

BASIC APPROACHES TO OD   The number of OD approaches is limited only by one's definition of OD. It may simply be a synonym for sensitivity training, in which case the topic is easily and quickly reviewed. Or it may encompass just about every possible idea that has been proposed to bring about change in individuals, groups, technology, or structure. In such a case, almost every topic we have covered in this book could be argued to be part of OD.

What we have tried to do is cull the more popular, interesting, and well-researched techniques for presentation here. For simplicity and clarity the techniques have been categorized as either structural or human processes.

Structural Techniques   The OD techniques that fall within the structural category affect work content and relationships among workers. To review these techniques in detail would repeat concepts discussed previously in Chapters 4 and 11, but a quick overview may be helpful.

Structural redesign options—job rotation, work modules, job enlargement, job enrichment, integrated and autonomous work teams, and quality circles—represent structural OD techniques. That is, they represent planned structural interventions with the objectives of increasing employee motivation and satisfaction and, eventually, organizational effectiveness. We chose to introduce them as redesign options that could increase employee motivation. They could, just as accurately, have been discussed here as structural OD techniques.

Certainly, management-initiated changes in the organization's formal structure—that is, altering its degree of complexity, formalization, and centralization—also represent structural OD interventions. For instance, departmental responsibilities can be combined, vertical layers removed, and spans of control widened to make the organization flatter and less bureaucratic. The number of rules and procedures can be reduced to increase employee autonomy. An increase in decentralization can be made to speed up the decision-making process. All of these concepts represent examples of structural approaches to OD.

Human Process Techniques   The vast majority of OD research has been directed at changing the attitudes and behavior of individuals and groups through the processes of communication, decision making, and problem solving. Popular techniques include sensitivity training, survey feedback, process consultation, team building, and intergroup development. For the most part, each emphasizes participation and collaboration.

Sensitivity Training.   It can go by a variety of names— laboratory training, sensitivity training, encounter groups, or T-groups (training groups)—but all refer to a method of changing behavior through unstructured group interaction. Members are brought together in a free and open environment in which participants discuss themselves and their interactive processes, loosely directed by a professional behavioral scientist. The group is process oriented, which means that individuals learn through observing and participating rather than being told. The professional creates the opportunity for participants to express their ideas, beliefs, and attitudes. He or she does not accept—in fact, overtly rejects— any leadership role.

The objectives of the T-groups are to provide the subjects with increased awareness of their own behavior and how others perceive them, greater sensitivity to the behavior of others, and increased understanding of group processes. Specific results sought include increased ability to empathize with others, improved listening skills, greater openness, increased tolerance of individual differences, and improved conflict resolution skills.

If individuals lack awareness of how others perceive them, then the successful T-group can effect more realistic self-perceptions, greater group cohesiveness, and a reduction in dysfunctional interpersonal conflicts. It will ideally result in a better integration between the individual and the organization.

Does sensitivity training work? Studies confirm that it can change individual behavior, but the specific characteristics of the change are unclear. There is no typical pattern of change that results from the sensitivity training experience. Therefore, since each participant's response is unique, and hence unpredictable, the value of sensitivity training for changing on-the-job behavior is almost impossible to spell out ahead of time.

Survey Feedback. One tool for assessing attitudes held by organizational members, identifying discrepancies among member perceptions, and solving these differences is the survey feedback approach.

Everyone in an organization can participate in survey feedback, but of key importance is the organizational family: the manager of any given unit and those employees who directly report to him or her. A questionnaire is usually completed by all members in the organization or unit. Organization members may be asked to suggest questions or may be interviewed to determine what issues are relevant. The questionnaire typically asks members for their perceptions and attitudes on a broad range of topics such as decision-making practices; communication effectiveness; coordination between units; and satisfaction with the organization, job, peers, and immediate supervisor.

The data from this questionnaire is tabulated with data pertaining to an individual's specific "family" and to the entire organization, and distributed to employees. This data then becomes the springboard for identifying problems and clarifying issues that may be creating difficulties for people. In some cases, the manager may be counseled by an external change agent about the meaning of the responses to the questionnaire and may even be given suggested guidelines for leading the organizational family in group discussions of the results. Particular attention is given to the importance of encouraging discussion and ensuring that discussions focus on issues and ideas, and not on attacking individuals.

Finally, group discussions in the survey feedback approach should result in members' identifying possible implications of the questionnaire's findings. Are people listening? Are new ideas being generated? Can decision making, interpersonal relations, or job assignments be improved? Answers to questions like these hopefully will result in the group's agreeing upon commitments to various actions that will remedy the problems that are identified.

What does the general evidence demonstrate about survey feedback? We find that survey feedback meetings can lead to attitudinal changes by participants. Satisfaction, positive attitudes toward work and one's supervisor, and involvement in the organization have been shown to increase as a result of group discussions surrounding the survey results.

While the survey feedback approach changes attitudes, long-term changes in behavior have not resulted from mere group discussions of the results. There is, in fact, little evidence that survey feedback alone leads to changes in individual behavior or organizational performance. Discussion and involvement will not bring about the desired changes if the discussion fails to initiate follow-up actions.

Process Consultation. No organization operates perfectly. Managers often sense that their unit's performance can be improved, but they are unable to identify what can be improved and how it can be improved. The purpose of process consultation is for an outside consultant to assist a client, usually a manager, to perceive, understand, and act upon process events with which he or she must deal. These might include work flow, informal relationships among unit members, and formal communication channels.

Process consultation (P.C.) is similar to sensitivity training in its assumption that organizational effectiveness can be improved by dealing with interpersonal problems, and in its emphasis on involvement. But P.C. is more task directed than sensitivity training.

Consultants in P.C. are there to give the client insight into what is going on around him, within him, and between him and other people. They do not solve the organization's problems. Rather, the consultant is a guide or coach who advises on the process to help the client solve his or her own problems.

The consultant works with the client in *jointly* diagnosing what processes need improvement. The emphasis is on "jointly," because the client develops a skill at analyzing processes within his or her unit that can be continually called on long after the consultant is gone. In addition, by having the client actively participate in both the diagnosis and the development of alternatives, there will be greater understanding of the process and the remedy, and less resistance to the action plan chosen.

Importantly, the process consultant need not be an expert in solving the particular problem that is identified. The consultant's expertise lies in diagnosis and developing a helping relationship. If the specific problem uncovered requires technical knowledge outside both the client's and consultant's expertise, the consultant helps the client to locate such an expert and then instructs the client in how to get the most out of this expert resource.

Team Building. Organizations are made up of people working together to achieve some common end. Since people are frequently required to work in groups, considerable attention has been focused in OD on team building.

Team building can be applied within groups or at the intergroup level where activities are interdependent. For our discussion, we shall emphasize the intragroup level and leave intergroup development to the next section.

228

As a result, our interest concerns applications to organizational families (command groups), as well as committees, project teams, and task groups.

Not all group activity has an interdependence of functions. To illustrate, compare a football team with a track team. The former requires a coordinated effort by members in order to be successful. Regardless of how good the quarterback is, he needs people who can successfully catch the ball if he is to be effective at developing a passing offense. Similarly, on defense, success is dependent on coordinating the interdependent activities of eleven men. On the other hand, with the exception of relay events, a track team's performance is merely the summation of the performance of its individual members.

Team building is like football because it, too, requires interdependence. The objective is to improve team members' coordinative efforts to increase the group's performance.

The activities that form team building can typically include goal setting, development of interpersonal relations among team members, role analysis to clarify each member's role and responsibilities, and team process analysis. Of course, team building may emphasize or exclude certain activities, depending on the purpose of the development effort and the specific problems with which the team is confronted. Basically, however, team building attempts to use high interaction among group members to increase trust and openness.

It may be beneficial to begin by having members attempt to define the goals and priorities of the group. This will bring to the surface different perceptions of what the group's purpose may be. Following this, members can evaluate the group's performance—how effective are they in structuring priorities and achieving their goals? This should identify potential problem areas. This self-critique of means and ends can be done with the total group present or, where large size impinges on a free interchange of views, may initially take place in smaller groups followed up by the sharing of their findings with the total group.

Team building can also address itself to the clarification of each member's role in the group. Previous ambiguities can be brought to the surface. For some individuals, it may offer one of the few opportunities they have had to think through what their job is all about and what specific tasks they are expected to carry out if the group is to optimize its effectiveness.

Still another team building activity can be similar to that performed by the process consultant; that is, to analyze key processes that go on within the team to identify the way work is performed and how these processes might be improved to make the team more effective.

How successful is team building in improving group effectiveness? The evidence is mixed. A large portion of the studies that have sought to measure team building effectiveness relies heavily on anecdotal data. Reports indicate that it is effective in increasing member involvement and participation in group activities and in improving the effectiveness of meetings. Participant attitudes are affected by team building, but it is unclear what effects group development has on actual task performance.

Intergroup Development.   A major area of concern in OD is the dysfunctional conflict that exists between groups. As a result, change efforts have been directed toward improving intergroup relations.

Intergroup development seeks to change the attitudes, stereotypes, and perceptions that groups have of each other. For example, in one company the engineers saw the accounting department as composed of shy and conservative types, and the personnel department as having a bunch of "smiley-types who sit around and plan company picnics." Such stereotypes can have an obvious negative impact on the coordinative efforts between the departments.

Though there are a number of approaches for improving intergroup relations, a popular method emphasizes problem solving. In this method, members of each group meet independently to develop lists of their perception of themselves, the other group, and how they believe the other group perceives them. The groups then share their lists, after which similarities and differences are discussed. Differences are clearly articulated, and the groups look for the causes of the disparities.

Are the groups' goals at odds? Were perceptions distorted? On what basis were stereotypes formulated? Have some differences been caused by misunderstandings of intentions? Have words and concepts been defined differently by each group? Answers to questions like these clarify the exact nature of the conflict. Once the causes of the difficulty have been identified, the groups can move to the integration phase and work to develop solutions that will improve relations between the groups.

Subgroups, with members from each of the conflicting groups, can now be created for further diagnosis and to begin to formulate possible alternative actions that will improve relations.

There is again little hard evidence upon which to evaluate the effectiveness of intergroup development methods like the problem-solving approach we have described. Reports of attitudes being positively influenced by the process exist, but little can be concluded as to the effect on individual behaviors or organization performance.

IMPLICATIONS FOR MANAGERS

Organizations and their members must change if organizations are to adapt and survive. Managers, because of their authoritative positions and their accountability for the organization's performance, frequently play the role of change agent.

Managers can use a wide range of structural and human-process techniques to bring about change in individuals, groups, technology, or the organization's structural design. Regardless of the change techniques used, managers should make use of the three stage, planned change model. By following this model, both the resistance to change and the need to stabilize and sustain the introduction of any changes will be directly addressed.

SELECTED REFERENCES

BOWERS, DAVID G., "Organizational Development: Promises, Performance, Possibilities," *Organizational Dynamics*, Spring 1976, pp. 50–62.

FRENCH, WENDELL L., AND CECIL H. BELL, JR., *Organizational Development: Behavioral Science Interventions for Organization Improvement* (3rd ed.). Englewood Cliffs, N.J.: Prentice-Hall, 1984.

GUZZO, RICHARD A., RICHARD D. JETTE, AND RAYMOND A. KATZELL, "The Effects of Psychologically Based Intervention Programs on Worker Productivity: A Meta-Analysis," *Personnel Psychology*, Summer 1985, pp. 275–91.

LIPPETT, GORDON, RONALD LIPPETT, AND CLAYTON LAFFERTY, "Cutting Edge Trends in Organizational Development," *Training and Development Journal*, July 1984, pp. 59–62.

WARRICK, DON D., AND J.T. THOMPSON, "Still Crazy After All These Years," *Training and Development Journal*, April 1980, pp. 16–22.

WOODWORTH, WARNER, GORDON MEYER, AND NORMAN SMALLWOOD, "Organization Development: A Closer Scrutiny," *Human Relations*, April 1982, pp. 307–19.

EPILOGUE

The end of a book typically has the same meaning to an author that it has to the reader: It generates feelings of both accomplishment and relief. As both of us rejoice at having completed our tour of the essential concepts in organizational behavior, this is a good time to examine where we have been and what it all means.

The underlying theme of this book has been that the behavior of people at work is *not* a random phenomenon. While employees are complex entities, their attitudes and behavior can nevertheless be explained and predicted with a reasonable degree of accuracy. Our approach has been to look at organizational behavior at three levels: the individual, the group, and the organization system.

We started with the individual and reviewed the major psychological contributions to understanding why individuals act as they do. We found that there are individual differences among employees. However, many of these differences can be systematically labeled and categorized, which allows for generalizations. For example, while not all employees respond positively to enriched jobs, the evidence indicates encouraging results when employees possess high growth needs. Similarly, it is true that people have different personalities, but placing them in jobs that are compatible with their personality types should result in higher performing and more satisfied employees.

Next, our analysis moved to the group level. We argued that the understanding of group behavior is more complex than merely multiplying what we know about individuals by the number of members in the group. Since people act differently when in a group than when alone, we demonstrated how roles, norms, leadership styles, power relationships, and other similar group factors impacted on the behavior of employees.

Finally, we overlaid system-wide variables upon our knowledge of individual and group behavior to further improve our understanding of organizational behavior. Major emphasis was given to showing how an organization's structure, performance appraisal and reward systems, and culture affect both the attitudes and behavior of employees.

Looking back on this book's fourteen chapters, it may be tempting to criticize the stress placed on theoretical concepts. But as a noted social-psychologist once said, "There is nothing so practical as a good theory." Of course, it is also true that there is nothing so *impractical* as a good theory that leads nowhere. To avoid presenting theories that led nowhere, this book included a wealth of examples and illustrations. Additionally, we regularly stopped to inquire as to the implications of theory for the practice of management. The result has been the presentation of numerous concepts that, individually, offer some insights into behavior, but which, when taken together, provide a complex system to help you explain, predict, and control organizational behavior.

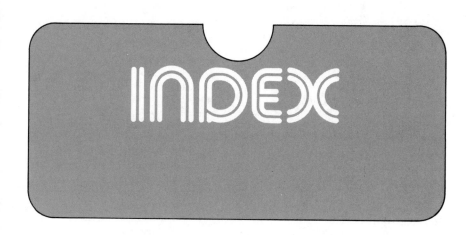